DESIRE UNLIMITED

Critical Studies in Latin American and Iberian Cultures

SERIES EDITORS
James Dunkerley
John King

This major series – the first of its kind to appear in English – is designed to map the field of contemporary Latin American and Iberian cultures, which have enjoyed increasing popularity in Britain and the United States in recent years.

The series aims to broaden the scope of criticism of Latin American and Iberian cultures, which tend still to extol the virtues of a few established 'master' works, and to examine cultural production within the context of twentieth-century history. These clear, accessible studies are aimed at those who wish to know more about some of the most important and influential cultural works and movements of our time.

DESIRE UNLIMITED

The Cinema of Pedro Almodóvar

Second Edition

PAUL JULIAN SMITH

VERSO

London • New York

First published by Verso 1994
© Paul Julian Smith 1994
Second edition first published by Verso 2000
© Paul Julian Smith 2000
All rights reserved

Verso
UK: 6 Meard Street, London W1V 3HR
USA: 180 Varick Street, New York, NY 10014–4606

Verso is the imprint of New Left Books

ISBN 1–85984–778–1
ISBN 1–85984–304–2

British Library Cataloguing in Publication Data
A catalogue record for this book is available from the British Library

Library of Congress Cataloging-in-Publication Data
A catalog record for this book is available from the Library of Congress

Typeset in 10/13pt New Baskerville by
SetSystems Ltd, Saffron Walden, Essex
Printed in Great Britain by The Bath Press

This second edition is dedicated to the Spanish friends who invited me to the Universities of Seville, Vigo, Pompeu Fabra, Alcalá, and País Vasco (Bilbao); and to the galleries at the Koldo Mitxelena (San Sebastián) and Bilbao Arte.

CONTENTS

CONTENTS

PREFACE TO THE SECOND EDITION

In the conclusion to the first edition of *Desire Unlimited*, written in 1993, I suggested that Almodóvar's position was uncertain and his future unpredictable. The long-lasting Socialist government in Spain seemed on the point of collapsing and with it the hedonistic culture of the 1980s with which he and they were associated. It is a great pleasure to report that Almodóvar responded to new circumstances with new cinematic solutions, re-establishing his position as the most artistically ambitious and commercially consistent film-maker in Europe.

Although perhaps the least successful of Almodóvar's films cinematically, *Kika* (1993) broached new topics for an uneasy era: the corrosive effects of the deregulated Spanish media and the decline into drug-related violence of Madrid, previously celebrated as the city of desire in such films as *La ley del deseo* (The Law of Desire, 1989). *La flor de mi secreto* (The Flower of My Secret, 1995) offered the familiar figure of an abandoned woman as central character. But, unlike in the earlier *Mujeres al borde de un ataque de nervios* (Women on the Verge of a Nervous Breakdown, 1988), bitter drama was barely sweetened by farce and personal narrative was placed in the context of a Spain and a Europe riven by political conflict. *Carne trémula* (Live Flesh, 1997) extended and intensified this new social bias, framing its complex sexual plotting (a full five characters driven by passion and jealousy) with an explicit historical commentary on Spain's transition from dictatorship to democracy. Finally, *Todo sobre mi madre* (All About My

Mother, 1999) revisited themes familiar from Almodóvar's earlier works, such as transsexualism, lesbianism, and drug addiction, but from a frankly emotional perspective. Such an uncompromising exploration of the work of mourning had never before been seen in Almodóvar's cinematic gallery of broken hearts and impossible relationships.

At the time of writing, *Todo sobre mi madre* is still successfully playing in eleven London theatres some three months after its release. In a period when foreign language films receive very limited distribution in English-speaking countries, this is a commercial triumph for Almodóvar and his production company El Deseo (not to mention the recently rebranded distributors Pathé), marking perhaps the first time that one of Almodóvar's films has truly connected with the British public at large. It is no accident that *Todo sobre mi madre* should achieve such commercial success internationally. Almodóvar's thirteenth feature serves as a kind of synthesis of his career to date, marrying as it does the marginal milieu of his early 'rose' period with the classical austerity of his later 'blue' period. It is the masterpiece of which Almodóvar's admirers knew he was capable.

The four films produced since the first edition have thus reconfirmed the main argument of the book: namely that beneath Almodóvar's genius for comedy and visual pleasure lies a film-maker whose works deserve to be taken with the utmost seriousness, both conceptually and formally. Certainly the recent films show a mastery of cinematic technique that is unparalleled in contemporary cinema. The indispensable contributions of such skilled collaborators as cinematographer Affonso Beato, composer Alberto Iglesias, and editor José Salcedo (who, unlike his colleagues, has accompanied Almodóvar since the days of *Pepi, Luci, Bom* (1980)), lend a high degree of artistic continuity to the recent films which deserve to be treated together.

If Almodóvar continues to show us that, as I wrote in 1993, there is 'truth in travesty', then that truth remains unwelcome to some. A minority of hostile critics in Spain and the UK (notably Carlos Boyero in *El Mundo* and Alexander Walker in the London *Evening Standard*) rejected Almodóvar's characteristic focus on women in *Todo sobre mi madre*, arguing that the true test for his talent would be the creation of convincing male heterosexual characters. Such an attitude betrays the continuing assumption that those who place themselves on the feminine side of gender difference are inherently inferior to those who do not. As I attempted to show in the first edition of this book, such prejudice has been a leitmotif of Almodóvar's critical reception. But these critics also display a willed amnesia: *Carne trémula*, just two years earlier, had revealed Almodóvar's sympathy for and empathy with strong, complex and troubled male figures. Just as the limits of heterosexuality require constant policing, so admission to the select ranks of auteurship is consistently denied to those who bravely attempt to call masculine prestige into question.

This second edition of *Desire Unlimited* contains, at the end of the original text, a Part II comprising four chapters on the new films, accompanied by an updated filmography and bibliography. These new chapters are adapted and expanded from features I wrote for *Sight and Sound* on each film's release and they include for the first time an interview with Almodóvar himself. While these new chapters do not contain the academic apparatus of footnoting I provided for the original chapters, they offer an immediacy of response and (I hope) a sense of zeitgeist which is fundamental to the experience of cinema. Indeed each of these new pieces was written immediately after the relevant film's premiere in Madrid or its first screening at a festival or press preview.

It thus falls to me, in my capacity as journalist, to thank the editors of *Sight and Sound* who commissioned these features: Philip Dodd and Nick James. At a time when it is widely believed that serious film culture is in freefall, *Sight and Sound* is unique in its attempt to create a space between academy and industry, between film scholar and film fan. Despite financial pressures on the British Film Institute, *Sight and Sound* continues to support foreign-language cinema and to review all films theatrically screened in the UK, whatever their origin. Leslie Felperin and Ed Lawrenson at *Sight and Sound* also helped me by commissioning reviews and providing illustrations.

Pedro Almodóvar himself was characteristically generous with his time, granting a second unscheduled session for the interview. He and El Deseo's chief press officer Paz Sufrategui have consistently supported my academic and journalistic writing without at any point attempting to intervene in its content or focus, an attitude relatively rare in the film industry and thus all the more welcome. Finally I thank my editor at Verso, Jane Hindle, for her support throughout.

Paul Julian Smith
London and Cambridge, November 1999

ACKNOWLEDGEMENTS

I would like to thank Agustín Almodóvar and Lola García of El Deseo, S. A. for kindly providing me with scripts and rare text and video material. Most of the research for this book was undertaken at the Filmoteca Nacional and Biblioteca Nacional, Madrid, and the British Film Institute, London, to whose staff I owe thanks. Andrés F. Rubio very kindly gave me access to the press archives of *El País*, Madrid.

The following kindly provided me with material from Britain, Spain, and the US: Teresa de Carlos, Josep Anton Fernández, Philip Martin-Clark, Barbara Morris, my parents Bert and Margaret Smith, David Vilaseca, and James S. Williams. Students and colleagues in the Faculty of Modern and Medieval Languages in the University of Cambridge helped to support my commitment to film studies; I owe a particular debt to David Forgacs. The students of Berkeley, University of California, who chose 'Spanish 248' in spring 1993, played a great role in helping me to finalize my 'take' on Almodóvar. I am grateful to the Department of Spanish and Portuguese (and most particularly Emilie Bergmann) for extending such a fruitful invitation. John King, one of the series' editors, first suggested I wrote this book and was consistently encouraging, as was Colin Robinson at Verso. Philip Dodd, Pam Cook, and (especially) Jonathan Romney kindly invited me to write on Spanish cinema and gender theory for *Sight and Sound*.

Material from this book was read as papers or lectures in 1993 at Queen Mary and

Westfield College, University of London; the Comparative Literature Conference in honour of Arthur Terry, University of Essex; the Berkeley conference on Gender, Sexuality, and the State; Johns Hopkins University, Baltimore; Pomona College, CA; and the School of Cinema-Television, University of Southern California, where I am most indebted to Marsha Kinder. Trinity Hall, Cambridge, kindly loaned me the flat in which the bulk of the book was written, from summer 1992 to summer 1993. Fiona Bing, departmental secretary, greatly lightened my load as Head of Department.

Earlier versions of chapters 4, 5, 7, and part of 9 were published in *Journal of Hispanic Research; New Hispanisms*, ed. Mark Millington and Paul Julian Smith, Ottawa 1993; catalogue to Almodóvar exhibition at the Venice Biennale 1993, ed. Christian Leigh; journal of the Consejería de Educación, Spanish Embassy. My thanks to the editors for allowing me permission to reprint this material here.

Paul Julian Smith
London and Cambridge, June 1993

LIST OF ILLUSTRATIONS

All stills are reproduced by permission of Pedro Almodóvar and El Deseo, S. A. Plates 3, 13, 15 and 19 to 27 are from the collection of El Deseo, S. A.; 1, 2, 5, 7, 8 and 9 from the collection of Metro Pictures, 79 Wardour St, London W1V 3TH; 4, 6, 10, 11, 12, 14, 16, 17 and 18 from BFI Stills, Posters and Designs.

My thanks also to Tartan Video for permission to reproduce Plates 1–12.

PART I

INTRODUCTION:

EL DESEO, S.A.

(DESIRE LTD)

TRUTH IN TRAVESTY

A young woman returns to a seminary in rural Extremadura dressed as Dietrich in *The Devil Is a Woman*. She has come to announce the death of her brother, aged twenty-four, to the priest who had taken a particular interest in him. When the priest complains of her 'excessive frivolity' she replies: 'I adore frivolity; I could not live without it.' And surely, she continues, the prostitution she practises is less harmful than the conduct of priests who violate children's bodies in the name of God? The priest blanches. Two endings: the 'sister' reveals s/he is the abused brother in drag, and swishes out, vengeance complete. Or, the priest kills the young 'woman', only to discover that it is his beloved student who has returned to him.

An elderly bourgeois lady answers an advertisement in a Madrid newspaper, asking for 'young, pretty' secretaries. It is but a cover for the white slave trade; and Doña Julia finds herself working as an exotic dancer in Marrakesh and succumbing, with some delight, to drugs, alcohol, and rough sex. Awakening in the interview room (she has failed to get the secretarial job), she realizes it is but a dream. The next day, however, she walks out on her husband: 'Having thought about it for forty years, I've decided to leave you and live my own life.' A new life begins for Doña Julia.[1]

These unpublished stories are amongst the first works of Pedro Almodóvar, deposited in typescript in the Biblioteca Nacional, Madrid, for the purposes of copyright

1

in 1975. It was the year of Franco's death and of Almodóvar's twenty-sixth birthday. 'The Visit' and 'The Advertisement' announce distinct but related aspects of Almodóvar's creative enterprise which will continue throughout his career to date. The first is a love of comic confrontation, which is inseparable from serious concerns: the ex-seminarist may be dressed in a crinoline, but his thirst for vengeance is no less deeply felt for all that; indeed the glitzy drag is part of that vengeance on the hypocrisies of a repressive male order. The second is a love of female fantasy, which is always situated in a precise social location: the humour of Doña Julia's position relies on a recognition of her banal background, of the stultifying boredom of her leisured existence. Both characters make unlikely heroines, who are now recognizable as typically Almodóvarian; both are vehicles for a female identification or projection, which inspires comedy and pathos in equal measure.

One argument of this book will be that the conspicuous frivolity of Almodóvar's cinema is intimately linked to serious concerns which have often gone unnoticed; and that the frequent dismissal of Almodóvar's work as 'zany' or 'kitsch' arises from a disrespect for a register coded as 'feminine' and for those men who identify themselves with women's concerns. To seek truth in travesty is dangerous business and one for which Almodóvar has paid a certain price. Moreover, as we shall see, faced by the horrors of Francoism or (more recently) the po-faced pieties of Socialism, frivolity can be seen in a Spanish context as a political posture whose effects are as potent as they are uncontrollable.

Almodóvar's nine features to date constitute a body of work which deals in a complex and sophisticated fashion with a number of vital issues: gender, nationality, homosexuality. And each of these issues is clouded by controversy. Thus Almodóvar is known as a 'woman's director' (an often back-handed compliment) who has consistently placed women centre frame in his cinema; yet he has been frequently accused of misogyny, of humiliating and fetishizing those same women. Secondly, he is often cited as the embodiment of post-Franco Spain, the representative of the new nation; yet his films studiously avoid debates such as those on regional independence which most preoccupy that nation, which threaten, indeed, to convulse it. Finally, he is known (outside Spain at least) as a gay-identified man, who appeals to the queer-coded registers of kitsch and camp; yet his filmic career can be read as a progressive disavowal of homosexuality, whether masculine or feminine.

All of these critiques come together in the charge often made by foreign critics that Almodóvar's work is 'apolitical' or 'ahistorical'. What I hope to show, however, is that such views arise from an ignorance of or indifference to the Spanish context in which that work has been produced. Foreigners cannot expect Almodóvar to subscribe to forms of resistance which evolved in response to the triumph of the British and North American Right in the eighties; and if they are serious about respecting cultural difference they must pay more attention to a nation whose understanding of such issues as gender, nationality, and homosexuality may well be more sophisticated than their own. In his celebration of fluidity and performance, in his hostility to fixed positions of all kinds, Almodóvar anticipates that critique of identity and essence that was later to become so familiar in academic feminist, minority, and queer theory.

If critics and audiences have refused to recognize the seriousness of Almodóvar's commitment to the analysis of social and psychic concerns (a seriousness which in no way contradicts the brilliance of his comedy), then they have also neglected questions of cinematic technique. An autodidact whose modest beginnings in provincial La Mancha made a film career almost inconceivable, Almodóvar's features trace a trajectory from the minimalist tabula rasa of *Pepi, Luci, Bom* (1980), with its eccentric framing and contempt for continuity, to the glossy professionalism of *Tacones lejanos* (High Heels, 1991), with its gloriously saturated colour photography by Alfredo Mayo. In this book I pay particular attention to mise-en-scène, cinematography, and editing, arguing that the idiosyncratic look or feel of Almodóvar's cinema is constructed from precisely observable filmic means. These means change from one film to another: the neo-realist *¿Qué he hecho yo para merecer esto?* (What Have I Done to Deserve This?, 1984) uses a grungy set and fixed tripod camera to reproduce the ghastly claustrophobia experienced by its characters; the sleek costumes and fluid camera movements of *Matador* (1986) reinforce the high production values of Almodóvar's most abstract and stylized murder melodrama. And if technique differs from one film to the next, then filmic means intersect with each other and with Almodóvar's deliriously complex plots in unpredictable ways. Thus the colour coding of costumes in *Mujeres al borde de un ataque de nervios* (Women on the Verge of a Nervous Breakdown, 1988) suggests from the start an alignment between the feuding characters played by Carmen Maura and Rossy de Palma which is confirmed in the narrative only in the final scene. Or again, the disconcertingly lush music for *¡Atame!* (Tie Me Up! Tie Me Down!, 1990) points to a romantic conclusion to a violent kidnapping well before the characters themselves are assured of such a fortunate result. It thus follows that Almodóvar's films cannot simply be interrogated for 'positive images' and dismissed if they fail to live up to progressive Anglo-American norms. In a cinema of saturation, in which vivid colour and costume compete for attention with outrageous narratives and dialogue, it is vital to examine the context of images or plot points and not to freeze them in censorious isolation.

Moreover, the discontinuities of Almodóvar's technique are not to be dismissed as the result of chance or incompetence; rather they form part of a critique of representation (of the relationship between film as presence and film as language) which is also manifest in a love of the reflexive ironies reminiscent of Sirk (a frequent point of reference), or even Godard.

USES OF ALMODÓVAR

The offices of El Deseo, S.A. are situated in an undistinguished residential street outside central Madrid. They seem far indeed from the glamorous capital which forms the stylized background to films such as *La ley del deseo* (The Law of Desire, 1987). Their anonymity, even invisibility (there is no identifying sign on the street or in the building itself) seem somewhat uncharacteristic when contrasted with the all-pervasiveness of the Almodóvar 'trade mark' and the flagrant visibility of the director and his films. Few visitors could fail to be impressed by the loyalty and industry of Almodóvar's 'family' of co-workers (most particularly his producer-brother Agustín) and by their determination to protect him from the unsympathetic critics (known as 'detractors') who have dogged him since the beginning. It would be difficult to underestimate the role of such a collaborative enterprise in the success of films identified, perhaps improperly, by the single name 'Almodóvar'. One specific advantage of El Deseo is Almodóvar's ability to shoot each film in sequence, thus following the natural development of character and narrative, an expensive option which would be denied him by other production companies.[2]

El Deseo has produced three of the top five grossing Spanish films of all time; and it has been the most profitable production company in Spain (often by a considerable margin) in the last four years for which figures are available.[3] And this achievement has to be seen in the context of a Spanish cinema in perpetual crisis, with the eighties marking a steep decline in the industry, in all three sectors of production (the falling number of domestic features), distribution (the increasing stranglehold of US-controlled multinationals), and exhibition (the collapse in the number of functioning theatres). In a period when Spanish cinema has become synonymous with tedious repetition to a youthful domestic audience,[4] it is little short of a miracle that Almodóvar should have achieved such commercial success with the odds so stacked against him. I argue in this book that the Almodóvar 'phenomenon' is inexplicable without a detailed knowledge of the history of the Spanish film industry in the eighties. To take a specific example once more, Almodóvar's second film *Laberinto de pasiones* (Labyrinth of Passion, 1982) could not have been made without the support of exhibitor-turned-producer Alphaville. And the later films profited from generous subsidies from a Spanish government anxious to change Spain's image abroad.

One secret of Almodóvar's success has been determination from the very beginning to devote as much time to promotion as to production. In this book I study the creation of a press 'persona' which is the product of a mutual exploitation by Almodóvar and the media. There is little doubt that Almodóvar, with his very photogenic female entourage (the famous 'chicas'), his love of the modern, so typical of contemporary Spain, and his scandalous hints of sexual heterodoxy, filled a gap in a journalistic world avid for novelty and celebrity. But Almodóvar was also put to other uses outside Spain. For art-house distributors and exhibitors, concerned by the deaths of Fassbinder and Pasolini, the decline of Godard and Fellini, and the unfulfilled promise of new French directors such as Beneix and Besson, Almodóvar was the one true auteur to emerge in the 1980s and a regular source of high-profile new product. For academics in the US (and, to a lesser extent, the UK), Almodóvar was a dream director, equally exploitable for courses on gender, ethnic, or lesbian and gay studies.[5] Hispanists found a topic which, finally, was attractive to scholars and students in other areas; generalists could flatter themselves that they were taking an interest in a 'minority' area, which proved to be more pleasurable than most. More importantly, however, I shall argue that in his love of fantasy and cross-gender identification, Almodóvar coincides with recent psycho-analytically inspired feminist film theorists.[6] Both he and they pose a challenge to an earlier view which read narrative cinema primarily as the sadistic or voyeuristic gaze which the male exercises over a passive female object. If desire is unlimited (if spectator positioning is mobile and labile), then opportunities for visual pleasure proliferate.

To juxtapose Almodóvar with US gender studies is perhaps incongruous; for his films have often been criticized by foreign feminists, or men claiming to speak on their behalf. My own position is that images can never be inherently transgressive or hegemonic, and must always be placed in historical debates around cinema, censorship, and sexuality. Exemplary here is the polemic around sexual violence in *¡Atame!* which (as I hope to show) arose from a cross-cultural incomprehension, in which adversarial positions were derived from national debates which shared no common basis for argument. To be more precise, Spanish libertarianism (which saw the absolute freedom of the artist as an inevitable consequence of democracy) came into conflict with US regulative pragmatism (which subordinated artistic autonomy to commercial well-being). Moreover, addressing a mass audience at home and a minority ('marginal') audience abroad, Almodóvar's films could hardly fail to provoke diverse responses. Indeed it could be argued that they carry within themselves multiple models of spectatorship which resist any simple resolution.[7]

One favourite technique of Almodóvar is cross-cutting. For example, in the opening sequence of *Matador*, students' bullfighting practice is interspliced with an unknown woman's seduction and murder of a male sexual partner. Cross-cutting can lead, as it does in this sequence, to confusion, to discontinuity. But it also promises the spectator access to simultaneous action in discrete locales and significant juxtapositions in montage. Switching between film history, theory, and technique (and not scorning to invoke the humblest or most frivolous of sources), this book also takes cross-cutting as a key to a privileged understanding of a complex and contradictory cinematic phenomenon. By naming his production company El Deseo, S.A., Almodóvar hints with typically sly irony at the intersection of the psychic and the commercial. His practice of cinema will also prove to be a model of libidinal economy, unprecedented in film history.

NOTES

1. 'Relatos', unpublished ms by Pedro Almodóvar Caballero, Madrid 1975 ('La visita', 'El anuncio'); see also the unproduced script, 'El anuncio (título provisional)', Madrid 14 June 1976. 'La visita' is clearly the model for the scene in *La ley del deseo* (The Law of Desire, 1987) in which transsexual Tina (Carmen Maura) confronts the spiritual guide who has proved such a disappointment to her.

2. Private conversation with Agustín Almodóvar, September 1992.

3. *Mujeres al borde* (1); *Tacones* (2); *¡Atame!* (5). See the tables in Emilio C. García Fernández, *El cine español contemporáneo*, Barcelona 1992, pp. 140, 146–7.

4. See John Hopewell, "'Art and a Lack of Money": The Crisis of the Spanish Film Industry, 1977–1990', *Quarterly Review of Film and Video*, vol. 13 (4), 1991, pp. 113–22.

5. One of the earliest foreign retrospectives of Almodóvar's work was held in an academic institution: Dartmouth College, New Hampshire. See Nuria Vidal, *El cine de Pedro Almodóvar*, Barcelona 1989, opposite p. 385. (I cite this collection of interviews hereafter as 'Vidal'.) Another important collection of essays and interviews was produced by the film clubs of a number of Colegios Mayores in Madrid: *Los fantasmas del deseo*, Madrid 1988, with the collaboration of Miguel Albaladejo, Mario Arias, Rafael Enríquez, José A. Hergueta, Jesús Martínez Romero, José María Mellado, Carmen Obregón, Miguel A. Presas, Tomás Reyes, José I. Sánchez Alvarez, and Rafael Villarreal (cited hereafter as 'Albaladejo'). I have also consulted María Antonia García de León and Teresa Maldonado, *Pedro Almodóvar: la otra España cañí*, Ciudad Real 1989 (cited hereafter as 'García de León and Maldonado').

6. I am thinking most particularly of Carol Clover, Gaylyn Studlar, and Linda Williams here. Similarly, lesbian and gay theories no longer limit themselves to the analysis of overtly homosexual images; Paul Burston claims that in *La ley del deseo* the 'performance of gender' and 'inappropriate acting styles' are 'queerer by far' than the explicitly sexual opening scene: 'Genre Bender', *Time Out* (London), 2–9 June 1993.

7. This is Judith Mayne's argument with relation to Fassbinder in *Cinema and Spectatorship*, New York and London 1993, p. 169.

PEPI, LUCI, BOM, Y OTRAS CHICAS DEL MONTÓN (PEPI, LUCI, BOM AND OTHER GIRLS ON THE HEAP, 1980)

Rhetoric and Reference

FUN, FRIENDSHIP, FEMINISM

> I went to a party last night . . .
>
> (Little Nell)

In North American films friendship is generally between men, but I enjoy the complicity which exists between women. . . . Women have been able to give themselves up unashamedly to friendship for cultural reasons, because they have been condemned to live out their private life [*intimidad*] in secret and that private life has only been revealed to female friends. . . . Men deserve to be deceived by women. I love the idea of a girl deceiving her husband with a girlfriend. It's an image which I find attractive and which forms part of the secret autonomy of women. . . . Now I'm aware that the fact that I like the private life of women may still be a reflection of machismo. But I hope not, because I'm interested in women and their world, not just when they go to gossip in the bathroom, but at all times. I believe I'm one of the least machista men in the world, one of the most authentically feminist. (Vidal, pp. 33–5)[1]

In this interview, given in 1987, Pedro Almodóvar reflects on the making of his first full-length feature, *Pepi, Luci, Bom*, at the start of the decade. Typically, the director not only makes a declaration of a certain female identification which will recur throughout his cinema; he also anticipates possible objections from hostile critics. Thus Almodóvar takes care to contrast his cinema with dominant Hollywood norms and defends himself against the accusation of misogyny which will frequently be made against him. Important here is his stress on the fact that the secluded spaces of feminine intimacy are historically constructed and not natural, the product of a marginalization ('marginación') which women have turned to their own advantage. However, by offering spectators privileged access to these secluded spaces, even those in which unsuspecting men are duped by witty women, Almodóvar risks reduplicating that voyeuristic male look implicit in much dominant cinema practice. The fact that he goes on to invoke male pleasure in 'lesbian' porn numbers as proof of women's relative freedom from machista disapproval is hardly reassuring.

How, then, are Almodóvar's three leading ladies established? After the cartoon titles accompanied by a blast of trashy pop from Little Nell (bit player in *The Rocky Horror Show* and New York nightclub hostess), the camera finds lewd adolescent heiress Pepi (Carmen Maura) sprawled on cushions pasting stickers of Superman into an album. Her flat is (according to the script)[2] 'an outrageous mix of pop, kitsch, and modern objects' (p. 1). Marijuana plants are visible on the terrace and behind them we glimpse the windows of an anonymous apartment building. Opening the door to an unsavoury, balding policeman played by Félix Rotaeta (who also arranged funding for the film), Pepi engages in pornographic dialogue with him and agrees to allow him anal intercourse if he agrees to ignore the drugs. But the (nameless) policeman enters Pepi's 'front door', not the back. An unlikely virgin who had been planning to sell her maidenhood to the highest bidder, Pepi is now (according to a cartoon intertitle) 'thirsty for revenge'.

This is the first of several rapes in Almodóvar's filmography; and it raises serious questions which are at once political and cinematic. For on the one hand the scene clearly alludes to a certain oppression of women: Rotaeta's policeman is a caricature Fascist, as brutal as he is corrupt. But on the other, the use of music, mise-en-scène, and most particularly modes of performance distance the spectator, daring us to take any of the action at face value. The portrayal of an adolescent virgin by the thirty-year-old Maura is particularly implausible. And the introduction of Pepi's female friends is equally problematic. Bom (Olvido 'Alaska' Gara) is a fifteen-year-old musician. She is first seen rehearsing in full punk gear with her spectacularly inept band (the real life Pegamoides); but in the next she is dressed as a *maja* (nineteenth-century Madrid low life) giving a vigorous beating to the policeman's twin brother (Pepi's vengeance has gone astray). Luci, on the other hand (played by the disturbingly unresponsive Eva Siva), is first shown in the typical uniform of a Madrid housewife: scarf on head, 'horrific, hand-made jersey' (script, p. 15), trailing a wheeled shopping basket behind her. Once enticed up to Pepi's apartment, however, she is soon revealed as an enthusiastic masochist, her jumper profusely christened with a stream of urine from the obliging Bom.[3]

It is around Luci that the film's parodic discourse on feminism circulates. Returning to the garish flat she shares with her policeman husband and his brother, the former attacks her for wearing trousers and failing to have his dinner ready. Luci responds: 'I think women have to find their true selves.' Her husband abusively replies that she should find herself in the kitchen, where she should be. But the importance of this scene is twofold: first its exposure of male ignorance (the policeman can only guess at the source of the stains on Luci's jumper); and second its presentation of female revolt as an ironic repetition of media cliché. Throughout the film the characters will mouth commonplaces (on feminism, politics, pornography) whose status is not clear, whose bizarre new context renders them undecidable. Thus when the policeman remarks at breakfast that Spain is going to the dogs 'with so much democracy', he is both parroting the views of the far right *Alcázar* newspaper which he is reading, and offering up those views to comic redirection.[4]

Hence, although *Pepi, Luci, Bom* begins with the violation of a woman, it continues with the deception of men by women and with a series of scenes in which women's intimacy is centre frame (Plate 1). Female friendship is thus a space from which men are excluded and one to which they aspire; physically such places will include the flat in which Luci and Bom set up home (real-life residence of gay painters Costus) and the mixed nightclub El Bo, where the three friends meet a vulgar provincial 'flamenco rock singer' (the first in a string of notably unsympathetic roles for Almodóvar by the shrewish *andaluza* Kitti Manver). The use of such authentic locations was of course required by the no-budget shooting schedule. But they have also been offered as evidence for the documentary nature of *Pepi, Luci, Bom* and its reputedly direct testimony to a brief moment in the cultural history of Madrid. Such readings are now veiled in a potent nostalgia, with many of the youthful participants (such as Costus) having met early deaths. But there is a certain paradox in the fact that Almodóvar's first film is not only the most dependent on a pre-existing 'scene' outside the frame, but also the most explicit in its account of the artifice of cinematic narrative. Referentiality and rhetoricity are thus mixed together to form a strange and potent brew.

THE DIFFICULTY OF REPRESENTATION

> PEPI: La representación es siempre algo artificial.
> PEPI: Representation is always somewhat artificial.

Luci and Bom are living together at the Costus's house. When Pepi drops in bearing cocaine and pornographic comic strips, the latter's paintings of *folklóricas* and of celebrities such as the Shah of Iran are visible on the the walls behind. Pepi lets slip her intention of making a video on the life of her friends. However, she advises them that they cannot simply be themselves but must rather play (*representar*) their own characters. Pepi knows that they are really a forty-year-old housewife and a teenage punk, but they will have to act up their true sadomasochistic roles if the spectator is to be convinced of the authenticity of their relationship. Luci essays a few improbable ecstatic groans.

Almodóvar has said in interviews that this sequence serves both as a distancing device and as a verbal explication of the plot: without this explicit supplement to the narrative, the audience might not accept the impassivity of Eva Siva or the antipathy of Alaska as adequate portrayals of the lurid creatures they claim to be impersonating (Vidal, pp. 25–6). The dialogue thus serves to make Almodóvar's vision of the characters perfectly clear. However, the necessity for this verbal surplus or excess, also typical of Almodóvar's later work, calls into question the capacity of the cinematic image fully to communicate that which it claims to represent. And the rest of the film invokes multiple forms of representation, none of which is privileged and all of which are juxtaposed randomly with each other.

One of these forms is the monologue. Cristina Sánchez Pascual (later to star in *Entre tinieblas*) stalks a chaotic flat in dressing-gown, high-pitched squeak, and three-week beard. Addressing her heedless husband, slumped apparently unconscious on the bed, she tells the story of how he married her as if in revenge on his best friend who came out as a gay man and started to see other men. She berates him both for abandoning the friend ('People are free to do what they like with their own bodies') and for neglecting her: after so many nights without sex she is like 'a cat on a hot tin roof'. Typically, this highly stylized sequence, with its burlesque echoes of Tennessee Williams, is cross-cut with a documentary-style scene elsewhere: the raucous party at which the display of penises ('General Erections') has been arranged for the voyeuristic pleasure of the bearded lady's husband: momentarily aroused, he watches the party through binoculars as his wife mounts him.

The bizarre narratives of *Pepi, Luci, Bom* are, however, no stranger than the lurid case histories of perversion and vagrancy detailed in juridical and sociological texts under Franco. Thus one legal manual on 'hooligans and homosexuals'[5] tells the story of a young lady who spies on her erstwhile suitor as he penetrates a female partner in the bushes outside their hotel, from behind and *inter menstruationem* (p. 211). It even warns husbands (such as Luci's) that given the intensity of desire amongst women they risk losing their wives to Sapphic predators (p. 209). Almodóvar's mini-narratives of pleasure and perversion could thus be seen as rereading these juridical novellas, reframing criminal scenarios within the more fanciful realm of farce.

The scene which seems perhaps to be most purely documentary is that in which Bom's band performs to an ecstatic audience a song called 'Murciana', which is dedicated to Luci. It begins: 'I love you because you're filthy'. The band are presented, as they were in real life, by drag queen Fabio or Fanny McNamara, who stumbles ecstatically through an incomprehensible English introduction. A performer in Almodóvar's first three films, Fabio is (like Alaska, Costus, and Almodóvar himself) a key figure in the Madrid *movida* which *Pepi, Luci, Bom* is thought to document. But the social movement, like the film, is riven with contradiction. In José Luis Gallero's affectingly eccentric oral history of the *movida*,[6] one witness cites Almodóvar as testimony to the 'typically Southern' spontaneity and superficiality of Spain, so different from the dogged seriousness of the Germans or Japanese (p. 15). But Almodóvar himself refers to the nightclubs of the period as 'vehicles of experimentation', even 'great universities' (p. 9). And while Fabio stresses that the *movida* should not be expected to leave tangible remains behind it, that it was not like entering a profession (p. 318), other participants stress how educated people were at the time (even Fabio himself). One campaigner against penal conditions in Spain, versed in Deleuze and Guattari, became a pop music journalist (p. 92); Santiago Auserón, lead vocalist with Radio Futura (the best known 'modern' pop group), returned to Madrid from Paris, where he had been studying for a PhD on Artaud (p. 95). Gallero asks philosopher Fernando Savater and novelist Francisco Umbral to add their stories to his collection (neither prove terribly helpful).

Far from being spontaneous, then, the *movida* was thus born out of a certain self-consciousness: tired of being subordinate to the hegemony of New York or London, artists and self-publicists in Madrid set out reactively to create a punk-style do-it-yourself culture in which home-grown locations such as the Costus house stood in for better known antecedents such as the Warhol factory (p. 152). As Vicente Molina Foix suggests (p. 59), *Pepi, Luci, Bom* was at once historic and prophetic in this process: it both harked back to traditional forms (*zarzuela* and even picaresque) and pointed forward to the new marginal figures (such as Alaska) who were soon to be stars of the mass media. In this complex evolution, as in British punk once more, the role of the media was ambiguous. On the one hand, a diverse group of people (who always denied that they belonged to a movement) were reduced to a more or less homogeneous group: subtlety and irony were lost. On the other hand, novice filmmakers or musicians benefited from the oxygen of early publicity. Carmen Maura recounts how the first script of *Pepi, Luci, Bom* was read by critic Diego Galán before shooting had even begun (Vidal, p. 17). When the completed film was finally released, some two years later, Galán duly proclaimed it in *El País* to be a 'unique work', displaying a freshness and comedy absent from all but a small number of Spanish films (Barcelona, 30 October 1980). There was thus a certain complicity between 'modern' artists and the newly democratic press, anxious for home-grown cultural product which might head off an increasingly dominant Hollywood. Galán ends his review by calling for greater financial support for Spanish films such as *Pepi, Luci, Bom*, the only defence against 'mediocre, Yankee melodramas'.

I would suggest, then, that the much remarked 'freshness' of *Pepi, Luci, Bom* resulted not only from its chronicling of a new sociological model 'beyond the camera', but also from its articulation, however unwitting, of new forms of representation. Just as Costus combined uncompromising subjects (the rawly sexual male nudes of the 'Chulos' series) with a variety of painterly techniques (from crude caricature to photorealism),[7] so Almodóvar offered a lurid account of a previously unknown subculture, but one couched in a knowing and ironic form. As Alberto Fernández Torres remarked in art-movie journal *Contracampo*, the film's overt break ('ruptura') with the past, its embrace of artificiality and caricature, its appeal to ugly aesthetics, ungainly camerawork, and disrupted continuity, its desire, finally, to appear 'a disconnected babble' and to 'break with the formal logic of cinematic discourse', all this is in fact itself artificial; for (argues Fernández Torres) the self-conscious inversion of artifice remains artifice.[8]

When the film was shown at the San Sebastián festival, Almodóvar claimed humor-ously that 'when a film has one defect, people say it's badly made; but when it has many, they say it has invented a new style' (Vidal, p. 38). The joke hides a serious point. For the difficulty of representation is twofold in *Pepi, Luci, Bom*: it suggests both the impossibility of being banal,[9] when error is recuperated as style; and the impossibility of being spontaneous, when arrant ugliness is read as the mirror image (as the same) of professional production values.

TRANSITION OR RUPTURE?

POLICÍA: Esto es para que veas como está el país.
POLICEMAN: This is so you'll see what a state the country's in.

The first general elections since the Civil War (resulting in a 'centrist' UCD government) were held on 15 June 1977. The attempted anti-democratic coup led by Colonel Tejero took place on 23 February 1981. The lengthy gestation of *Pepi, Luci, Bom* is framed by these two historical milestones: the script was developed in 1977, while the film was shot at weekends when finance permitted over a period of eighteen months, and was finally released on 27 October 1980. It would clearly be foolish to look for direct connections between discrete events in that period and a work as chaotic and corrosive as *Pepi, Luci, Bom*. But it is surely legitimate to ask what ideological investments are to be found in the comic cacophony of a film made at a time characterized by such dramatic historical changes.

One answer is that the film's very existence testifies to a new-found and short-lived delight in freedom of expression. Revisions to the censors' code as late as 1975 (shortly before the death of Franco) included amongst a list of forbidden topics: suicide; the use of violence as a means of solving social or human problems; prostitution, sexual perversions, adultery and illicit sexual relations; abortion and anything tending to undermine the institution of marriage and the family; drug abuse and alcoholism.[10] Nudity was now permitted, as long as it was justified by the context of the whole film and was not intended to arouse passion in 'the normal viewer' (pp. 470–1). The following year a renewed edict, justified by 'the proliferation of obscene spectacles and publications' in Spain, reasserted that the production or exhibition of pornography fell under the jurisdiction of the notorious *Ley de Peligrosidad y Rehabilitación Social* (also used to harass gay men) (p. 473). In 1976 and 1977 the obligation to submit scripts for advance vetting was rescinded and replaced by mere notification to the authorities that shooting was about to commence (pp. 481, 483). Finally a new classification system of 1978 proposed the setting up of special theatres for 'S' films, defined as those which 'might offend the sensibility of the average viewer' (p. 499).

It may be more than a coincidence, then, that Almodóvar's first film should consist of a string of vignettes devoted almost exclusively to topics banned from cinema screens only a few years earlier; or that the film might seek consistently and shamelessly to offend the sensibility of the average viewer. Indeed that challenge remains potent in the nineties: on the film's belated release in the US, trade journal *Variety* reported that distribution would be hampered in many territories by the film's graphic image and soundtracks.[11] Moreover, faced with the po-faced seriousness of Francoists in newly 'democratic' guise, the frivolity of Almodóvar came to be read in itself as a political posture (Gallero, p. 12). Thus if we return to the film itself, we find an oscillation between parodic versions of historical events in linear time and utopian moments which tend to break out of any chronological sequence. For example, when the policeman confronts Luci after she has abandoned him for Bom, he demands her ID, claiming that a law passed on 1 July obliges citizens to carry their card or risk a fine of four thousand pesetas. When Luci replies that a 'real husband has no need of laws to control his wife' she is beaten to a pulp, uttering groans of pleasure all the while. The penis size competition earlier in the film, compered by Almodóvar himself, is called 'General Erections'. This is clearly a parodic pointer to the plebiscite recently celebrated when the script was written; but it is also a blatant assertion of the autonomy of pleasure and of the triumph of libidinal anarchy over the pieties of political progressives (known as *progres*). Ironically, one of the most improbable scenes of the film, the least anchored to any verifiable social context, is one Almodóvar claims to have copied from a scene he witnessed in real life: Julieta Serrano (who was to play the Mother Superior in *Entre tinieblas*) runs after a child outside El Bo nightclub at three in the morning dressed as Scarlett O'Hara (Vidal, p. 33).

Such feminine frivolities recur in the scene where Fabio McNamara, as an idiosyncratic Avon Lady decked out in blonde wig, black beret, and glitter miniskirt, drops in at the Costus's house extolling the virtues of a face mask made of fruit salad and ambushing an innocent postman as he vainly attempts to deliver a telegram. As a (literally) screaming queen, Fabio, like Scarlett O'Hara, knows no law but desire, no time but the present. It is perhaps significant that the confrontation between past oppression and modern licence is acted out only within the context of heterosexual marriage: glorious eccentrics such as Fabio encounter no such restrictions. In their flagrant unconcern for social or political arguments, such utopian scenes thus point intermittently to a definitive break with a still-pervasive Francoist inheritance, a break which is itself to be read within a political context.

Unlike in the case of Portugal, Spain had been denied a cathartic revolution at the end of its long dictatorship. As Paul Preston notes,[12] the *ruptura pactada* or negotiated break between the Francoist Movimiento and UCD had forestalled the widely expected *ruptura democrática* or swift and complete break with the dictatorship (pp. 17, 80). The transition was thus 'less a fundamental change than a political re-adaptation of certain élite forces' (p. 120). And since the new government believed that political reform, far from transforming society, rendered social reform unnecessary, disillusionment was almost immediate (p. 121). It was thus that *desencanto* and democracy were born simultaneously.

Pepi, Luci, Bom suggests initially a utopian rupture with the (heavily censored) cinema that had preceded it. As late as 1977, scenes linking the military with prostitution or homosexuality and soft-core lesbian or transsexual sequences (one involving Victoria Abril's revelation of a prosthetic penis) had been cut from Spanish-language releases (González Ballesteros, p. 348). Playing mercilessly on taboo, *Pepi, Luci, Bom* marked a new level of verbal if not visual explicitness. Moreover, technically the film seemed to mark a clean break with existing cinematic norms: when the camera pans shakily over Pepi's building, when successive sequences cheerfully flout continuity, it is as if (as in the case of Almodóvar's most often cited precedent, Warhol) the most basic syntax of cinema (of cinematography and editing) is being invented anew.

However, it might be better to read *Pepi, Luci, Bom* as a *ruptura pactada*, a negotiated break with the past. In its celebration of earlier forms of hispanicity (the *maja*, the *zarzuela*), in its fond homage to international camp (Scarlett O'Hara, the Avon Lady), the film suggests that the modernity which it proclaims so shamelessly is inextricable from the dead forms which precede it and which it claims, nonetheless, to have superseded. Just as the disenchantment of democratic Spain arose from a realization that the promised change had proved to be merely a re-adaptation, so the studied political indifference of Almodóvar's cinema derives from an acknowledgement that there could be no *tabula rasa* (on or off screen), that the traces of tradition were the very condition of possibility for future art, future lives.

READING THE BACKSTORY

PEPI: Ante ti se abre una nueva vida.
BOM: Ante ti también.
PEPI: Eso espero.
PEPI: A new life is dawning ahead of you.
BOM: Ahead of you too.
PEPI: That's what I'm hoping.

Almodóvar could hardly have picked a less auspicious moment to begin his feature career. As Antonio Vallés Copeiro notes, legislation aimed at reducing cheap and tawdry film production had led to a sharp decline in the number of domestic features made in Spain since 1977.[13] In the three years to 1980 (the year in which *Pepi, Luci, Bom* was released) the number of operative cinemas in Spain had fallen by more than 10 per cent and, more importantly perhaps, the share of the gross taken by domestic films had plummeted from almost 30 per cent to just over 20 per cent (p. 178). The considerable increase in the box office taken by the smaller remaining number of cinemas was deceptive: it was achieved only by a near-doubling of the average ticket price. While some of this decline could be attributed to transnational factors whose effect in Spain had been somewhat delayed (the increasing penetration of television and video, the 'domestication' of leisure habits), another factor was unique to Spain: the sudden influx of foreign films previously prohibited by the Francoist censor. Ominously, this disastrous scenario seemed unaffected by a considerable increase in state support for the industry, which rose from 458 to 1,165 million pesetas (p. 179). It was a pattern of expenditure and decline which would be reversed only temporarily throughout the course of the eighties.

Pepi, Luci, Bom was far indeed from receiving state support. Unlike most Spanish directors, the self-taught Almodóvar (coming as he did from a modest, provincial background) had not had the opportunity of attending the state film school. The film was initially funded by the 'cooperative' who made it (and who received no salary for doing so) and was completed only with the financial support of independent producer Pepón Coromina, who insisted on taking a hefty share of the profits. Almodóvar himself claims to have made nothing from a film which was subsequently shown on Spanish television and in many foreign markets (Vidal, p. 24). It was a perilous financial position which would end only with the setting up of El Deseo, S.A. to produce his sixth feature in-house.

What Almodóvar had indeed understood, however, was that if cinema attendance was no longer a mass phenomenon, more marginal audiences would become increasingly important, both commercially and aesthetically. Like Malcolm McLaren and Vivienne Westwood in Britain in the previous decade, he was in a position to exploit a subculture which (like the punk which was its greatest influence) 'interacted with the media, music, and fashion industries'.[14] *Pepi, Luci, Bom* thus anticipated Almodóvar's subsequent career not only in the development of its themes (female friendship, the impossibility of the couple), but in its placing of cinema within a multi-media context undreamt of by mainstream Spanish film.

The historical moment which gave rise to such potent mixtures is now heavily mythologized: when *Pepi, Luci, Bom* was recently shown on network television the preview writer spoke of an 'orgy of fun and creativity', a 'jewel of freshness and spontaneity', a time when Almodóvar 'was still free'.[15] But if the key note is one of mourning for a time and place now definitively lost, it seems important to stress what remains of the *movida*. One survivor is Alaska, the teenage punkette who has continued to pursue a successful musical career and is now the owner of one of Madrid's most fashionable nightclubs. At thirty, Alaska still serves as a focus for 'alternative' discourses in the capital and provides evidence of cultural connections inconceivable in Britain or the US. For example, a recent interview appearing in Barcelona-based monthly *Ajoblanco* shares space with a lengthy posthumous text by philosopher Félix Guattari.[16] And there are curious coincidences between the two figures. Both reject the 'passivity' of media-hypnotized audiences; both call for a renaissance of active subjects who will speak back to technology; both decry racism and homophobia. While Alaska's current concern for ecology and animal rights may seem a long way from *Pepi, Luci, Bom*'s cult of urban squalor, it bears witness nonetheless to what she continues to call a 'punk' ethos which bases creativity on found materials, on the marshalling of whatever resources are available for cultural intervention: 'The punk principle of "Do it yourself": what you want doesn't exist, you don't have what you want, just do it . . . the [technical or financial] means matter less than the way in which you act' (p. 46).

It was a principle that Almodóvar turned to good use in *Pepi, Luci, Bom*. But it is also a model of political and cultural intervention which (as in the case of punk) has no means of negotiating the alliances it seeks between multiple, minimally competent subjects or groups. It is significant in this context that Bom, the character played by Alaska, has no visible family. Of the motley cast of the film only Carmen Maura's Pepi is provided with a father, and he is but an occasional, nagging voice on the telephone. Triumphantly devoid of 'backstories' (of the imaginary histories constructed for film and television characters to give them 'depth') Almodóvar's fabulous eccentrics live only for the moment and revel in their superficiality. In this they are akin to Spaniards of the transition, miraculous orphans deprived of a dreaded and ridiculed Father, whom they would prefer to disavow.

But Almodóvar's cinema is also founded on another exclusion and one much less visible to foreign audiences: his rejection of the leftist critics of Franco, known contemptuously as *progres*. In one of his very first interviews he is anxious to point to the difference between the liberal, bourgeois protagonists of mainstream Spanish film of the time (the example of Carlos Saura comes to mind) and his own preference for suburbanites and hooligans.[17] In the final shot of *Pepi, Luci, Bom*, Carmen Maura and Alaska, gaudy in pink tights and poodle haircuts, walk across an urban motorway, arm in arm, promising each other a new life after their recent misadventures. It is a new beginning also for a somewhat staid and worthy Spanish cinema. It will have some trouble assimilating a defiantly contemporary filmmaker as contemptuous as his characters of aesthetic conventions and political pieties.

NOTES

1. A sympathetic review by 'A.F.' in the Spanish trade journal *Cineinforme* (no. 46, November 1980) agreed with Almodóvar that the film was feminist. It was reviewed next to an Italian import released as *Reprimidos y cachondos* (Repressed and Randy), typical of the soft-core exploitation films flooding the Spanish market at the time.

2. 'Guión original', Madrid 1981. None of Almodóvar's scripts has been published; I cite each of them in the original typescript.

3. Almodóvar's graphically scatological depiction of sexual relations between women is thus far indeed from the aestheticizing tendencies of English-language art movies of the same period criticized by Mandy Merck: '*Lianna* and the Lesbians of Art Cinema', in *Perversions: Deviant Readings*, London 1993, pp. 162–76.

4. The Francoist identification of family and state was of course all-pervasive. A moral manual for Guardia Civil entrants develops an extended metaphor between the 'patria' and the 'mother' from whose innards men draw sustenance: Academia Faro, *Curso de aspirantes a oficial (primera fase): educación moral*, Madrid 1971, p. 5.

5. Antonio Sabater Tomás, *Gamberros, homosexuales, vagos, y maleantes: estudio jurídico-sociológico*, Barcelona 1961. I would like to thank Jorge Salessi for very kindly giving me a copy of this work.

6. *Sólo se vive una vez: esplendor y ruina de la movida madrileña*, Madrid 1991.

7. See the catalogue to the travelling exhibition edited by Jeremy Lewison, *New Spanish Figuration: Paintings by Chema Cobo, Costus, Luis Gordillo, Guillermo Pérez Villalta*, Cambridge 1982.

8. *Contracampo*, no. 18, January 1981, p. 73.

9. I take the phrase from Gianni Olla, 'L'impossibilità di essere banale', in Sergio Naitza and Valeria Patané, *¡Folle, folle, folle, Pedro!*, Cagliari 1992, pp. 25–32. I would like to thank Agustín Almodóvar for very kindly giving me a copy of this book.

10. Teodoro González Ballesteros, *Aspectos jurídicos de la censura cinematográfica en España*, Madrid 1981.

11. 'Suze.', 3 December 1990. The reviewer claims that 'archivists, cinephiles, and hardcore Almodóvar fans [are] the only ones likely to ever see the pic.'

12. *The Triumph of Democracy in Spain*, London 1986.

13. *Historia de la política de fomento del cine español*, Valencia 1992, p. 177.

14. Jon Savage, *England's Dreaming: Sex Pistols and Punk Rock*, London 1991, p. 69.

15. Anonymous, *Guía El País*, 19 December 1992.

16. José Ribas, 'Alaska', *Ajoblanco*, 47, December 1992, pp. 40–50; Félix Guattari, 'Por una refundación de las prácticas sociales', pp. 32–9.

17. Juan I. Francia and Julio Pérez Perucha, 'Primera película: Pedro Almodóvar', *Contracampo*, no. 23, September 1981, 5–7 (p. 6).

2

LABERINTO DE PASIONES

(LABYRINTH OF PASSION, 1982)

Cult Film Experiences

SEXUAL INDIFFERENCE

Madrid es la ciudad más divertida del mundo.
Madrid is the most amusing city in the world.

SCENE 1. RASTRO. EXTERIOR. DAY.

General view of a Sunday morning in the Rastro. . . . Riza Niro admires the extraordinary variety of objects and people he comes across. He is a young Arab, dressed so as not to appear a tourist, but without success. In spite of his European clothing his Arab origins are apparent. . . . It is also obvious that he is trying to pass unnoticed. Amongst the multitude of admirable things on his way one particularly attracts his attention: the crotches of the guys he encounters. Riza's eyes watch nothing else. (Cross-cuts between crotches and his eyes.) A few yards behind him Sexilia is also walking. Big dark glasses, pinkish, pale complexion, young, sensitive, blonde, exceptionally attractive, as modern inside as she is outside. Her eyes, behind the glasses, go from crotch to crotch, with identical admiration to those of Riza.[1]

The playful first sequence of Almodóvar's second feature not only serves to establish the two main characters (Riza, the gay exiled son of the ex-Emperor of Tiran; Sexi, the nymphomaniac pop star); it also suggests immediately the question of sexual indifference.[2] Cross-cutting between the man's and the woman's 'identical' looks at anonymous male bodies, the editing suggests that there is no distinction between the two, that the crotches are offered indifferently to heterosexual and homosexual voyeurs, in the market or in the cinema. A graphic match between the two characters serves to identify them further: both hide their lascivious glances behind dark glasses. Riza pauses for a moment to examine a stall loaded with mirror shades, and his image is repeated and fragmented in them. It is a telling image in a film which will stress the multiplicity of identities and their tendency to uncontrollable reproduction.

Riza is next shown at the terrace of a bar, whose clientele is described in the script with characteristic promiscuity as 'drug addicts, dealers, high-class queens who've just got out of bed, trendy kids from the provinces etc.' (p. 1). Reading *El País*, Riza focuses on three articles, shown to the spectator by inserts: the first announces the flight of the Emperor of Tiran to Paraguay; the second reveals that a Spanish biogynaecologist has succeeded in cloning canaries; the third advertises a new opus by 'world-famous porn star Patty Diphusa'.[3] In the deliriously complex plot which follows these three fragments will prove to be intimately linked. By an extraordinary coincidence, Patty her/himself (played by Fabio or Fanny McNamara) is sitting at a neighbouring table, where he enjoys simultaneously two drinks and snorts of nail varnish. He cries exultantly '¡Qué overdose!' Catching sight of the darkly handsome Riza, he loudly asks the waiter to take over a note for him. The note promises to make Riza happy this evening, playing on Spanish *feliz* and 'Liz Taylor': 'Me guxtaría hacerte feLiz (Taylor) exta noche.' It is an offer the smirking and straight-acting Riza cannot refuse. As he walks out of frame with the perilously camp Fabio tottering beside him, the camera lingers once more on 'modern girl' Sexi, who is making arrangements to take home a dozen or so men for an orgy. Riza and Sexi thus share the frame for a moment, but will not meet until much later in the film. It is a technique of which Almodóvar makes significant use in this crazy comedy.

Homo- and heterosexuality are thus juxtaposed and rendered equivalent: in the crowded streets of what the film calls 'the most amusing city in the world' there is infinite opportunity for sexual encounters. The gay-coded activity of cruising is thus extended to straight women: indeed, nymphomaniac Sexi's conquests are yet more anonymous and random than those of the gay characters in the film. The question unanswered by this opening sequence is whether Almodóvar can account for the specificity of gay, male experience in the city, or whether it is assimilated into a ubiquitous and generalized jouissance. The biogynaecologist proves to be Sexi's father.

And like the cloned canaries, the multiple partners of *Laberinto de pasiones* suggest replication without differentiation, reproduction without difference.

Iván Zulueta's poster for *Laberinto de pasiones* features a big red heart, curiously reminiscent of a pair of buttocks; and this anatomical anomaly is combined with a collage at the bottom of the poster of cartoon characters.[4] And throughout the film the heterogeneity of collage works against the uniformity of replication. Thus in the English-language press book synopsis Almodóvar himself warns the spectator that the film is made up of 'music, oral violence, persecutions [i.e. chases], changes of image, obesity . . ., remedies for people with dry lips and weak fingernails'. In an interview also in the press book, he claims there are some fifty characters in the film, thus enabling him to 'give the impression of possessing a tremendous imagination' without having to 'go too deeply' into any single one of them. The fact remains, however, that the two main characters (who are later to fall in love) are indeed endowed for the first time in Almodóvar with psychological motivation for their joyfully anarchic promiscuity. Thus when Toraya the ex-Empress of Tiran (and thus stepmother of Riza) visits Sexi's gynaecologist father (Plate 2) the latter reveals (in flashback) that Sexi's nymphomania derives from a childhood trauma which took place when he (the father) rejected his daughter on the beach in order to meet with the Emperor, who had a particular interest in his work. The full story of this primal scene is revealed only at the end of the film; and it is clearly parodic, citing similar 'complexes' in Hitchcock or (less evidently) Bertolucci's melodrama of incestuous romance *La Luna* (Vidal, p. 59).

Having identified her father with the sun, Sexi can no longer face daylight. The meaning of her condition is explained to Sexi by her obese Argentinian psychoanalyst, who claims to be 'of the Lacanian school'. But here performance is of the essence. For at no point in the film does Cecilia Roth's Sexi appear disabled by her condition; indeed she assumes it with some relish. Ofelia Angélica's psychoanalyst is a figure of fun, tossing sweets into her mouth or ironing as she conducts the session, vainly pursuing a hopeless attempt to get Sexi's sexless father into bed. The provision of 'deep' psychology is thus burlesque; but Almodóvar asks us, nonetheless, to identify with the central couple in their odyssey towards therapeutic catharsis and heterosexual monogamy. It is a journey which could hardly be considered characteristic of Almodóvar or his films.

MECHANICAL REPRODUCTION

HASSAN (a Sadec): ¿Crees que tus mariconadas son más impor-
tantes que el destino de todo un pueblo?
HASSAN (to Sadec): Do you really think your queer affairs are
more important than the fate of an entire nation?

Sexi's father has devoted his life to seriality: but he has produced only cloned canaries that cannot sing and a 'monstrous' test-tube baby, who is verbally abused by her far from doting mother (the caustic Eva Siva). And as the film develops, this playful critique of reproductive technologies is extended to other characters. Thus Queti (Marta Fernández Muro) is the gawky and wimpish daughter of the dry cleaner to whom Sexi brings her extravagant costumes. Abandoned by his wife, her father confuses Queti with her mother; and armed with aphrodisiac ('Vitapens') he rapes Queti every other day, tying her to the bed before he does so. When she protests that she is his daughter not his wife, he replies that she has a split personality: but even if she had four personalities instead of two he would love them all equally. In spite of the jaunty music playing over this scene, it remains disquieting. The sequence not only announces the theme of incest which will recur later; it also confirms the sense of endless replication in *Laberinto de pasiones*, of the multiplication of relationships and identities both inside and outside the family. The process will only come to a halt when Queti has chosen to exchange her tawdry life for that of another and undertake a more glamorous, yet equally incestuous, romance.

Another early scene confronts the technologies of heterosexual reproduction with more spontaneous homosexual structures. Toraya, the ex-empress, makes a telephone call from a booth in the street. Its purpose is to procure a sample of her former husband's semen now she has been rendered fertile by Sexi's doctor father. As she discusses this delicate transaction with her agent in the emperor's entourage, we see Riza walk past Sadec (a youthful Antonio Banderas) behind the phone booth. Riza is wearing a curly wig, the ostentatious sign of anonymity. Almodóvar cross-cuts in medium close-up between the pick-up and the telephone call, and then cuts to a long shot of all three in the frame together. Just as in the opening scene at the Rastro Riza and Sexi are juxtaposed but do not coincide, so here Riza and his stepmother are brought together unawares: the script specifies that the men's encounter takes place 'behind the princess's back' (p. 19). And as in the previous scene, once more the axis of difference between the characters is homo- and heterosexual. But here there is also a hint of complicity between the two milieux juxtaposed on screen. When her informant advises her to look for Riza in the queer bars and saunas of Madrid, Toraya does not register shock but rather displays a delighted, even simpering smile on her well-glossed lips. Behind her Riza and Sadec set off for the latter's flat.

After they have had sex, Riza flees from Sadec's flat (which boasts posters of Julio Iglesias, Bruce Lee, and the Ayatollah Khomeini) when he discovers that Sadec and his companions are Tiranian terrorists, and thus sworn enemies of his father. Toraya is thus joined by Sadec in a parallel but separate search for Riza. Glamorously cross-dressed in blue suit and fedora, Toraya cruises gay Madrid in search of her stepson. In a montage sequence she is shown checking out the men in a park and along the central Castellana avenue. The script, however, goes further with the ex-empress venturing into a crowded gay disco and even an equally well-attended public lavatory (p. 54). In this unfilmed sequence Toraya and Sadec meet outside the cottage, and both confess they are 'looking for someone'. The quest for lover and (step)son is once more compared, rendered indifferent.

In *Tearoom Trade*, his classic sociological study of gay public sex in the US, Laud Humphreys describes his adoption of the role of 'watch queen'.[5] Aware that a hostile heterosexual observer would have no hope of examining the subculture he was studying, he chose to take up a position within that subculture. The watch queen has two looks. The first is internal and is directed to the spectacle of gay male sex within the toilet; the watch queen does not participate in the action but derives pleasure from looking and intensifies the pleasures of those looked at. The second look is external and is directed to the straight world outside the toilet; here he acts as lookout, anticipating and forestalling incursions by police or queer-bashers (pp. 26–30).

The duality of the watch queen (both voyeur and lookout) suggests a model for Almodóvar's oblique attitude to homosexuality in *Laberinto de pasiones*. For on the one hand, he represents for the pleasure of a gay audience sympathetic and naturalistic scenes of same-sex encounters between, say, Riza and Sadec (the latter played by Antonio Banderas as boyishly innocent and attractive). On the other hand, he antici-pates and disarms potential hostility from a straight audience, suggesting through cinematography and editing that hetero- and homosexuality are identical (sexually indifferent), and declining to film those unambiguous scenes of gay gratification he allowed himself in the private space of a script which remains unpublished. Just as the tearoom is a space in which (in Laud Humphreys's words) one can be 'in private in public' (p. 11), so the hermetic space of Almodóvar's city of eccentrics offers a public forum for the performance of private (gay) preoccupations at the same time as it screens (protects) that performance from unsympathetic eyes.

Riza will prove to be bisexual and is 'cured' of his love of men by Sexi. While Anglo-American critics have taken this as being somehow atypical of Almodóvar,[6] it is in fact characteristic of the scepticism towards the idea of homosexuality as a discrete libidinal territory which recurs throughout Almodóvar's work. As gay Valencian novelist Lluís Fernández warned in a text published in the same year *Laberinto de pasiones* was released,[7] the new tolerance officially marked by the abolition of the *Ley de peligrosidad social* threatened to erase ('tachar') the only identity history had offered Spanish gay men, that of illegality. In *Laberinto de pasiones* Almodóvar reconfirms that critique of identity politics found in Catalan and Castilian gay liberation of the 1970s;[8] and moreover he reproduces, in burlesque mode, topics of the old disciplinary model of homosexuality current under Franco. Thus Spanish doctors of the 1960s claimed that gay relationships were 'unviable';[9] and were precipitated by male disgust with 'the degraded state of [Spanish] womanhood'.[10] (In *Laberinto de pasiones* Riza's love of men, we learn, is caused by a childhood disappointment with future nymphomaniac Sexi.) Fortunately, however, 'a proportion of homosexuals can return to normality if they are pushed [*empujar*] by the friendly hand of a psychotherapist or priest' (p. vii). In the unlikely guise of a confessor or doctor, Almodóvar manipulates his characters, causing them to crisscross the divide between the perverse and the normal with bewildering rapidity and conspicuous pleasure.

José Luis Gallero's oral history of the *movida* notes time and again the importance of gay men in the emergence of that cultural scene of which *Laberinto de pasiones* is so clearly a part. But it also reconfirms the hostility of that scene to any political intervention whatsoever. One witness recounts that when confronted in a bar by a request to sign a petition proffered by the 'typical bearded [activist] queen', Fabio McNamara tore up the paper, proclaiming enigmatically 'Killer, tío, killer'; a phrase interpreted as meaning 'Stop all that queer stuff [*mariconadas*] with signatures'. Fabio's mix of theatricality and audacity is said to be a typical 'gesture' of the *movida*.[11] Whether the anecdote is true or not, the word 'gesture' is significant here. For in *Laberinto de pasiones* it is Fabio once more who embodies a gestural homosexuality which may prove to be an oblique locus of subversion. Buck-toothed and skinny, barely covered by skimpy patches of fun fur and a diamante g-string, Fabio as Patty Diphusa is in one sequence shown reaching ecstasy with an electric drill. It is a shoot for a porno photonovel in which Almodóvar himself plays 'the director'. When Riza comes to the studio seeking Fabio's advice on how to change his image the latter, claiming implausibly to be a skilled 'esthéticienne', gives pointedly useless guidance on women's hair-styles of the 1950s. Fabio also pretends to speak French (the sequence defeats the subtitlers). But what is important (what is comic) about this sequence is not simply its stress on the virtuality of identity, which the characters change as easily as their wigs. It is also the conflict between modes of performance exemplified by the actors. Almodó-var has spoken of Imanol Arias's overly conscientious approach to his craft, of his intense pursuit of naturalistic behaviour and motivation (Vidal, p. 50). Fabio, on the other hand, is so unskilled an actor that he must be directed from within the frame, and even then he adopts a uniquely stylized monotone. The clash of acting styles thus implies a conflict of modes of identity within the film with Arias-Riza playing straight (in all senses) as the sympathetic, traumatized lover and Fabio-Patty barely acting at all, and yet offering a grandly gestural performance which is gloriously comic. It is a performance which in its gleeful repetition of found materials (its energetic mimicry of foreign languages) points up the generic confusion of *Laberinto de pasiones*, its tireless collaging of diverse media.

BEYOND ALL REASON

Seven–7 Up/Eight–After 8/Nine–9 to 5
('Suck it to me')

When *Laberinto de pasiones* was released in September 1982 Spanish critics found it difficult to place. Diego Galán in *El País* called it 'confused', and argued that aesthetic effects which resulted merely from a low budget should not be mistaken for genuine artistic innovation.[12] Using a culinary metaphor characteristic of critics' response to the film, Jorge de Cominges in *El Noticiero Universal* called it a 'spicy dish, but somewhat indigestible, seasoned with an adopted "gay" sensibility' (23 October 1982). Also bracketed off by scare quotes in his review are the words 'moderno' and 'punk'. Confronted by a defiantly chaotic and aggressively heterogeneous work, critics sensed that it was the product of a contemporary subculture, but were unable to decide which one. As the film receded into a cultural history which changed in Spain by the moment its context was further obscured: previewed for its first showing on network television (at the significant time of 1 a.m.), it is described by J. Batllé Caminal as 'pasota'. The term is, however, more characteristic of the immediate post-Franco disillusion with politics some years earlier.[13]

Scenes which retain the strongest impression of actuality are those filmed in the Carolina nightclub (Plate 3). Two musical numbers are featured in this location. 'Suck it to me' stars Almodóvar and Fabio, the former in fish-net stockings, the latter in glitter drag. The second is lip-synched by Imanol Arias's Riza, resplendent in streaked hair and punkish tartan trousers. It is called 'Gran Ganga' (Big Bargain). 'Suck it to me' contains a paean to drug abuse and (more importantly perhaps) a parody list of random associations with English numerals: 'Seven–7 Up' etc. Just as Fabio the pretend make-up artist mimics French beauty terms, so here Fabio the would-be pop star plunders North American consumerism. But as in all bricolage, elements change their meaning when placed in a new context; and it would be naive to take such overt references as denoting a wholesale rejection of indigenous Spanish culture. The trace of punk, conspicuous in the music, costumes, and even graphic style of the film, is a case in point. Gallero's oral history repeatedly returns to the British example of spontaneous cultural intervention which preceded the *movida*. But his sources confess that their movement lacked the fierce social critique of punk: Spaniards were just too amiable for their own good. More frivolous and more readily coopted than punk (or so its survivors claim here) the *movida* was the product of a period of economic and cultural expansion and was not born out of a British-style reaction against mass unemployment and national decline (p. 12). Almodóvar himself notes that the amiable anarchy of the time was the result not of resistance to authority, but (on the contrary) of a celebration of *desgobierno* or lawlessness: the so-called centrist UCD government, discredited inheritors of Franco, staggered to electoral defeat at the hands of the Socialist PSOE soon after *Laberinto de pasiones* was released (Vidal, pp. 39–40). The relentless good humour of the film (which confronts rape, incest, and terrorism with disconcerting equanimity) thus testifies to a historical moment which could not be further from punk pessimism.

And precedents for *Laberinto de pasiones*'s sunny pop style are Spanish as well as foreign. *Movida* veterans mention the trip to Madrid by Barcelona-based cartoon artist Nazario as decisive (Gallero, p. 155). And Nazario's short graphic narratives (*historietas*) clearly share a sensibility with Almodóvar.[14] Thus Nazario is indiscriminately eclectic, citing sources as diverse as Greek mythology and cookery books. Yet he also bears witness to specifically Spanish gay concerns: a notably graphic 'Pansies' Alphabet' ('Abecedario para mariquitas') includes not only icons well known to English speakers such as Monroe and Dietrich, but less familiar Hispanic figures like Juana Reina and the Virgin of the Rocío. And in his love of 'odd women' ('mujeres raras') Nazario shares Almodóvar's use of female figures as vehicles for his own concerns. He thus produces a pornographic *mélange* quite alien to his opposite numbers outside Spain (such as Tom of Finland), whose more conservative gay male clientele would be unlikely to welcome such detailed and profuse exploration of female bodies. One *historieta* even features a glamorous mother in search of a perverse child who (like Almodóvar's Toraya) speaks in a delirious mixture of Romance languages.[15]

It is at the concert in the Carolina that Sexi finally falls for Riza: his performance is cross-cut with her rapturous reaction shots, signalling the eventual triumph of an (ironized and qualified) straight gaze over the perverse spectacle of the first half of the film. *Laberinto de pasiones* thus appears to contradict the emphasis of other cult films or midnight movies which tend to reveal an enduring fascination with sexual ambiguity.[16] Fabio and Sadec are abandoned by the end of the movie when Riza and Niro, finally free of their neuroses, consummate their true (heterosexual) love for one another on a flight to Panama. But the cult movie is the one genre flexible enough to accommodate a film as wilfully diverse and perverse as *Laberinto de pasiones*. As J. P. Tellotte suggests, the cult movie is a 'supertext', lacking fixed limits and favouring 'boundary crossings or territorial "violations"'.[17] And those who love films such as *The Rocky Horror Picture Show* 'beyond all reason' (the phrase is Andrew Sarris's) take their transgressive pleasure in a 'blurring of genre forms' (p. 8). The cult movie's impoverished conditions of production (its appeal to spontaneous bricolage in mise-en-scène or art design) help define an audience who find in the privileged knowledge they share a certain promise of freedom as an improvised pseudo-religious community (pp. 11–13). Tellotte thus finds dual impulse in the cult, linked etymologically to both cultivation and worship: the audience must first labour to create the experience themselves, but once the film's cult status is confirmed they must submit to its aura. The cult movie thus cannot be thought outside its conditions of production and consumption, can exist only as 'experience' (p. 16). Testifying to the irrational territory beyond good taste and mainstream mechanisms, it thus promotes both transgression and containment, taking up a fragile and provisional place 'at the heart of the limit' (p. 16).

Timothy Corrigan compares the cult film to an 'adopted child'; it was not destined from birth for its final form, but rather suffered a certain deviation from its natural course.[18] And it is perhaps no accident that *Laberinto de pasiones* is also the story of a stepson: Riza finally encounters and is seduced by his father's first wife, Toraya. Certainly, the wayward paths of *Laberinto de pasiones*'s many characters are matched only by Almodóvar's indiscriminate generic allusions, which recognize no borders, no violations of good taste. Similarly, the history of the film's production has become public property and has come to be savoured by its audience: Almodóvar has often told of how he was forced to paint the sets himself to the designs of artist Guillermo Pérez Villalta. The choice casting of Helga Liné, veteran of innumerable B movies, also establishes a link with cult tradition and works to engage a select audience's sympathy. With its frequent explicit references to sex, drugs, and pop music *Laberinto de pasiones* set itself up as marginal, implacably opposed to the timorous mainstream of Spanish film. Indeed, apparently threatened by Almodóvar's very conspicuous trendiness, Diego Galán is moved to claim in his review that established auteurs Carlos Saura and Manuel Gutiérrez Aragón remain the most 'modern' of Spanish filmmakers. Yet that marginality, that transgression for which the film so clearly strives, is vitiated by the very self-consciousness of its quest for amorality. Destined all too clearly for culthood, it was rejected by established critics and achieved its final status only when taken to its heart, like an adopted child, by later, more sympathetic audiences.

MAKING AN EXHIBITION

TORAYA: La historia di questo secolo ha sido molto ingiusta con me.

TORAYA: The history of ce siècle has been très injuste with moi.

Unlike the shoestring finances of *Pepi, Luci, Bom*, *Laberinto de pasiones* had a workable if modest budget given by Peter Besas as \$175,000.[19] And its production values were higher. Where *Pepi* was notorious for its poor-quality sound, the engineer on *Laberinto* was Martin Müller, known for his work with Wim Wenders.[20] *Laberinto de pasiones* was initially a modest commercial success, grossing almost sixty million pesetas in the first year of release, and being seen by almost a quarter of a million spectators.[21] By way of comparison, the biggest-grossing film of that year was *La colmena* (The Beehive), Mario Camus's reverent adaptation of a period literary classic, which reached an audience of one and a half million.

However, it would be unjust to claim with hostile critics such as Caparrós Lera that *Laberinto de pasiones* 'did not please the public' (p. 224); for it has played continuously at late-night showings in Madrid throughout the ten years since its release. And here exhibition is of the essence. For *Laberinto* could not have been made without the participation of the Alphaville cinemas in central Madrid. Javier Garcillán and Mariel Guiot had opened two screens in 1977 and two more in 1979. A bar was added in 1980 (a vital resource in a city as sociable as the Spanish capital).[22] Initially intended as a home for the US independents and French new-wave films imported by Musidora, the couple's distribution company (and dedicated, uniquely in Madrid, to showing such films in subtitled versions), the Alphaville, established a unique setting for the exhibition of non-mainstream cinema, avoiding the dull pieties of earlier art houses (known in Spain as *cines de arte y ensayo*).

Guiot compares the business of exhibition to the rag trade: the finished film, which may appear complete to the public, still requires to be 'dressed', tricked out in the proper apparel to promote itself and attract its own audience. *Laberinto de pasiones* was Alphaville's first venture into production; and there is no doubt that Almodóvar's early films benefited enormously from the loving treatment they received at Guiot's hands. Moreover, it was Alphaville which initiated the late-night screenings hitherto unknown in Madrid, thus securing almost unlimited runs for both *Pepi, Luci, Bom* and *Laberinto*, now redefined (reclothed) in the garb of a previously unknown genre: the midnight or cult movie. Almodóvar has generously admitted the debt, comparing Alphaville to an old-fashioned book shop to which one went not only to buy merchandise but also to enjoy and to discuss it; and he claims that the cinema was quite literally his home. As a refuge from the commercial concerns of the mainstream, the Alphaville retains for Almodóvar the 'possibility of adventure' in a cinematic Madrid full of dead ends.

The significance of the Alphaville is thus that it helped to create a shared cinematic sensibility which engaged both novice filmmakers and spectators. And its continued existence at a time when the art circuit in the US and UK is struggling to survive helps to nurture an audience important for Almodóvar, one which shares a love of both North American and European cinema, and is responsive to both high and low culture. But Almodóvar's reference to Alphaville as 'home' is perhaps particularly significant. For his films have, from the beginning, focused on a sense of family which is (in all senses of the word) incestuous. *Laberinto de pasiones* ends with multiple incest: Riza sleeps with Toraya and the unfortunate Queti (raped by her father) is transformed by plastic surgery into her heroine Sexi, thus enabling her to consummate her passion for the latter's gynaecologist father. The film thus offers a parody of both maternity and paternity. But Almodóvar has suggested that the Oedipal scenarios burlesqued here make some genuine reference to his personal position as a son in search of an absent father: the female character with whom he claims to identify is Queti (Vidal, p. 49). As in the Patty Diphusa texts which are contemporary with the film (and in which the first-person pronoun is invariably capitalized as 'YO'), *Laberinto de pasiones* gives off a whiff of egotism which is not always pleasurable even to devoted fans. It is perhaps significant that few of the actors in *Laberinto* recur in Almodóvar's later films: the director appears to have less sympathy for them than for his other creations. This is the one film in which the characters' insistence on making an exhibition of themselves proves wearisome.

It would be a mistake, however, to suppose that *Laberinto de pasiones*'s narcissism deprives it of historical resonance. Francisco Umbral, the best known chronicler of the cultural scene at that time, has left an evocative account of the film's premiere at the Alphaville called 'Los punkis'.[23] He begins:

> They come with their hairstyles like feather dusters; they come with male rouge on scandalous lips, with thistles on their lapels and . . . dark glasses, sun glasses on a cloudy night in September – darkly, brightly they come.

Umbral displays an indulgent fascination with the glittery *Zeitgeist* of the period. But he also makes some perceptive remarks on the fashionable crowd whose names he enumerates with mock reverence. He notes that everything here is 'pre-': all is so new, so impatient, and so mobile that modernity is the sole value to be recognized. And in this modernity the psychologism and sociology of the old school of Spanish cinema are simply abandoned: there is neither reverence for psychic trauma nor concern for social injustice. Noting that everything is treated directly and openly, Umbral cites Queti-Sexi's final phone call to her psychoanalyst: 'Excuse me for hanging up: I'm in bed with my father.' Umbral describes the 'punk children' of the premiere as 'young Martians', so alien do they seem to any previous generation. But he also notes that in their eclectic thrift-shop clothing they reflect in spite of themselves the history of their mothers. Spectacular exhibitionism thus lends them a certain 'truth in [their] falsity'. Shimmering in bargain-basement lamé, they are greeted by the night, but (Umbral claims) ignored by a Madrid on the verge of the elections which are to change the face of the nation.

Umbral's ironic chronicle of the city posits a stark contrast between the self-absorption of Almodóvar's cultist crowd at the Alphaville and the momentous historical change facing Spain at that same moment. But, as we have seen, in its unwitting testimony to the collapse of governmental authority in Spain (to what Almodóvar called 'desgobierno') *Laberinto de pasiones* cannot be separated from the time which produced it. Indeed, it is in its very insistence on modernity, its refusal to contemplate the psychic, cinematic, or political past, that the film's historical dimension is to be found.

NOTES

1. 'Guión original', Madrid 1981, p. 1.

2. I borrow the term from Teresa de Lauretis, 'Sexual Indifference and Lesbian Representation', *Theater Journal*, 40, May 1988, pp. 155–77.

3. The character was created by Almodóvar for *La Luna* magazine; the texts are collected as *Patty Diphusa y otros textos*, Barcelona 1991; and translated by Kirk Anderson as *The Patty Diphusa Stories and Other Writings*, London 1992. The name is a pun: 'patidifusa' is the feminine form of an adjective meaning 'aghast' or 'nonplussed'.

4. Zulueta's posters are collected in *Pausas de papel: carteles de cine de Iván Zulueta*, Valencia 1990.

5. My edition, London 1970.

6. See the review by Gary Giddins in *Village Voice*, 23 January 1990.

7. See his prologue to the Spanish translation of Richard Dyer's *Gays and Cinema: Cine y homosexualidad*, Barcelona 1982, p. 8.

8. See my *Laws of Desire*, Oxford 1992, p. 5.

9. L. Frutos Carabias, introduction to A. M. Krich, *Los homosexuales vistos por sí mismos y por sus médicos*, Madrid 1966, p. 4.

10. A. Alvarez Villar, prologue to Krich, p. vi. Other medical accounts include Fernando Chamorro Gundín's chilling *Resultados obtenidos con técnicas proyectivas en una muestra de 200 delincuentes homosexuales españoles*, Madrid 1970; and Juan Masana's reformist *El fenómeno de la homosexualidad*, Barcelona 1971.

11. *Sólo se vive una vez*, Madrid 1991, p. 274.

12. Barcelona edition; 1 October 1982.

13. 'Pasotismo' derived from the verb *pasar*, pronounced with a sibilant 's' and meaning 'to be indifferent'; e.g. 'Yo paso de política' = 'I couldn't care less about politics.'

14. See the collection *Mujeres raras*, Barcelona 1988. My thanks are due to Josep Anton Fernández for providing me with a copy of this book.

15. 'La hija de Copi', pp. 47–53.

16. Gaylyn Studlar, 'Midnight S/Excess: Cult Configurations of "Femininity" and the Perverse', in J. P. Telotte, *The Cult Film Experience*, Austin 1987, pp. 138–55.

17. 'Introduction', *The Cult Film Experience*, p. 2.

18. 'Film and the Culture of Cult', pp. 26–37 (p. 26).

19. *Behind the Spanish Lens: Spanish Cinema under Fascism and Democracy*, Denver 1985, p. 215.

20. José Luis Guarner, review of *Laberinto de pasiones*, *El Periódico*, 22 October 1982.

21. J. M. Caparrós Lera, *El cine español de la democracia*, Barcelona 1992, p. 233.

22. Maite Rico, 'Mariel Guiot: dueña de los cines Alphaville', *El País*, 22 June 1992; Pedro Almodóvar, 'El callejón con salida'.

23. *El País*, 23 September 1982.

3

ENTRE TINIEBLAS

(DARK HABITS, 1983)

Out of the Convent

THE SUSPENSION OF INCONGRUITY

SOR RATA: Es lógico que se asuste. Es la primera vez que ve a un
tigre en un convento.

SISTER RAT: Of course she's frightened. It's the first time she's
seen a tiger in a convent.

Entre tinieblas, Almodóvar's convent comedy, was released in the UK and US as 'Dark Habits'. There could be no more telling example of the impoverishment of meaning effected by the crossing of linguistic and cultural borderlines than this (literal) travesty of the original title. For the Spanish phrase is a sombre reference to Catholic ritual: *tenebrae* are the days before Good Friday when candles are successively extinguished in church. The phrase thus implies a reinscription of religious dynamics (of sacrifice and redemption) which will prove to be typical of the film as a whole.

In the opening sequence junkie nightclub singer Yolanda (Cristina S. Pascual) returns to the chaotic apartment where her gruffly unsympathetic boyfriend dies from a heroin overdose. His livid face is reflected in the shiny surface of the floor, with Yolanda far off in the frame behind him. This mirror shot is repeated in the flashback that follows in which Yolanda is visited in her dressing-room by two nuns who claim to be devoted fans. Yolanda's red-nailed fingers use scissors to cut her boyfriend out of the photograph she autographs for the grateful sisters, who invite her to visit their convent whenever she wishes. Reflection and excision: *Entre tinieblas* is thus based on the mirroring of images of women, a symmetry which bears within it nonetheless the trace of a male principle already amputated at the start of the narrative and consistently disavowed throughout the film.

Entre tinieblas has no major male characters; and Almodóvar has spoken of his refusal to allow men to become the centre of attention in a 'women's picture' (Vidal, p. 88) and of the absolute autonomy of the nuns in the film, whose freedom is uncompromised even by God.[1] However, such (phantasmatic) liberty is not uncontested in a film whose comedy is at first articulated in the form of a series of oppositions. Thus the Spanish poster for the film (designed by cineaste Iván Zulueta) shows a tiger in nun's clothing, with a sacred heart pierced by syringes and surrounded not by the traditional flames, but by hairs. Human and bestial, secular and religious are fused in this 'clash of two worlds'.[2] And a still used for the cover of the UK press kit shows an elegantly coiffed and made-up Marquesa (veteran Mari Carrillo) gesturing extravagantly as she addresses the glum and glowering Mother Superior (Julieta Serrano) in her habit and cowl (Plate 4). In this early sequence the Marquesa, liberated by the death of her 'Fascist' husband, has come to inform the Mother Superior that she will no longer support the convent financially, but will devote her considerable income to satisfying her own pleasures. The contrast between the 'two worlds' of the worldly woman and the cloistered cleric is reinforced graphically through costume once more when Yolanda, accused of her boyfriend's murder, seeks refuge in the convent dressed in the scarlet lurex gown and gloves which she wears on stage. There is thus an additional opposition here between the spectacular exhibitionism of the sexual woman and the rigorous renunciation of visual pleasure of the woman whom we initially presume to be asexual. Yolanda's arrival would thus seem to signal an opportunity for comedy of incongruity in which the perceived opposites of sensual pleasure and spiritual asceticism are contrasted with and transformed by one another.

This is not to be the case. For the nuns (supposedly innocent of social changes outside the convent) already embody the sensual obsessions of contemporary Spain. Thus the Mother Superior is a lesbian and junkie; Sor Estiércol ('Sister Manure': Marisa Paredes) is a reformed murderess with a taste for acid-induced visions; Sor Rata ('Sister Rat': Chus Lampreave) is the author of sleazy novels (Plate 5); Sor Perdida ('Sister Sinner': Carmen Maura) has a pet tiger and a cleaning fetish; finally, Sor Víbora ('Sister Snake': Lina Canalejas) delights in designing avant-garde costumes for mannequin-like Virgins. The turn to pleasure typical of both Almodóvar and Spain of the transition is thus firmly installed within the convent before Yolanda's arrival. Hence, while much of the comedy derives from the Sisters' failure to coincide with the self-denial and discipline which might be expected of them, that distance from type is wholly taken for granted, its incongruity suspended throughout the film.

This is not to deny the shock value of certain scenes when viewed in certain contexts: *Entre tinieblas* has yet to be shown uncut in Argentina, even since the restoration of democracy.[3] But in stressing the similarities between the two main characters (as when the Mother Superior and Yolanda are both stricken by heroin-induced vomiting at their first meal together) Almodóvar chooses to sacrifice simple comedy of contrast in favour of a more complex and unsettling comedy of merger or fusion. As the Mother Superior claims at the end of the film, she has admired fallen women so much that she has become one of them herself. It is a blurring of desire and identification which will frequently recur in Almodóvar's mature cinema. The spectator, like Yolanda, is thus 'led in' to the convent and sutured into identification with her point of view through a newly sinuous and mobile camera; but, again like Yolanda, he or she is then abandoned within a space whose crazy rationale remains inexplicable. Surprised by a tiger in a convent, we can only agree with Sor Rata that fear is a logical reaction.

On its release in Britain critics were unanimous in proclaiming that *Entre tinieblas* recycled old jokes about 'naughty nuns', jokes which would only prove shocking and titillating to Spaniards accustomed to Francoist censorship.[4] This somewhat patronizing verdict not only neglected the contributions of music and performance in rendering 'naughtiness' highly serious, it also misread Spanish history. For Catalan and Spanish critics were equally unanimous in claiming that the film was not simply anti-clerical, and was more humorous than scandalous or sacrilegious.[5] An examination of successive versions of the script[6] and of the final cut of the film itself shows that parodic or farcical elements are progressively cut from the film, crucially (as we shall see) with regard to the ending.

There is little doubt that Almodóvar is, in *Entre tinieblas*, reworking traditional Spanish cinematic genres. Thus the three kinds of films sponsored by the victorious Nationalist government after the Civil War were a militaristic 'cinema of the crusade', an escapist musical 'cinema of folklore', and a pious and sentimental 'cinema of priests'.[7] Typical of the last category were Luis Lucía's *La hermana San Sulpicio* (Sister San Sulpicio, 1951) and Ladislao Vajda's *Marcelino, pan, y vino* (Marcelino, Bread, and Wine, 1954), the first a discreet account of female sexuality and spirituality, the second an unselfconsciously homoerotic tale of a small boy raised by a community of monks and rapt to heaven by a naked Christ. A certain sexual equivocation was thus already implicit in the genre of the religious film of the 1950s, as is confirmed by the testimony of a young, gay spectator such as novelist Terenci Moix.[8] Almodóvar's 'theology of trivialization' (the phrase is from Francisco Marinero's review) at once respects the conventions of the genre and adopts frivolity as a form of opposition to the official machismo which reinforced religious orthodoxy.[9] There is thus a certain irony in Almodóvar's vindication of religiosity as a sphere of autonomous feminine sexuality, an irony which can be retained only by preserving the dead forms of Catholic practice in the aspic of a respectful simulacrum. For example, when Yolanda arrives in the convent (a scene iconographically reminiscent of the Annunciation) the nuns are at mass and are singing a hymn dedicated to the Lord of life and of love, urging him to open the 'wound' in the heart. *Entre tinieblas* thus lesbianizes the patriarchal Word not by inverting or opposing it, but by suggesting that a certain space for autonomous female desire has already been opened by that Word itself. It is a tricky technique, and one which is inseparable from non-verbal resources of cinematography, costume, and music.

DIEGESIS AND RAPTURE

YOLANDA: Es la música que habla, que dice la verdad de la vida.
YOLANDA: It's the music which speaks, which tells the truth about life.

In his sympathetic review of *Entre tinieblas*, José Luis Guarner claims that, as Spain's unique pop art cineaste, Almodóvar goes beyond questions of style to fashion some perfect moments of filmic 'magic'. There is little doubt that technically *Entre tinieblas* is far more proficient that Almodóvar's two earlier features; and in addition to a carefully crafted screenplay, Almodóvar skilfully exploits the non-verbal resources of cinema to varied ends. Moreover, rapturous or 'magical' qualities absent from the dialogue are allowed to resurface in highly stylized and excessive use of mise-en-scène and music.

One resource to which Almodóvar's characters cannot have access and which cannot be acknowledged within the diegesis is camerawork. As Almodóvar noted to Nuria Vidal, this was the first film in which he made use of sinuous tracking shots (as when the camera follows the Mother Superior down the aisle of the chapel or moves slowly over the expressive faces of the nuns in chapel) (p. 67). In general, however, the shooting style is characterized by close-ups and high angles, which were at once determined by the limited spaces of the authentic location in which filming took place and intended to call attention to the characters' claustrophobia and their psychological interiority. When the Mother Superior is visited by the youthful Merche (Cecilia Roth), an ex-inmate on the run from the police, the tight framing and sharp camera angles reinforce a sense of tension and oppression: the Mother Superior stoops gravely to replace Merche's shoes as she is led away to prison. José Luis Téllez's subtle review article in *Contracampo*[10] also pays particular attention to framing. Téllez, who reproaches Almodóvar for not running what he sees as the risk of naturalism, singles out three scenes characterized by the 'preeminence of filmic enunciation', all related to the doomed love affair between the Mother Superior and Yolanda. The first is a tracking shot announcing Yolanda's arrival in the convent; the second a conversation in which the two women are framed by separate windows; the third a bolero sequence in which cinematography is matched to the rhythm of the music (p. 110). Téllez finds 'a certain intensity' in such sequences, analogous perhaps to Guarner's 'magic'. When formal device exceeds what is strictly necessary to advance the plot it thus creates the possibility of what Téllez calls a 'productivity' of the image which breaks free of its avowed referent.

The role of costume in *Entre tinieblas* also seems to participate in this productive surplus of meaning. Thus at one level costume is acknowledged by the characters and addressed within the diegesis: homely Sor Rata swoons over Yolanda's glamorous dress; matronly Sor Víbora shows off her extravagant costumes for the Virgin as if in a 'fashion show' (script, p. 59). As Yolanda remains in the convent and withdraws from heroin her clothes become less extravagant, more sober. But beyond this strictly denotative level, costume serves as a stimulus to fantastic association and identification. Thus Yolanda, Merche, and the young drug dealer who visits the Mother Superior share the colour red, contrasting with the shadowy locale of the convent. And red is also used as a visual 'hook' establishing non-verbal, associative links between separate strands of the narrative. Thus Almodóvar cuts from Yolanda's red-nailed hand clutching the nuns' visiting card, to a scarlet lipstick trace on a black and white photograph of the nuns, and to an extreme close-up of the Marquesa (who is, we are told, trained as a make-up artist) vigorously applying lipstick. The Mother Superior's renunciation of visual pleasure is thus counterbalanced by a fetishistic overvaluation of specular display in secular women: in her office are displayed as if for an altar-piece a lavish selection of photos of 'famous sinners' from Brigitte Bardot to Marilyn Monroe.

This opposition between despecularization and hyperspecularization corresponds to roles gendered as male and female in dominant cinema practice, a gendering which

Kaja Silverman relates to the historical renunciation of ornamental costume by men in the eighteenth century.[11] In a typically masculine projection, the Mother Superior spies on Yolanda as she dresses and buys her a gown to wear for a special function. Almodóvar's characters thus repeat that division of labour between voyeurism and exhibitionism conventionally equated with the gender divide; but those roles, once redistributed amongst women, prove surprisingly fluid. Hence although both women remain subject to patriarchal constraints (Yolanda to the police; the Mother Superior to her Mother General), the power play between them is flexible and reciprocal. For example, the Mother Superior uses her knowledge of the death of Yolanda's boyfriend to insist Yolanda remain in the convent; but Yolanda addresses the Mother Superior using words that her boyfriend had previously spoken to her: 'You are only a tool I am using for my own purposes.' And as Yolanda is despecularized, reduced to a modest blouse and slacks, the Mother Superior is quite literally illuminated, spotlit in the darkened chapel as she battles her pharmaceutical and amorous addictions.

If the role of costume in the film is at once denotative and connotative (pragmatic and associative) then the role of music is equally problematic. *Entre tinieblas* marks the transition between the caustic punk and pop of *Pepi, Luci, Bom* and *Laberinto de pasiones* and the sentimental boleros which dominate Almodóvar's later films. And, like costume, music looms large within the diegesis. Thus Yolanda is a nightclub singer and the Mother Superior a fellow fan of Latin American ballads. And one of the scenes singled out by critics as diverse as Téllez and Marinero is the one in which the two women sing along to a bolero called 'Encadenados' (In Chains) in the Mother Superior's office. I have written elsewhere of the cinematography in this sequence, where repeated reverse-angle close-ups in frontal position confront the spectator with an unequivocally lesbian look (Plate 5).[12] The effect is somewhat more muted in the dialogue. But also significant here is the relation between image and soundtrack. For when the music begins, Yolanda is seen in the corridor outside the Mother Superior's office and the source of the sound (the Mother Superior's record-player) has yet to be established. It is thus initially read as extra-diegetic (or 'incidental') movie music and not an intra-diegetic element emerging from within the space of the frame. When the song is repeated over the final credits it recuperates that lost extra-diegetic status, serving as a definitive and authoritative commentary on a love which has proved to be a 'martyrdom', which permits neither conclusion nor satisfaction.

There is thus a certain suspension in both the status of the music (diegetic/non-diegetic) and in the rapturous space it opens up for repetition without end: the singer tells his beloved it would be better if she did not return, better that she forget him; while insisting nonetheless that there can be no goodbyes between them, that they are chained together for ever. In his description of this scene in the 1983 version of the script Almodóvar writes: 'The music floods the room. Without speaking, both women sing along to the song, forming an operatic duo loaded with hidden meanings [*intenciones*]. Yolanda is subtly flirting with the Mother Superior' (p. 53). What interests me here is Almodóvar's insistence on the non-verbal character of music, even when it involves (as here) the use of the voice. There can be no clearer example of the way in which music and mise-en-scène serve as the ecstatic medium for powerful drives (for *intenciones*) which resist overt verbal expression, whose rapture threatens to overflow the fixed frame of diegesis.

ELOQUENT GESTURES

> MOTHER SUPERIOR (a Yolanda): Mi único pecado es quererte demasiado.
> MOTHER SUPERIOR (to Yolanda): My only sin is to love you too much.

On *Entre tinieblas*'s release in Spain, critics focused on the performances of the film's cast. Trade journal *Cineinforme* called attention to the fact that the film featured 'excellent figures of our cinema' and suggested that the sometimes scandalous ('fuerte') material was mitigated by the presence of an exceptional cast.[13] From the liberal *El País* to the rightist *ABC*, critics agreed that the intelligence of the acting style made up for deficiencies in direction.[14] In *Diario 16*, Francisco Marinero stressed the 'seriousness' of the actresses' performance, claiming that they avoided caricature by matching the roles to their own unique styles ('especialidades'). Acting styles were thus 'read' against the audience's knowledge of previous performances by the same cast, and of their current roles' conformity with or divergence from the character types with which they were associated.

It is thus significant that foreign critics should fail to recognize the seriousness perceived by Spaniards and keep silent on acting styles whose context they were unable to address. Press kits also set the parameters of critical response. In Britain, Metro Pictures (the distributor and exhibitor) described *Entre tinieblas* in a press release as 'wacky' and the Mother Superior's love for Yolanda as a 'raging crush'. The fact that the film was shown with *Dick*, 'a non-pornographic short film that humorously explores women's thoughts on the penis', was hardly conducive to a measured response.[15]

However, even Spanish critics were disconcerted by the unclear generic markers of Almodóvar's new brand of 'modern' comedy. Angeles Maso in *La Vanguardia* (23 October 1983) wrote that in spite of her skill as an actress Julieta Serrano as Mother Superior did not 'find the tone' in her performance, 'plac[ing] herself outside Almodó-var's parodic context'. It could be argued that it is precisely this disturbing inconsistency of tone which is Almodóvar's innovation as a director of actors. But first we should examine the very possibility of analysing performance style in cinema, which is by no means self-evident. In *Eloquent Gestures* (Berkeley 1992), Roberta E. Pearson gives a detailed account of shifting codes of acting in early cinema. Stressing the relative neglect of performance by film historians and theorists, she defines it in a restricted sense (after Richard Dyer) as 'facial expression, voice, gesture, body position, body movement' (p. 7). Even when thus delimited, performance remains complex with each 'bodily' element subject to varied interpretations which remain culturally and historically specific. It is thus inadequate to fall back on a perceived duality between melodrama and naturalism, because these terms mask an unacknowledged normativity (p. 8). If we are to avoid the 'triviality of the judgmental' (p. 9) we must thus seek intertextual evidence as to the values attached to gesture in a given place and at a given time.

In the case of *Entre tinieblas* Pearson's approach would suggest that we cannot simply distinguish between, say, the grand gestures of the Marquesa (who clutches her breast in the publicity still) and the reticence of the Mother Superior (who looks on in scorn). Such images should be addressed within both generic and historical contexts. And one ambiguous form of intertextual evidence to such a context is Almodóvar's own record of the shoot, as told to Nuria Vidal. Almodóvar claims that Cristina S. Pascual (then wife of the head of the film's production company, Tesauro) was miscast as Yolanda. When she refused to give him the extravagant and passionate performance he required, he rewrote the script to shift emphasis onto Julieta Serrano's Mother Superior (pp. 94, 95). *Entre tinieblas* is thus stranded between the somewhat reserved and distant persona of Pascual and the grave sentimentality of Serrano, who becomes the identification character in the second half of the film.

The final script provides mixed testimony to this conflict. Reaction shots stress the seriousness with which characters accept such potentially comic scenes as Sor Rata's presentation of Yolanda at a bizarre party for the Mother Superior (p. 152). Sometimes gesture remains unspecified, as when in the depths of her dark passion the Mother

Superior is said to be either kneeling with her arms crossed over her breast or simply leaning against the wall of the chapel (p. 104). Yolanda's backstory (in which she claims to have been brought up under the shadow of the Virgin in her mother's home) is absent from the film, thus reinforcing the audience's withdrawal of identification with her. Inversely, Almodóvar retains the most potentially ludicrous sequence (in which the Mother Superior as a 'new Veronica' receives the imprint of Yolanda's face on a handkerchief), rescuing it from absurdity by shooting subjectively from the Mother Superior's point of view: 'inflamed with mystical pleasure' (p. 155). Likewise Julieta Serrano herself claims the film is 'a very serious story told in a way which makes the audience laugh' (Vidal, p. 98). While clearly the testimony of director or actor cannot delimit the meanings of a performance style (which always surpass conscious intention), it does point or gesture towards a cultural and historical context which remains to be established even for a European film of the recent past.

Further intertextual evidence is provided by *Entre tinieblas, la función*, a stage version of the film adapted by Fermín Cabal and performed on a national tour ending at the Teatro Infanta Isabel in Madrid in autumn 1992. The commercial success of the play testifies to Almodóvar's diversification into other media and to the generalization of a sensibility still perceived as marginal in 1983 when the original film was released. During the play's run as many as four commercial theatres in Madrid were showing plays featuring actors well known from their roles in Almodóvar's films;[16] and the audience for *Entre tinieblas, la función* included such diverse constituencies as teenage girls, young gay men, and older women in the fur coats typical of the Spanish bourgeoisie. While lesbianism still proved shocking (with an audible intake of breath greeting the Mother Superior's line to Yolanda 'My only sin is to love you too much'), a broadly gestural performance, more suited to live theatre than cinema, served to neutralize some of the disturbing or unrealized elements of the original. Thus Rossy de Palma (in the role previously played by Marisa Paredes) is shown in *El País Semanal* (9 August 1992) brandishing a large knife over her head; and much play was made in the theatre with this prop. Yet even such eloquent gestures are more complex than they might appear. For de Palma, described in *El País* as 'Ugly. And strange [*rara*]. And charming', received an ecstatic welcome from the mainly female audience in the theatre. While the complexities of the film were reduced to farce (ending with a song and dance in which the public was encouraged to participate), as the only actress in the cast also to be featured in Almodóvar's cinema, de Palma provided an ambiguous focus for a Spanish audience. *El País* reverently reports her international renown (a video clip for George Michael; an advertising campaign for The Gap). The commercial and artistic success of Almodóvar's 'strange women', their unmistakable shift from margin to centre, thus serves as an eloquent example of the social changes possible in contemporary Spain, at least in so far as they are restricted to the entertainment industry.

PRODUCING THE AUDIENCE

Frente a frente, y nada más.
Face to face, and that is all.

(ENCADENADOS)

Entre tinieblas was Almodóvar's first film to appear after the so-called Miró Law established a generous system of advanced subsidy for 'quality' Spanish cinema. As Vallés Copeiro notes, the initial effect of the reform was a sharp decrease in the number of films produced, as genre films such as farces and pornography struggled to survive.[17] Released late in the year, *Entre tinieblas* failed to make the top ten grossing domestic films, but a list of the fifty Spanish successes of 1983–85 places it at number thirty, with an audience over that period in Spain of over four hundred thousand viewers. The biggest-grossing film of 1983 was Eloy de la Iglesia's violent melodrama *El Pico* (The Shoot, with six hundred thousand viewers in one year); the greatest success over the three years Mario Camus's tasteful literary adaptation *Los santos inocentes* (The Holy Innocents, with almost two million viewers).[18] If, as Francesc Llinàs claimed, Almodóvar was one of only three Spanish directors who established himself at this time (*Cuatro años*, p. 155), his audience remained relatively small.

When *Entre tinieblas* was shown on network television on 31 October 1987, J. Batllé Caminal wrote in *El País* that it was a transitional film, linking Almodóvar's early fragmentary beginnings to his later, more 'solid' work. He also notes the 'visual elegance' of the film, worthy of Hitchcock, and its emotional charge, similar to Sirk. Press clippings from the time of the film's production, however, tell a somewhat different story. And it is worth taking a little time to examine the narrativization of Almodóvar's career in Spanish and Catalan print media.

A location report and interview by Carlos Ferrando[19] are clearly sensationalist, focusing on the director's alleged drug abuse (he insists he is bored with the theme). References to the film's success with the audience (but not the critics) at the Venice film festival leave space for a lengthy account by Almodóvar of the traumatic effects of religious education in Spain and his attempt to recuperate Catholic tradition after acknowledging the definitive absence of God.[20] One review notes that the film served to demonstrate to foreign festival audiences the freedoms enjoyed by a permissive Spain.[21] Accounts of the lavish parties marking the premieres in Madrid and Barcelona also leave ample space for 'the director's opinion' (on female autonomy, seriousness of intent, and his own status as auteur[22]) and stress the fashionable glamour of the ambience, a 'Spanish version of Hollywood, brought up to date with a dash of punk'. It was also widely reported that the 'modern' crowd at Barcelona was joined by a group of handsome young men dressed as nuns.[23] Even columnists who disliked the film, claiming it was destined for 'a very small audience, Pedro Almodóvar's audience',[24] devoted full pages to the premiere, lavishly illustrated with celebrity snapshots.

It is possible to trace in these diverse materials the production of an audience for Almodóvar's cinema, based on the coming together of a number of disparate groups: gay men and transvestites or transsexuals are joined by established media stars and personalities familiar from the weekly gossip magazines. Almodóvar thus comes, slowly, to crystallize that 'modernity' and 'internationalism' which would typify society under the Socialists. Representing Spain not only to foreigners but to Spaniards themselves (somewhat dazzled perhaps by his perverse reappropriation of Hollywood), Almodóvar embodies in his career the historic shift (or *cambio*) whose effects were almost universally assumed to be beneficial. And in a stream of interviews he not only recasts the national migration to the city as his own ('young villager triumphs' in Madrid); he also confesses to an intimate narrative of disappointment in love which at once coincides with films such as *Entre tinieblas* and encourages a growing audience to identify with his predicament. The press persona constructed in this way is thus (like the films once more) both ironically distanced and flagrantly sentimental.[25]

Entre tinieblas ends with the Mother Superior deserted by Yolanda. As Sor Estiércol cradles her in her arms the camera pulls out of the window to leave the two women enclosed by this frame within the frame. The bolero 'Encadenados' plays a last time (extra-diegetically) on the soundtrack. However, in both versions of the script the film had ended with Yolanda, the Marquesa, and Sor Rata leaving to start a new life together. And the final freeze frame was to show the Marquesa and a chimp complacently watching the 'happy couple' of Yolanda and Tarzan (sic) frolic in a swimming-pool. The jettisoning of this final sequence no doubt coincided with the shift of identification from Yolanda to the Mother Superior which Almodóvar decided on halfway through the shoot. It also responds, however, to codes of performance, costume, and music which serve to restrain the farcical elements of the film by placing them within a context whose seriousness is transparent to any sympathetic observer. It is a shift of emphasis which will prove symptomatic of Almodóvar's future films.

In Emile Ardolino's Hollywood comedy *Sister Act* (1992), Whoopi Goldberg plays a nightclub singer who hides out in a San Francisco convent after witnessing a murder. While Almodóvar received no credit for the film, the plot is clearly reminiscent of *Entre tinieblas*; and the Spanish press claimed that Almodóvar was originally slated to be the director.[26] The difference between the two films throws the distinctiveness of Almodóvar's sensibility into perspective. For, as its tag line suggests ('No sex, no booze, no men. No way.'), *Sister Act* is a simple comedy of opposition or incongruity in which desire is contrasted with law, vital energy with stultifying repression. Moreover, that promise of transgression offered by the Goldberg character is fully contained by a patriarchal frame: in the final sequence the nuns' choir sings for the Pope who has come to visit their inner-city mission. The women's voices are thus reduced to the interior of the diegesis, legitimized by male authority. Moreover, the one taboo that cannot be transgressed is that of love between women: Goldberg is provided with a cursory, male love interest and Maggie Smith's Mother Superior remains frigid throughout. While the pious normativity of the narrative is somewhat mitigated by Goldberg's style of performance (which hints at an ironic and intelligent distance from her character), *Sister Act* denies the very possibility of female autonomy or of social change even as it places women in centre frame and makes them responsible for narrative agency. By contrast, Almodóvar, for all his inconsistencies and confusions, leaves a certain space in *Entre tinieblas* for women to play new roles in narrative cinema, to serve as subjects and objects of lesbian love, to come out of the convent and into the street. It is an achievement of which Hollywood has proved incapable and one which is not to be minimized.

NOTES

1. Pedro Almodóvar, 'La opinión del director', *Gaceta Ilustrada*, 19 October 1983.

2. The phrase is Joaquín Luqui's in his *Treinta años de diseño gráfico en el cine español*, Madrid 1987, p. 57.

3. José Comas, 'Censurada en Argentina la película de Almodóvar, *Entre tinieblas*', *El País*, 29 September 1990.

4. See brief reviews by Alexander Walker, *Evening Standard*; Tim Pulleine, *Guardian*; Sheila Johnston *Independent*, all published on 23 August 1990.

5. Francisco Marinero, '*Entre tinieblas* de Pedro Almodóvar', *Diario 16*, 6 October 1983; J. M. López i Llaví, 'Irreverència entre l'humor i el melodrama', *Avui*, 12 October 1983; José Luis Guarner, '*Entre tinieblas*', *El Periódico* (Barcelona), 28 October 1983.

6. 'Guión original', Madrid 1982; 'Guión original: título provisional', Madrid 1983.

7. Virginia Higginbotham, *Spanish Film Under Franco*, Austin 1988, p. 18.

8. See his autobiography *El peso de la paja*, Barcelona 1990, p. 155.

9. John Hopewell, *Out of the Past: Spanish Cinema after Franco*, London 1986, p. 32.

10. 36, summer 1984, pp. 108–10.

11. *The Acoustic Mirror*, Bloomington 1988, pp. 24–7.

12. *Laws of Desire*, Oxford 1992, pp. 184–5.

13. 'A. F.', no. 116, October 1983, p. 19.

14. Diego Galán, '*Entre tinieblas*, monjas alucinadas', *El País*, 3 October 1983; César Santos Fontenia, '*Entre tinieblas* de Pedro Almodóvar', *ABC*, 4 October 1983.

15. Press release, 25 June 1990.

16. The listings in *El País* for 15 December 1992 feature vehicles for Loles León, Angel de Andrés López, and Kitti Manver, in addition to *Entre tinieblas* itself.

17. *Historia de la política de fomento del cine español*, Valencia 1992, p. 203.

18. Francesc Llinàs, *Cuatro años de cine español*, Madrid 1986, pp. 95, 98.

19. 'Pedro Almodóvar: "Las drogas están bien para alternar, pero no para trabajar"', *Diario 16*, 17 November 1982.

20. Pérez Abellán, '*Entre tinieblas*, irreverente, escandalosa y muy, muy divertida', *Diario 16*, 28 August 1983.

21. Angeles Maso, 'Pantalla abierta: *Entre tinieblas*', *La Vanguardia*, 23 October 1983.

22. Inés Prat, 'Un estreno de lo más progre', *Gaceta Ilustrada*, 19 October 1983.

23. Bru Noya, 'L'estrena del film *Entre tinieblas* va convocar els "moderns"', *Avui*, 12 October 1983.

24. Antonio Sánchez Carrillo, 'Se estrenó la película de Pedro Almodóvar, *Entre tinieblas*', *Pueblo*, 5 October 1983.

25. Angel S. Harguindey, 'Pedro Almodóvar: Toma la fama y corre', *El País Semanal*, 29 September 1984.

26. M. Torreiro, 'Interior de un convento', *El País*, 16 December 1992.

4

¿ QUÉ HE HECHO YO PARA MERECER ESTO? (WHAT HAVE I DONE TO DESERVE THIS?, 1984)

Gender, Space, Representation

A MODEL HOUSEWIFE

> Bien pagá fuiste mujer.
> Woman, you were well paid.

In *¿Qué he hecho yo . . .?*'s pre-credit sequence the camera glides down on a crane through a wintry Madrid square in which a film crew go about their work. A dowdy middle-aged woman in the background picks her way gingerly through the crew. Jaunty mandolin and accordion music fades in on the soundtrack. The camera moves in on the woman (Gloria: Carmen Maura) who looks back at the crew as she enters a martial arts academy. Crew members are nailing up the sign which is to be used in the film.

This sequence, described by Almodóvar himself as 'Godardian' (Vidal, p. 136), brings together some of the problems and paradoxes of the director's fourth feature. On the one hand, this is Almodóvar's most naturalistic film, one in which the action unfolds within a recognizable city space afflicted by the familiar malaises of urban life in the Spanish capital: overcrowding, illiteracy, crime, and drug abuse. On the other, this is a film in which representation is not taken for granted, in which social issues are not simply re-presented for the camera, but are rather inextricable from the various cinematic means (mise-en-scène, lighting, performance) on which they are dependent if they are to appear on screen. And frequently, as here, this hesitation between re-presentation and representation (between ontology and language) registers as an unresolved incongruity between the various cinematic resources of which the film is composed: thus the wintry mise-en-scène clashes with the incidental music (by Bernardo Bonezzi). And by placing a woman, once more, at the centre of the frame, Almodóvar raises tricky questions of desire and identification in relation to dominant cinema practice: for if the economic subordination of women is as absolute as the film suggests, a feminine point of view cannot be achieved without a struggle, cannot simply be assumed to exist.

Gloria is a working woman. The script tells us she is 'ruined' ('ajada') by her labour;[1] and in Maura's brave performance the glamorous actress of other films is barely recognizable. When we first see her she is on her knees scrubbing the floor, but looking up to where the kendo students in their costumes and masks are practising moves with a club. In the next shot, we are shown the students and Gloria together, the latter in a room behind the men where, invisible to them, she imitates the blows they are making to their partners' heads, but using her mop rather than the martial club. It is a comic scene and one in which the spectator is given access to a woman's actions which remain invisible to the men on screen.

Cinematically, what is interesting about this shot is the use of a technique infrequent in Almodóvar's earlier films: depth of field. And in the shot which follows we also find the use of a static camera and of a contrast between the foreground and the back-ground of the mise-en-scène. Gloria appears to be stealing from a cabinet in the left foreground, when in the right background a naked man moves into shot behind her and stands under the shower. Turning to face her (and the spectator) he beckons for her to join him. She does so, fully clothed; and the couple's frantic attempt at copulation is shown first from a high angle, looking down on the shower, and then from the side, through distorting glass bricks. Gloria attempts to arouse the man but (as is clearly visible) it is all to no avail. Disturbed and disgusted, she leaves the shower and returns to the exercise room: grabbing one of the kendo clubs, she repeats the moves made by the students, this time aiming the club straight to camera. As the man (Polo: Luis Hostalot) leaves, the two exchange rueful glances. His is a look of frustration and discomfort (script, p. 5).

In his review of *¿Qué he hecho yo . . .?* in *El País* (26 October 1984), Diego Galán writes that Almodóvar has yet to develop a properly cinematic style, and is too dependent on an excessively complex and wordy script. While this may be the case elsewhere in what is (as so often) a fiendishly intricate plot, what interests me about these opening sequences is that they are wholly lacking in dialogue. Maura's eloquent looks, her futile imitation of the stylized gestures of male violence, establish with subtle economy her predicament and her doomed attempts to relieve her frustration. As David Denby wrote in his review for *New York* magazine (29 April 1985), this tiny vignette encompasses the whole film: male vanity and incompetence; female victimization; and the release of revenge. But it is the very lack of dialogue which problematizes the spectator's response to the shower scene. Almodóvar instructed Maura to 'act normally' during the shooting, as if such an episode happened every day; and the actress herself has testified to her discomfort while filming the scene (Vidal, p. 128). However, if the outrageous or the incongruous is presented as normal (and this is, of course, one foundation of Almodóvar's comic technique) then how is the spectator to respond to the everyday tragedies of a woman's life, to the daily drudgery of domestic labour?

Back home Gloria sniffs detergent before loading the washing-machine and putting a chicken in the oven (both of these activities are shot from inside the domestic appliance). The walls of the tiny flat are covered in paper whose colours and designs clash furiously with each other and with kitsch prints of idealized rural scenes (white horses at play). The script calls the set 'suffocating' and (a significant word) *cutre*, 'squalid and vulgar'; perhaps best translated by the word used by Denby: 'grungy'. Crammed into this space are Gloria's loutish taxi-driver husband (Angel de Andrés López); her eccentric mother-in-law (Chus Lampreave); and her two sons: Toni, a teenage drug dealer, and Miguel, an even younger male prostitute. The evening meal is a disaster: the chicken is burnt and, with no money for wine, Gloria's husband is obliged to buy a bottle of mineral water from his mother, who hoards bottles in a locked cupboard. Miguel vomits up his dinner over his grandmother who (in a visual echo of the earlier shower scene) gets into the shower fully dressed to clean up; Toni arrives to find nothing but mouldy tomato sauce in the refrigerator; and his mother scolds him for not ensuring he is fed by his older male lovers.

In an important interview on the release of *¿Qué he hecho yo . . .?*,[2] Almodóvar claims that his interest in housewives stems from the fact that they transcend genre, could be the heroine of almost any kind of film; moreover, if, like Gloria, a housewife is also a cleaning lady, she is the ideal witness of various social milieux. However, the choice of a housewife as protagonist is not simply a pragmatic one. The opening sequences in the flat suggest rather that Gloria represents a grotesque deformation of the Catholic ideal of the married woman. Francoist marriage manuals suggested that a perfect *casada* must combine the roles of woman (happy, tender, and compassionate by nature); selfless companion to husband; tireless homemaker; and ideal mother.[3] As María

Teresa Gallego notes in her study of women in the Falange, women were allowed no self-realization except in domestic labour; and their fundamental characteristic was submission.[4] It was only on the death of Franco in 1975 that *permiso marital* (the husband's power to control his wife's affairs) was abolished;[5] divorce was not legalized until 1981 and abortion (under limited circumstances) in 1985. Even in 1987 (three years after the film's release), Spain had the lowest percentage of working women and the highest ratio of housewives in the European Community.[6]

To some extent, then, *¿Qué he hecho yo . . .?* bears witness to the material conditions of working-class women's oppression in Spain. But it does so in an idiosyncratic manner, typical of Almodóvar. Thus we are shown not only the brutal insensitivity of Gloria's husband towards her in, say, his imperious requests that she cook or iron for him. We are also shown the reproduction of male privilege through writing. While Gloria is illiterate, her husband teaches their son to copy his own signature exactly; this, he claims, is as important as the surname. But this talent for imitation, typically, plays a part in the plot: the family become involved in an abortive scheme to forge letters written by Hitler.

Equally idiosyncratic is the insertion of a video clip in which Almodóvar himself lip-synchs to the traditional *tonadilla* (Andalusian popular song) 'La bien pagá' (The well-paid woman). Dressed as a hussar, he is accompanied by his habitual musical accomplice Fanny (or Fabio) McNamara, disguised as Scarlett O'Hara. This is clearly a gratuitously camp distraction from the vulgar brutalities of Gloria's domestic regime. But it is in such unlikely moments that Almodóvar's interventions into history and politics are to be found. Watching the clip on television, the grandmother comments nostalgically on the beauty of the songs 'of her time'. As the custodian of the family's history she embodies a certain (perhaps phantasmatic) continuity in Spanish culture. What is more, the song is cross-cut with Gloria's husband's brutally selfish attempt at lovemaking. The montage thus points ironically and without dialogue to a parallelism between prostitution and marriage. Just as the kisses of the woman in the song have been bought 'for a handful of coins', so Gloria has thrown away her life for the meagre income provided by her husband. She has hardly been well paid for the sexual services she offers.

But there is yet another historical reference here. The high, plangent voice to which Almodóvar mimes in the clip belongs to Miguel de Molina, a Republican singer who specialized (as here) in songs associated with and often sung by women (Vidal, p. 144). Thus apart from the glitzy drag of Fanny in the video, there is also a hidden acoustic transvestism in the soundtrack, one which bears witness to a certain cultural history of crossing over from one genre to another. It is an important precedent for Almodóvar, who also seeks truth in travesty, has a weakness for female identification and ventriloquism.

CITY/SPACE

ABUELA: ¡Qué frío hace en este Madrid!
GRANDMOTHER: How cold it is in this Madrid of yours!

In extreme long shot the tiny figures of the grandmother and Toni are silhouetted against a gloomy sky. No buildings are visible, only a leafless tree and a telegraph pole. Suddenly Almodóvar cuts to a camera position 180 degrees from the first. Once more the figures are overwhelmed by their background; but this time it is the fortress-like tower blocks of workers' housing which fill the screen, leaving no space for sky.

This sequence suggests at once the determining influence of environment on character and the liminal nature of that environment: the exteriors are filmed on location in the eastern suburb of Concepción, a setting which combines the crowded alienation of the big city with the anxious solitude of the periphery. *¿Qué he hecho yo . . .?* stresses throughout that Madrid is inseparable from provincial life, composed as it is of migrants from the diverse villages of Spain (Vidal, p. 108). In typically burlesque mode, the odd couple in this sequence are searching the squalid park for branches to take to the flat, only to discover a lizard which follows them home.

The towering flats and glowering sky also point to the primacy of mise-en-scène in the film. We have already noted how Gloria's class and economic position are defined by her *cutre* taste in interior decoration. And, as the script reveals, the other characters in the film are also defined by the decors they inhabit. The Barbie-like prostitute next door (Verónica Forqué) has an exotic backdrop, replete with exotic costumes and wigs; the houseproud neighbour Juani (Kitti Manver) glories in a flat which 'looks like a furniture warehouse on the outskirts of Madrid', so kitsch are its contents (script, p. 129). Outside the block, the house of the bourgeois Lucas (where Gloria cleans) is described as 'the typical home of a nonconformist, drunken writer. Ornaments from foreign countries, magazines, women's shoes, serviettes, newspapers, pictures' (p. 57). Lucas's brother, a psychiatrist, is shot against a severe monochrome painting in the style of Penck.

What is important about the mise-en-scène here is not simply the ranking of characters according to class and profession. It is also the incongruities embodied in these sets, incongruities which generally go unnoticed or unstated by the characters. Thus the teenager Toni shares a bedroom with his grandmother; it is (according to the script) 'a mix of each of them. A print of Saint Anthony shares the wall with a heavy metal poster' (p. 17). Such details are likely to pass unnoticed by the spectator. But they point to a certain layering of history (within the family, in the city), to the coexistence of different cultures and stages of development which go unreconciled, which are simply juxtaposed in their comic or pathetic incongruity.

The sense of space in the city links mise-en-scène to camerawork. Almodóvar himself has drawn attention to four techniques more frequent here than in his other films: the use of a fixed camera on a tripod; the prevalence of medium shots over close-ups or long shots; the constant movement of actors in and out of the frame; and, finally, the variable height of the camera, which moves up and down according to the characters' changing moods (Vidal, p. 119). Most of these techniques are determined by the restricted nature of the sets, which did not permit the luxury of tracking shots. And they serve to increase the claustrophobia of desperately confined characters. But they also communicate a certain sense of space which might be called ideological: thus the 'subjective' shots from inside domestic appliances suggest Gloria is observed by the objects to which she is enslaved. Celebrated here is an impossible tracking shot in which the camera shadows Gloria and Juani as they trek past shop windows disconsolately in the rain, shooting from *inside* the shops. The sequence is in fact composed of a number of still shots edited together. As Almodóvar himself notes, this is an inversion of a normal tracking shot in which it is the camera and not the location which moves. In thrall to consumer goods she cannot afford to buy, Gloria does not so much look at them as they look at her, in her isolation (Vidal, p. 121). She stands, finally, mesmerized before an electric hair-curling iron.

If space enforces social difference between the characters, it also brings them together: the bourgeois Lucas comes to Gloria's neighbourhood because he is visiting her prostitute neighbour. As Philippe Rouyer notes in his review of the film, the complex relations of an ensemble cast are linked by the crossing of their paths in the same building.[7] But there is little sense of the space *between* buildings. Gloria claims at one point that, with no money for the bus, she had to walk home from her cleaning job. But we are not shown that movement between locations. Indeed, the only journeys shown are Lucas's trip to the airport (a favourite Almodóvarian location) and his trip in Antonio's taxi to the latter's building. This journey is shot on the M-30, the monstrous ring road which passes by Concepción. It is thus motivated by the diegesis (the taxi would plausibly follow that route). But the M-30 seems to take on a totemic or emblematic status. The ring road is an uncanny interspace, a means to gain access to more domestic and familiar city streets. But it is also a symbol of modernity. When Gloria's husband is planning to meet his ex-lover (a Nazi chanteuse) he tells Gloria, with smug satisfaction, that he'll take Frau Müller for a spin on the M-30; she'll like that. Opened just before the death of the dictator in 1974 (and christened 'the Avenue of Peace'), the ring road was the last of the grandiose Francoist projects of modernization, widely seen as part of the 'inauguration syndrome' whose massive social costs went unrecognized.[8] As an ironic symbol of urban development, the M-30 thus suggests not only the shifting space of the modern city, but also a specific historical attempt to impose a monumental vision on a Madrid whose roots remained obstinately provincial. Indeed, in a city not lacking in grandiose memorials to its various rulers, it is significant that the M-30 is the only recognizable public work the spectator is permitted to see.

Almodóvar's treatment of space is thus at once archaic and postmodern. On the one hand, his characters are primitive subjects (like the mother) 'grounded' in the landscape they inhabit and nostalgic for the origin (the provincial village) they have lost. On the other, they are detached or dissociated from the cityscape, materializing (like Gloria) in a plurality of locations in which they have no immediate connection and which are disconnected from each other. If, as Mary Anne Doane argues in *Femmes Fatales*,[9] modern technology, including cinema, has effected a 'despatialization of subjectivity' (which is no longer joined to the landscape, which accedes to a non-space of anonymity), Almodóvar conserves and reproduces stages prior and subsequent to that development. But just as his building contains discrete, irreconcilable spaces placed side by side (family home and brothel), so these differing modes of relation to space are also juxtaposed without explanation, are simply offered to the spectator in their incongruity.

Yet this coexistence of different modes is by no means a denial of history and geography, which return insistently at the level of language. Thus Almodóvar tells us that he chose Kitti Manver for the part of the shrewish Juani because of his love of her provincial accent (from Jaén) (Vidal, p. 2): the accent goes unmentioned in the diegesis; yet it constantly reaffirms the presence of the country in the city. Or again García de León and Maldonado have drawn attention to the grandmother's complaint of how cold it is in 'this' Madrid (as opposed to the village she longs for) (p. 86). The idiomatic use of the demonstrative adjective epitomizes the grandmother's character, and her longing for the *pueblo* to which she returns at the end of the film. Dialogue thus combines with mise-en-scène to produce an oblique and subtle account of urban life in the 1980s, of its perils and fragile pleasures.

HYPERREALIST COMEDY

POLO: El lagarto conocía al asesino.
POLO [police inspector]:   The lizard knew who the murderer was.

Let us consider three publicity stills from *¿Qué he hecho yo . . .?* (Plates 6, 7, 8). In the first, Gloria, her hair wet and scraggly, is seen at the bus station, struggling to cope with plastic bags full of shopping. In the second she sits on a bed gloomily, clutching her precious hair-curling iron as the prostitute and a client show every sign of reaching extravagant orgasm beside her. In the third the grandmother looks down tenderly at the lizard which is crawling up her bosom. These three images show the range of modes of representation in the film: from straight neo-realism (the documentation of working-class life) to surrealism (the unmotivated irruption of the grotesque and extreme into the real) by way of an uneasy compromise between the two (the incongruous juxtaposition of the banal and the exceptional). The reconciliation of comic and tragic is hard to achieve; and Almodóvar's uniqueness in Spanish cinema is quite evident here. It is curious indeed to come across the dishevelled Maura, clutching her bags, amongst the stills of bare-breasted women and randy priests reproduced in a recent study of Spanish comedy.[10]

Almodóvar has frequently referred to the influence of neo-realism on his filmic practice, citing both Rossellini and the 'ferocious and funny' Spanish version of the school in the 1960s.[11] Nuria Vidal's chapter on *¿Qué he hecho yo . . .?* is prefaced by an epigraph from Rossellini on the 'tension' and 'hysteria' of the modern world, which is particularly apt (p. 108). Almodóvar himself claims here, as on the film's release, that he was aiming not for a John Waters-style parody of the domestic milieu but a presentation of the housewife exactly as she is ('tal cual') (p. 115). But where neo-realism saw shooting on location as an approximation to concrete reality or truth, Almodóvar chose to shoot all his interiors in a studio. Cinema, he claims, is not reality (p. 118). Almodóvar thus follows some neo-realist precepts in this film, in his use of working-class protagonists, vernacular dialogue, and implied social criticism.[12] With his frequently immobile camera he also coincides with a favourite neo-realist tendency: the primacy of mise-en-scène over editing. Exemplary here are the scenes mentioned at the start of this chapter in which depth of field substitutes for cross-cutting between different locations (the exercise room and the shower). But where theorists such as Bazin argued that neo-realists 'respected the ontological wholeness of the reality they filmed' through such techniques,[13] Almodóvar deprives them of any such transcendent quality. Similarly, where the neo-realists assumed a certain community of interest inspired by the moral statements of their films, Almodóvar's vision of a fragmented and atomistic society admits of no such consensus in its audience.

It thus follows that even where ¿Qué he hecho yo . . .? refers to concrete issues grounded in a recognizable historical predicament (drug abuse, prostitution, migration) it assumes no consistent attitude towards those issues. Toni may be a drug dealer, but on leaving Madrid for the country he gives his mother the money he has earned; the prostitute neighbour may have the proverbial heart of gold, acting 'like a sister' to Gloria; but she is also as consumerist as her neighbours, fretting over the (kitsch) 'objects of value' accumulated in her flat. Almodóvar thus rejects the ethical responsibility and commitment to social change of the neo-realists, but preserves and enhances their respectful attention to the everyday detail of human lives.

What is more, those touches of crazy comedy typical of Almodóvar sometimes involve 'issues' of which the neo-realists fought shy, such as homosexuality. Thus when Miguel returns home late for dinner he replies to his mother's accusation that he has been sleeping with his schoolfriend's father with the assertion that '[his] body belongs to [him]'. As Vicente Sánchez-Biosca notes, the humour relies on the child's repetition of a phrase derived from feminism.[14] The reframing of the phrase's context thus leads to a distanced or 'secondary' realism, not wholly divorced from social practice but floating somewhere above it. Gloria, of course, is concerned only by the fact that her son has not been fed by his lover. And the acceptance of Miguel's behaviour within the diegesis thus makes an implicitly political point. Where Rossellini depicted homosexuals as monsters who threatened the working-class family (the Nazi officer in *La città aperta*), Almodóvar shows them wholly, if not happily, integrated into it. The disavowal of sexual preference as taboo (the child's nonchalant vindication of his choice) thus makes a social comment precisely in so far as it deviates from plausible behaviour in that milieu. As Sánchez-Biosca notes, the relation between character and behaviour is unpredictable in Almodóvar; but if his world refuses to function like the real one, still it refers to it.

The ambiguity of the relation between character, dialogue, and setting is confirmed in another scene of homosexual declaration. When Gloria takes Miguel to the dentist she knows she cannot pay for her son's fillings. As the dentist (played by the extravagant Javier Gurruchaga) examines him, she asks whether he likes children ('niños'). As the script suggests, 'the question can be understood in various ways. The double meaning floats in the air, but none of them is embarrassed by it. They treat it with absolute simplicity' (pp. 78–9). By the end of the scene, Gloria has 'placed' her youngest child in the dentist's consumerist heaven (complete with Sony hi-fi); there is one less mouth for her to feed at home. Although this scene could be read once more as a disavowal of the real position of gay men in contemporary Spain, in its uncompromising assumption that material needs take precedence over sexual integrity it displaces the burden of guilt onto those who are responsible for poverty and deprivation. And here the mode of performance specified by the script is of the essence. Just as the double meaning hangs undecided and disregarded over the characters, so the spectator is suspended between Carmen Maura's grave and hopeful mother and Javier Gurruchaga's comic, tongue-flickering seducer.

This is not, of course, to argue that any deviation from realist or neo-realist norms is inherently transgressive or serves in itself to denaturalize social and sexual inequalities.[15] Rather it is to suggest with one Italian reviewer that Almodóvar points the way to a new European cinema, less auteurist, richer in objects, more visceral and attentive to viewing pleasure.[16] As Gianni Vattimo suggests in his notes on Madrid as the postmodern capital, we find in Almodóvar's utopian attitude to homosexuality a 'fantastic sociology' in which emancipation can lead to immediate pleasure without passing first through revolutionary violence. It is a 'weak' revolution which acts through a slight distortion of social mediations, such as consumerism.[17]

This slight distortion is seen in the substitution of a cat or dog by a lizard as the family pet. When Gloria finally kills her husband with a ham bone (using the kendo chop she has learned in the academy), the lizard is the only witness to the crime. It is splattered with blood. The incompetent detectives arrive and one of them stamps on it and throws it off the balcony. It is worth citing the script at this point, although it does not coincide exactly with the finished version:

> Outside it is still raining. The lizard falls next to the kerb, a little current of water washes away the blood stains which had stuck to the animal's body. The blood of Antonio, of Gloria, and of itself. The grandmother and Toni come down the street protecting their heads with sodden branches. They discover the crushed lizard next to the kerb. (p. 152)

Previously we have been given a subjective shot from the lizard's point of view as the policeman's foot squashes it to the floor. It is in such minute details, in such curious and painterly combinations of the aesthetic and the grotesque, that Almodóvar's hyper-realist comedy is to be found.

CROSSING OVER

GLORIA (a Toni):   No olvides nunca que soy tu madre.
GLORIA (to Toni):   Never forget that I'm your mother.

¿Qué he hecho yo . . .? was a cross-over film for Almodóvar in several ways. It was the first time he was given a substantial budget (some seventy million pesetas) (Vidal, p. 124); and the Spanish trade paper *Cineinforme* announced that it would be premiered simultaneously throughout the country and was likely to gain a wider public than the specialist audience who attended the earlier films.[18] In France the film helped to establish Almodóvar's reputation, somewhat ironically, at a time when the Spanish abandonment of protectionism had led to a new and extreme imbalance between the number of French films shown in Madrid and Spanish films in Paris (forty to two in 1985).[19] The trade papers in the US stressed, for once, the seriousness of Almodóvar's concerns: his commitment to the analysis of sexism, the position of women, and the family.[20] *¿Qué he hecho yo . . .?* also won high praise in influential quarters: the *New York Times* critic called it 'a small masterpiece'.[21] Even in Britain where a later release date found critics sated with Almodóvar's work, *¿Qué he hecho yo . . .?* had varied admirers. The *Guardian* critic stressed (like the Americans) Almodóvar's 'sympathy with the downtrodden';[22] the Communist *Morning Star* proclaimed it 'a cry from the heart of working-class Spain'.[23]

This is one case, then, in which foreign critics seemed to take Almodóvar more seriously than his compatriots. The latter were generally hostile, and unwilling to allow Almodóvar any real concern for social and sexual inequalities in the film.[24] Where critics of all nationalities coincided was in their indecision as to how much of the film was intended to be as it was. Was the mise-en-scène meant to be as tacky as it looked? The lighting as flat and dead as it was? Were the non-naturalistic sequences caused simply by Almodóvar's inability to induce his actors to play scenes straight? Coincidentally, this question of self-awareness is one that can also be posed of the film's housewife heroine. Thus, as Laura Mulvey suggests, in Douglas Sirk 'characters are not allowed transcendent awareness or knowledge'; there is a conflict in his films (present also in Almodóvar) between the mise-en-scène, to which characters can respond within the diegesis, and those techniques, such as lighting style or camera movement, which are accessible only to the spectator.[25] Likewise in psychoanalytic theory the mother's knowledge and the mother's desire generally go unexamined.[26] Here there is evidence of Almodóvar's supposed empathy with feminism. For although Gloria's knowledge of her position is necessarily limited (she can respond to her surroundings but not to the immobile camera which traps her within the frame) she is clearly the identification figure throughout the film; and she is never blamed for the way her sons turn out. Struggling to feed her children, but frequently hostile or inattentive towards them, Gloria is the 'good enough mother'[27] of psychoanalysis who neither destroys nor coddles her progeny. If Almodóvar cannot represent for her a female desire outside patriarchy (she remains sexually frustrated throughout the film), he at least shoots consistently from her point of view, refuses to make her responsible for her family's predicament.

When, after the death of her husband, the grandmother and Toni set off from the bus station, Gloria tells her son never to forget that she is his mother. The camera follows her in close-up as she walks away, tearful and distressed. It is a long take. She returns to the now empty flat and a slow 360-degree pan from her point of view registers the emptiness of the home. As she leans over the balcony, tempted by suicide, the screen behind her is filled one final time by the flats opposite. Suddenly she makes out below her younger son Miguel, who has returned from the dentist to take his father's place. He tells her: 'This house needs a man.' They embrace.

Almodóvar has proclaimed the authenticity of this scene of reconciliation between mother and son, saying the film as a whole seeks to praise motherhood (Albaladejo, p. 75). *¿Qué he hecho yo . . .?* is also the first film in which his own mother makes an appearance (as an ex-neighbour of the grandmother from the *pueblo*). While the son's phrase reads ironically in the context, there can be little doubt that this melodramatic moment is meant seriously. Albaladejo calls it 'a transparent declaration of principles . . . personal and shamelessly intimate' (p. 22). And noting that Bonezzi's music for this sequence recurs in love scenes of *La ley del deseo*, Albaladejo sketches out an Oedipal scenario which is repeated in the later film: after the loss of the hated father, the gay son returns to the mother figure and the plot circle is closed. The analogy does not quite hold. But in its critical account of gender roles, its problematization of urban space, and its investigation of representational modes, *¿Qué he hecho yo . . .?* stands as the most consistently comic and moving of Almodóvar's early films.

NOTES

1. 'Yo maté a mi marido' (unpublished typescript), Madrid 1983, p. 2.

2. Angel S. Harguindey, 'Pedro Almodóvar: toma la fama y corre', *El País Semanal*, 29 September 1984.

3. See Dr A. Clavero Núñez, *Antes de que te cases . . . .: un texto de formación prenupcial* (1946), 12th edn, Madrid 1961, pp. 282–96.

4. *Mujer, Falange, y Franquismo*, Madrid 1983, pp. 198, 200.

5. John Hooper, *The Spaniards*, Harmondsworth 1986, p. 197.

6. Ian Gibson, *Fire in the Blood*, London 1992, pp. 90, 97, 105.

7. 'Qu'est-ce que j'ai fait pour mériter ça?: L'immeuble en folie', *Positif*, no. 317–18, pp. 102–3.

8. Ayuntamiento de Madrid, *Madrid: Cuarenta años de desarrollo urbano*, Madrid 1981, pp. 1–6, 220.

9. New York and London 1991, p. 190.

10. Florentino Soria and Jesús González Requena, *La comedia en el cine español*, Madrid 1986, p. 187.

11. John Hopewell, *El cine español después de Franco*, Madrid 1989, p. 445.

12. Millicent Marcus, *Italian Film in the Light of Neorealism*, Princeton 1986, p. 22.

13. Peter Bondanella, *Italian Cinema from Neorealism to the Present*, New York 1983, p. 32.

14. 'El elixir aromático de la postmodernidad o la comedia según Pedro Almodóvar', in José A. Hurtado and Francisco M. Picó, eds., *Escritos sobre el cine español 1973–87*, Valencia 1989, pp. 111–24 (p. 121).

15. Cf. Linda Williams, '"Something Else Besides a Mother": *Stella Dallas* and the Maternal Melodrama', in *Home is Where the Heart Is: Studies in Melodrama and the Woman's Film*, Christine Gledhill, ed., London 1987, pp. 229–325 (p. 304).

16. Federico Chiacchiari, *Cineforum*, no. 289, November 1989; cited in Sergio Naitza and Valeria Patané, eds., *¡Folle folle folle Pedro! Il cinema di Pedro Almodóvar*, Cagliari 1992, p. 304.

17. Preface to the Spanish edition of *La sociedad transparente*, Barcelona 1990, pp. 70–1.

18. Anon., 'Un nuevo estreno', *Cineinforme*, no. 140, October 1984, p. 12.

19. Jean-Pierre Jeancolas, 'Paris-Madrid aller retour: une conférence de presse espagnole', *Positif*, no. 304, June 1986, p. 61.

20. See reviews by 'Strat.' in *Variety*, 29 August 1984; and Kirk Ellis in *The Hollywood Reporter*, vol. 286, no. 14, 22 March 1985, p. 15.

21. Richard Grenier, 'New Directors/New Films: "What Have I Done" Depicts a Funny Unfamiliar Spain', 30 March 1985.

22. Derek Malcolm, 3 August 1989, p. 23.

23. Jeff Sawtell, 4 August 1989, p. 8.

24. See the edited reviews in García de León and Maldonado, pp. 255–9.

25. 'Notes on Sirk and Melodrama', in Christine Gledhill, ed., pp. 75–9 (p. 77).

26. Naomi Segal, 'Motherhood', in *Feminism and Psychoanalysis: A Critical Dictionary*, Elizabeth Wright, ed., Oxford 1992, pp. 266–70 (p. 269).

27. For this term, derived from Winnicott, see Segal, p. 267.

5

MATADOR (1986)

Power, Pleasure, and the Frenzy of the Visible

VOYEURISM

M. de matador y m. de mirar.
M. for matador and m. for looking.[1]

A woman is drowned in her bath. The blood balloons over her face as her throat is cut. The head of another woman is severed by a circular saw. Cut to an extreme close-up of a male face, feverishly agitated. The next shot comes from behind the man's chair: his legs are placed astride the TV screen on which the earlier images appear and he is furiously masturbating (just out of frame). With no transition, we are then shown the same man (Diego, played by Nacho Martínez) lecturing a class of students on the correct way to kill a bull. The camera lingers on one student, who seems particularly absorbed (Angel, played by Antonio Banderas). This pedagogic scene is cross-cut, once more without explanation, with a scene of desire in which a dark-haired woman (María, played by Assumpta Serna) picks up a muscular man in a location which has not been established. In a sequence of graphic rhymes or visual echoes the woman undresses the man, pulling him to the bed by his belt (Plate 9), while the students practise their passes with a *carretón* (a horned trolley, substitute for the bull). As a student closes in for the kill, María mounts the man, dressed only in a tight corset and (coinciding with the student's lunge) presses the jewelled hairpin she has taken from

65

her phallic coiffure into the hollow beneath the nape of his neck. She achieves a solitary orgasm with her dead partner; Angel, in the bullfighting academy, looks up to the cloudy sky as if in a daze.

This first sequence of *Matador* (1986) raises tricky questions of voyeurism, fetishism, and disavowal. Is the spectator of narrative cinema necessarily male? Is female exhibitionism inevitably the object of his gaze? Is this heterosexist spectatorial regime always based on the negation of the homosexual fantasy which subtends it? These general questions raised by feminist and gay psychoanalytic theory are to some extent anticipated by and played out in Almodóvar's most abstract melodrama. But at the end of this chapter I will also consider, briefly, the problem of historical context and the relation between this the director's fifth film and the particular circumstances of its production, distribution, and exhibition in Spain and abroad.

In *Hard Core: Power Pleasure and the Frenzy of the Visible*, Linda Williams has examined the supposed connection between pornography and the 'slice and dice' genre to which Almodóvar seems to be alluding here.[2] Calling attention to conflicting theorizations of cinema as either realist ontology or linguistic structure and divergent accounts of graphic sexual violence as either the perversion of a cinema deemed to be ethically positive or as the exemplification of a cinema held to be innately perverse, she shows how some spectators have seen horror films (and their chimerical cousins the 'snuff movies') as a displacement of hard-core pornography: penile penetration is substituted by another, more definitive piercing of the flesh; and the involuntary spasm of female orgasm, stubbornly invisible, yields to a new frenzy of the visible, which culminates in death (pp. 192–4). Citing Carol Clover, Williams argues against those theorists who see such spectacular sadism as simply an extreme example of the normalized perversions inherent in dominant cinema practice and claims that such global accounts of spectatorship repress both feminine agency and male masochism. Even the male adolescents who are the target audience for slasher films may participate in a spectatorial bisexuality, a certain oscillation between positions gendered as masculine and feminine, active and passive, sadistic and masochistic (pp. 204–6).

Matador was labelled 'pornographic' by some critics on its release in Spain;[3] and distribution in Britain was held up by concern over its graphic combination of sex and violence.[4] And, as the opening sequence suggests, its central character Diego is a case study of the pornography consumer whose arousal leads to dehumanized sadism: the retired bullfighter acts out the sex murders he enjoys on video. His passionate voyeurism (repeated later in the film when he glimpses María on the video screen) reveals a desire for mastery over and for knowledge of others. From the texts in

Matador's Spanish press book, however, it would seem that Almodóvar has incorporated a certain psychoanalytic self-consciousness into the film itself. Punning on the film's title, he claims that 'matador' equals 'mata d'or'; that is, long, golden tresses, 'the symbol of danger'. This feminine fetish (reversed in the film, in which the normally blonde Serna is dyed brunette) recalls to Almodóvar Buñuel's *L'Age d'or*, made fifty years earlier. The director goes on to claim that the 'm' of matador also stands for 'looking' and for 'death' (*mirar*, *muerte*). The connection between voyeurism and mortality is thus quite explicit. But who looks and who dies? Almodóvar's own synopsis stresses identifications between the characters in their search for substitute objects which will fit ever more closely their exorbitant desires. Thus María Cardenal (the woman with the hairpin in the first sequence) is driven to murder by her compulsion to repeat or 'imitate' the mode of killing employed by Diego Montes, the bullfighter who has retired to his school after being gored in the groin. María and Diego, we are told, belong to the same 'species'. But Diego's pupil Angel, whom we also saw in the first sequence, identifies equally with the torero, taking on himself the blame for the murders committed by both Diego and María. In the final line of the synopsis, Almodóvar tells us that when Diego and María meet, neither Angel nor they themselves will be able to avoid 'the inevitable'. And 'Lo inevitable' was the working title of the film.[5] But, as we shall see, the play of reflections (of repetitions and reversals) in the film is such that the outcome is by no means predetermined. For, as we saw in the first sequence once more, the central, heterosexual narrative (in which a woman and a man take up alternately the voyeuristic and sadistic positions gendered as male) is mediated by the ambiguous third term of the youth Angel, from whose privileged point of view the spectator is first given access to the couple's passionate crimes. As the unwilling recipient of the frenzy of the visible (a telepathic who cannot distinguish between his own actions and the murders committed by others which are projected on the screen of his imagination), Angel is the epitome of voyeurism, proof that the irruption of unmediated fantasy leads both to rapture and to psychosis.

FETISHISM

DIEGO: Este es el lavabo de hombres, ¿no has visto el letrero?
MARÍA (con sorna): No te fíes de las apariencias.
DIEGO: This is the men's lavatory. Didn't you see the sign?

MARÍA (scornfully): Don't put your faith in appearances.

In an early sequence Angel, inspired by Diego's advice that women should be treated 'like bulls', is spying on his young neighbour Eva (Eva Cobo), who happens to be Diego's girlfriend. We first see Eva dressing after a shower, as if through a pair of binoculars. A quick cut to Eva's bathroom reveals, with a change of focus, that the previous shot is from Angel's point of view: we can now see him peering from the window opposite. The two young people are then shown leaving the building and a hand-held camera follows Eva from behind as she walks down the Madrid sidestreet. The dark shadows thrown by the streetlamps contrast with her vivid pink jacket and his red sweater. The camera then tracks alongside her as she strolls, unconcerned, flicking through a magazine. Suddenly, Angel comes into shot on the left and drags her into an alleyway behind them. Bending her back over a car, we see him attempt (in alternating close-ups of the two faces and abdomens) to remove Eva's panties. He menaces her with a Swiss army knife, which at first produces a corkscrew, rather than the desired blade. Suddenly, we cut to a full body-shot of the (clothed) couple from the side; and a vivid blue flash of lightning marks Angel's orgasm. As torrential rain falls, Angel apologizes to his victim, who slaps him around the face. Eva turns to go and slips, gashing her face on the wet ground. As she stumbles off into the distance, the camera tilts down to discover Angel unconscious on the ground, having fainted at the sight of her blood.

One British critic of *Matador* registered surprise that a scene of attempted rape could be played for laughs.[6] It seems likely, however, that Almodóvar is not simply aiming for humour in this sequence. He is concerned not with the victimization of the woman, but rather with the internal conflict of the man: Angel identifies with his master Diego, but is unable successfully to imitate his actions. Hence while feminism has taught us to see rape as a social conflict *between* individuals, Almodóvar here disavows the problem of male domination (Eva is considerably more self-possessed than Angel) and focuses on the psychic conflict *within* individuals produced by the impossible demands of fantasy.[7] As we shall see, Angel will come to figure an impossible bisexuality, to which the other characters can only aspire.

Moreover, if cinema is (as Williams suggests) not ontology but language, not the representation of entities anterior to the medium, but the representation of events constituted by that medium, then cinematography and mise-en-scène must be part of the meaning of such a sequence and not simply the vehicle for a pre-established content. Thus although the camerawork at first suggests a vérité depiction of sexual violence (the brief tremor of the hand-held shot), the gaudy palette of the art design and the expressionist lighting design point rather to a stylized and anti-realist register. Although the location is authentic, the effect is as distancing as any studio set. As Almodóvar says of this sequence, he has made the 'concrete location' a 'metaphorical space', transforming the single city into a thousand cities, simply through the process of shooting in it (Albaladejo, p. 79).

This is not, however, to claim that such stylization somehow transcends the material fact of male domination outside the cinema. And *Matador* would seem at first to reconfirm the fetishistic and exhibitionistic roles which much feminist film theory has taken to be the essence of narrative cinema. Thus there is great emphasis on female costume: María alternates between ostentatiously feminine creations and virilized business suits; Eva spends much of the film in a crimson wedding gown; even her mother (played by veteran Chus Lampreave) takes her turn on the catwalk at an unlikely fashion parade (see final section). This female fetishization immobilizes the film, serves to distract the male spectator from the dangers of castration by offering a seductively aestheticized avenue of escape. One scene from the middle section of the film is exemplary here. As Diego pursues María out of an incongruous old people's home, she pauses on an overpass high over a busy street. Shot from below, her scarlet cape billows around her. It is one of the most flagrantly iconic sequences of the film. The location is the 'Segovia Viaduct' in southern Madrid, a notorious suicide spot since the nineteenth century. Femininity and death: the supposed association between the two at this brief moment of suspension in a film of complex and often fast-moving action points to the fetishization of the woman whose very visible 'glamour' ensures the continuity of the male spectator's relation to the phallus.

Elsewhere María's figure is cut or veiled in classic screen-goddess style, exciting and relieving male castration anxieties. Thus when Angel first sees her, only the red lips are visible, the top half of the face masked by the prison bars. Or when Diego first sees María, she is wreathed in exhaust smoke, an urban icon. Mary Ann Doane has suggested that the veil of the femme fatale (which suggests both closeness and distance, surface and depth) reveals the limits of an illusory female power, which may pose as a challenge to the phallus, but cannot elude it.[8]

But if Almodóvar seems merely to reconfirm the fetishizing impulse of narrative cinema, which fragments and obscures the female body only to project it as an 'enigma' for the male imagination to solve, at other points in the film female castration and exhibitionism 'bleed over' into the male domain. Thus Diego is the object of María's fetishistic impulses: she preserves memorabilia associated with him at a 'temple' to the torero in her country house. And if she is shot, as we have seen, from below in a position of phallic mastery, then Diego (and Angel) are often shot from above in the high angles known appropriately in Spanish as *picados* (from *picar*, 'to dive'; but also to 'prick' or 'pierce'). In a number of sequences, Diego remains immobile (he has a limp) and the camera pans over him; María, however, tends to irrupt vertically into the frame (as when she mounts her first victim in the opening sequence).[9]

But to celebrate a pre-Oedipal phallic femininity is not, of course, to escape fetishism; on the contrary. *Matador* points rather, and more frequently, towards a fantastic abolition of sexual difference in a graphic code of contagion or reversibility. Thus María marks the place of her penetration with a lipstick trace on the male neck; and it is to the men's toilet that she retreats in a cinema to wash off a red lipstick stain on her black and white business suit.[10] If sexual difference is, as María sarcastically claims to Diego in this sequence, merely a matter of appearances, then subjects may choose to place themselves on whichever side of the phallic divide they wish. It is symptomatic that the whole of this exchange is shot in a mirror. In a later sequence the figure of the police inspector (Eusebio Poncela) interposes in the frame between Diego and Angel as they converse in the garden of the academy; but in the very next shot, it is María who interjects between Diego and the inspector, providing the third term which disrupts homosocial mirroring.[11] Less evident than these graphic symmetries is the use of sound bridges (the staggering of dialogue or effects from one sequence to another). Thus towards the end of the film we see María facing the camera through a shop window with Diego watching her outside. As his head moves gradually to obscure hers, a voice on the soundtrack offers a definition of an eclipse: when two stars come together their light appears to be extinguished; but in their brief convergence both acquire a new brilliance, which is dark and fiery. As the next shot reveals, the voice is that of Angel's psychiatrist (Carmen Maura), who is reading to him in the hospital. The image is not simply a fine example of that 'abstraction' which Almodóvar seeks to lend his amorous role play. It also suggests in its visual and auditory overlap the fantastic dissolution of sexual difference, the pleasures and perils of an intersubjective fusion that is both desired and feared. Feminine fetishization in *Matador* thus points, finally, to the fragility of sexual difference. When the bloody wound of the woman is passed to the man, we are shown (in Elizabeth Grosz's words) 'not only how men may objectify women, but also the threat posed for phallic masculinity in the very conception of woman as castrated.'[12]

DISAVOWAL

ANGEL: Vengo a denunciar una violación.
COMISARIO: ¿Te han violado?
ANGEL: No. Yo he sido el violador.
COMISARIO: ¿Estás seguro?
ANGEL: I've come to report a rape.
POLICE INSPECTOR: Have you been raped?
ANGEL: No. I was the rapist.
POLICE INSPECTOR: Are you sure?

Matador is Almodóvar's most rhapsodic treatment of love between a man and a woman. Yet the director has claimed that the film is a love story not between a male and female but between two people of the same 'species': in spite of the superficial heterosexuality of the protagonists the relationship is really one of 'homosexuality' between a pair of identical beings (Albaladejo, p. 81). But if here heterosexuality is disavowed, elsewhere it is compared to necrophilia. Diego instructs his girlfriend Eva to 'play dead' when he penetrates her; and in the original script it is only when she emits a 'sigh of pleasure' at his orgasm that the audience knows she is not merely feigning death (p. 43). The involuntary spasm of Eva's body is thus made to speak the truth of Diego's autoerotic and pornographic voyeurism, which becomes indistinguishable from his practice of alloeroticism.

Angel's attempted rape of Eva is motivated by homosexual panic: he attempts to prove to Diego and himself that he is not queer ('maricón'). However, the question of homosexuality is constantly reasserted in the film, only to receive equally vehement denials. Thus the wounded Diego, who figures castration to María's deadly, virilized femininity (acting, Almodóvar suggests, 'like a ballerina' (Albaladejo, p. 81)), represents the phallus to the virginal Angel: in an early scene in which the pair confront each other over a billiard cue, the latter confesses that he 'doesn't know how to play' and that he has never slept with a woman (Plate 10). But Angel is not simply sexless, as his name might suggest. Although he defiantly rejects Diego's proposal that he might prefer men, Angel is the centre for a constellation of disavowals which go beyond his character to contaminate the film as a whole.

Graphic matches point to an identification or merging between men which anticipates that between Diego and María. Thus when Angel first visits the police station, his face is seen through the window alongside the reflection of the watching police inspector: though they are facing different directions their images coincide. The inspector seems unwilling to believe Angel is a rapist and asks rather if he has been raped. Angel thus provokes a certain disturbance in representation, serves as an unwitting pointer to the actual reversibility of 'active' and 'passive' relations between men, which can be achieved only in fantastic disavowal by Diego and María.

Disavowal is linked to fetishism. Just as in the latter female castration is at once affirmed and denied, so in the former repressed material is allowed to enter consciousness even as that repression is maintained. And, as D. A. Miller has argued, the question of homosexuality can never be indifferent in cinema, cannot be dismissed as an 'offhand reference'.[13] Diego's question to Angel remains open throughout the film. And the torero describes the younger man to the police inspector as a 'mystery', someone 'difficult to define'. Angel is shot consistently tighter in the frame than other characters; he is stripped naked and dressed in red; and his eyes look up to the sky in a form of mystic jouissance. And as a character who is defined by inaction (unable to perform either sex or murder; fainting at the sight of blood) he corresponds more consistently than María to the fetishized, feminine object of narrative cinema. The script confirms this quality, citing the 'strange excitation' that takes hold of him when he sees photographs of the murder victims, an excitation which reaches 'an almost hypnotic state' (p. 35). Confined to the hospital, Angel speaks like a 'visionary', his words taking on 'an apocalyptic meaning' (p. 92). The sexual difference abolished between the male and female 'of the same species' is here reasserted between the (intermittently) phallic man (Diego) and his pallid, ethereal admirer. But Angel's feminization leads to psychosis. Unable to distinguish between self and world (between his own desires and his telepathic hallucinations), he displays involuntary spasms or 'excitations' of the body, betraying that frenzy of the visible which speaks to the spectator of mystic or orgasmic pleasure.

Angel, the script tells us, could be very attractive, if it were not for his shyness and lack of self-confidence (p. 1). In a typical gesture of disavowal, the possibility of a homosexual gaze is (even here in the private space of an unpublished manuscript) at once revealed and denied. But the film does contain one minor character, the police inspector, who offers the spectator visual knowledge of homosexual pleasure. In one sequence in the middle part of the film (a sequence absent in the script) we are given a montage in which the camera pans slowly over the crotches of young male students as they practise their balletic bullfighting passes (the female students seen in previous sequences at this location are absent). Like the slasher images at the start of the film, the viewpoint of this voyeuristic scene has not been established. Eventually we are shown a reverse shot of the ironic and amused figure of the police inspector, who is partially screened behind foliage. It is significant that Diego, who is directing the students, cannot at first see the observer: the set-up thus points to an involuntary revelation of the body in motion staged to a concealed spectator (behind the tree or in the cinema).

Almodóvar has suggested that the minor characters in the film are 'zombies', circling around the main couple (Albaladejo, p. 83). But the inspector's subjectivity has already been eloquently emphasized in the film through his mode of looking. Thus, as the script confirms, he is by nature 'sober, sceptical, and dispassionate'; yet finds himself 'attracted by the defenceless and mysterious beauty' of Angel (pp. 26, 35). A voyeur (like Diego), the inspector is also veiled (like María), the object of dark desires which must be drawn into visibility. He thus participates in that reversibility we saw in the bisexual Angel. The dwelling of the camera on the young students' bodies is significant, moreover, because it raises two questions infrequent in film theory. The first is that of male exhibitionism (which is, of course, clinically far more frequent than female). Is it possible to think a narrative cinema in which men rather than women form those fetishes in the presence of which action must succumb to glamorous stasis? The second question is that of female, heterosexual fetishism. Naomi Schor has recently argued that 'female fetishism is invisible, untheorizable because it coincides with the norm of phallocentrism, which is to say the fetishization by the culture of the phallus *on men*.'[14] She also notes, as mentioned earlier, that the female form of fetishism is the collecting of memorabilia, an activity much stressed by the film in María's cult of objects associated metonymically with Diego (the ritual instruments and costumes of the corrida). It thus seems possible that to fetishize the male body as partial and passive object of an active, desiring look is only possible by positing a gay, male observer, whose point of view is obliquely related to a dominant regime of visibility. It is telling that Pauline Kael, in her generally positive review, should criticize the 'timing' of this sequence.[15] Yet in *Matador* that possibility, that chance (which will always remain untimely to a heterosexual audience) is raised, only immediately to be denied. The police inspector is one of the few characters in Almodóvar's work to whom no sexual activity (other than looking) is attributed: he even refuses the female psychiatrist's offer of a comradely night in bed, with a guarantee of no sex.

Just as fetishism is at once a defence against female castration felt to be all too real, and a denial of that castration through displacement of the woman's phallus onto substitute objects, so homosexuality can be affirmed only to be denied, allowed to enter consciousness only on condition that repression be maintained. Hence if Diego and María stage a dance of reciprocity in which the bloody wound of the woman is repeated and reversed, and if Angel poses the necessity and the impossibility of a bisexual position which would fuse active and passive; the police inspector (with his ironic and dispassionate gaze) represents that loss and pathos by which gay men are reconciled to a dominant regime of visibility, are permitted brief and untimely access to the normalized perversions of narrative cinema.

NATIONALITY

Esp
a dividida.
Spain divided.

The first titles before *Matador*'s credit sequence state that the film is subsidized by the Ministry of Culture and co-produced with Spanish state television. According to official figures, half of the film's recognized budget of seventy million pesetas was covered by state subsidies granted before production began and offset against box office receipts after the film's release. This figure included a 25 per cent subsidy granted only to films of 'special artistic quality'.[16] In 1986, the year of its release, *Matador* was the third most successful Spanish film in the domestic market, grossing almost one hundred million pesetas and seen by over three hundred thousand people.[17] It was beaten only by a popular farce and a reverent adaptation of a literary classic, which starred the two most bankable actors of the day.[18] Of the films which were granted advance subsidy during filming in 1985, *Matador* has the fourth highest balance in favour of the producers after the deduction of the proportion of gross owed to the state, almost thirty million pesetas. By way of comparison, Saura's *El amor brujo* (Love the Magician), with both budget and subsidies twice that of Almodóvar's film, gave a negative balance (owed to the state) of nearly fifty million (Gómez B. de Castro, p. 252).

It is clear, then, that more than Almodóvar's earlier works *Matador* struck something of a chord with Spanish audiences at a particular historical moment, when other films on national themes (such as Saura's) did not. Although the director himself denies it and professes indifference to bullfighting (Albaladejo, p. 80), there appears to have been a revival of interest in the corrida in that period. Coincidentally, at the same time *Matador* was being filmed, Catalan Antoni Ribas was shooting a sex comedy, *El primer torero porno* (The First Porno Bullfighter). While on *Matador*'s belated release in the UK and the US critics tended either to stress its 'Iberian' pedigree[19] or to warn that English-speaking audiences might not appreciate Spanish jokes or subtexts,[20] for Spaniards the question of nationality was much more complex. The more perspicacious reviewers (such as Vicente Molina Foix and José Luis Guarner) suggested that Almodóvar had transformed 'racial tradition' into fantasy, elegantly denaturalizing the *españolada* and creating an 'admirable piece of nonsense [*disparate*] for Hispanists'.[21] Hence, while foreign critics tended to see the film as re-presenting (and thus reconfirming) national traits assumed to transcend both cinema and history, Spanish critics (whether favourable or not) saw the film as representation, as the reworking of a cultural tradition that carried within it, necessarily, a certain social history.

One scene that is particularly relevant here is the fashion show at which Almodóvar himself plays the part of the designer. Enthusing over model Eva's face wound (the result, we remember, of Angel's attempted rape) and over the vomit accidentally splattered over another model's dress, he tells scatty reporter Verónica Forqué that the show is called 'Spain divided', because Spaniards are either envious or intolerant. Almodóvar thus invokes, parodically, the topos of 'the two Spains', of the painful divisions notorious in Spanish history, but in a playful register which deprives such clichés of their continuing resonance. For the essence of fashion is modernity, a modernity which participates in psychic rather than historic realities. Thus the fashion show is in general the site of active and passive scopophilia, an arena for women to act out both voyeurism and exhibitionism to each other. And it is the place in which the fetish proclaims itself as substitute for an original femininity which is itself an illusion. Finally, it is a scene of disavowal, in which feminine castration is affirmed through its negation. In this sequence María sports a long braid of hair which swishes backwards and forwards between the two edges of the split back of her dress. It is an appropriately playful and suggestive image of loss and possession, castration and phallus.

But the trace of history in this scene is not only in the modernity of the costumes. It is also in the setting itself: an abandoned slaughterhouse in the southern suburb of Legazpi, which the script tells us is a 'gloomy place which . . . still preserves the traces [*huellas*] of ancient sacrifices' (p. 67). And history is also embodied in Eva's mother (Chus Lampreave), who, sitting beside Diego, asks him if he would like some *pipas* (the traditional dried sunflower seeds, unlikely fare at a swish fashion show).

Caught in the light on the catwalk, Eva's mother does a brief turn before returning to her seat. It is one of those inspired moments of craziness typical of Almodóvar's comedy. But I would suggest, finally, that Eva's very modern mother shares with the major characters a love of performance which should not be trivialized. Indeed, she points to a third approach to the question of nationality in *Matador*, one which avoids both the idealist shibboleth of the 'Iberian character' and the sterile impersonality of a joyless internationalism. That possibility is that nationality is neither essence nor absence but performance.[22] Let us examine the final scene of the film for evidence of this.

Diego and María have retreated to her house in the country to which they are followed by the other characters, led by the telepathic Angel. The camera pans over the lovers' naked bodies stretched out on Diego's cape, as the torero brushes a rose (held in his teeth) against María's pubic hair and up to her nipples. The couple are back-lit to give their bodies a soft glow. 'Espérame en el cielo, corazón' (Wait for me in heaven, darling), a song sung by Mina, is heard on the soundtrack. As Diego penetrates María, she plunges a hairpin into the nape of his neck and, entreating him to look at her, fires a gun into her mouth.

As Almodóvar himself suggests in the press book, this is a unique moment of reciprocity for the characters who have till then 'made love alone'. It is also the 'hardest' of the film's soft-core sex scenes, with its glimpse of female (if not male) genitalia. More important perhaps is the combination of abstraction and hispanicity: the lovers' orgasms coincide with a total eclipse outside the house, the ultimate fusion of celestial and terrestrial bodies;[23] yet their scene of desire is also ostentatiously folkloric, dense with the iconography (flowers, music, costume) of the españolada. For Thierry Cazals this 'fetishist' decor is a 'museum' of past mise-en-scènes in which nothing new can be born, an 'empty arena' in which it is no longer possible to die of love, but only of not seeing oneself love.[24] I would suggest, however, that in this 'cinema of anti-memory' the repetition of pre-existing motifs need not mean sterility or narcissism. The 'artist of modern life'[25] can allow himself only fetishized allusions to a threatening national history. Just as the sexual fetish is a defence against female lack and a disavowal of that lack, so the historical fetish protects the subject from the wounds of history, while abolishing that history, confining it to the hermetic, aestheticized space of the cinematic mise-en-scène. If it is the role of narrative cinema to resolve the male castration crisis precipitated by the sight of the woman by fetishizing that woman, converting her into a glamorous object, then it may be the role of national cinema to resolve historical crises of division in a similar way. Hence the unprecedented success of Matador, a 'racial' Spanish drama with a 'Japanese' style (press book).

In the article on modernity whose title I have just cited, Vicente Molina Foix has called attention to a paradox in Almodóvar's cinema. On the one hand, he is a Baudelairean flâneur, at home anywhere in contemporary society and acutely attentive to the particularities of his time. On the other, he specializes in curiously deracinated characters, whose misfortunes are never the result of social injustice or political oppression (pp. 18–19). Molina Foix relates this paradox to Almodóvar's wary relation to a Francoist heritage, which he denies the power to determine either himself or his films; and we have seen that this mechanism of disavowal (of reference and repression) is also present in Almodóvar's treatment of the voyeurism and fetishism characteristic of the cinematic apparatus. But to claim, as Almodóvar does, that the subject (of history, of cinema) is not determined by the past is not to deny that past a more subtle and mediated role in the construction of subjectivity and desire. In its lush critique and celebration of power and pleasure, in its final fascination with the involuntary spasm of death, *Matador* speaks in spite of itself of a crisis of division which is as much national as it is libidinal, which must also find its place in the frenzy of cinematic visibility.

NOTES

1. Spanish press book, Madrid 1986.

2. My edn, London 1991. For more recent feminist anti-censorship perspectives on pornography, see Lynne Segal and Mary McIntosh, eds., *Sex Exposed: Sexuality and the Pornography Debate*, London 1992.

3. Pedro Crespo, review in *ABC*, 8 March 1986; Eduardo Gil de Muro, *Vida Nueva*, 22–9 March 1986, p. 58; Víctor Vadorrey, *Hoja del Lunes*, 16 March 1986.

4. See Christopher Tookey, review in *Sunday Telegraph*, 8 December 1991.

5. Pedro Almodóvar and Jesús Ferrero, 'Lo inevitable', Madrid 1986.

6. Anne Billson, review, *New Statesman and Society*, 6 December 1991.

7. See Margaret Whitford, 'Rape: Political Perspectives', in Elizabeth Wright, ed., *Feminism and Psychoanalysis: A Critical Dictionary*, Oxford 1992, pp. 364–6.

8. *Femmes Fatales*, New York 1991, pp. 49–56.

9. See Doane for similar framings of Glenn Ford and Rita Hayworth in *Gilda* (pp. 99–101).

10. See Peter Evans, 'Almodóvar's *Matador*: Genre, Subjectivity, and Desire', *Bulletin of Hispanic Studies* (forthcoming) for an account of this sequence with reference to María's assertion of a 'pre-Oedipal masculinity'.

11. Compare the triangular framings in *Gilda* once more analysed by Doane (p. 113).

12. 'Fetishization', in Elizabeth Wright, ed., *Feminism and Psychoanalysis: A Critical Dictionary*, Oxford 1992, pp. 117–18.

13. 'Anal Rope', in Diana Fuss, ed., *Inside/Out: Lesbian Theories, Gay Theories*, London 1991, pp. 119–41.

14. 'Fetishism', Elizabeth Wright, ed., *Feminism and Psychoanalysis: A Critical Dictionary*, Oxford 1992, pp. 113–17.

15. *New Yorker*, 16 May 1988.

16. Ramiro Gómez B. de Castro, *La producción cinematográfica española: de la transición a la democracia*, Bilbao 1989, p. 252.

17. Francisco Llinàs, *Cuatro años de cine español*, Madrid 1987, p. 99.

18. The films are *Sé infiel y no mires con quién* (Be Unfaithful with Anyone You Like) and *Tiempo de silencio* (Time of Silence), respectively, the latter starring Imanol Arias and Victoria Abril.

19. See Philip French, review, *Observer*, 8 December 1991.

20. See reviews by Peter Besas, *Variety*, 9 April 1986; and 'Rich.', *Variety*, 26 November 1986.

21. Molina Foix, *Fotogramas*, April 1986, p. 6; Guarner, *La Vanguardia*, 15 March 1986.

22. For nationality as performance, see Fernando Savater, 'Teoría del nacionalismo performativo', in *Impertinencias y desafíos*, Madrid 1981, pp. 68–80.

23. See Cristina Piccino's review in *Filmcritica*, vol. 40, no. 394, April 1989, pp 272–4 for a reading of this scene which stresses the 'fusion' of bodies into a 'new object' which liberates desire and surpasses codes.

24. Review in *Cahiers du Cinéma*, 407–8, May 1988, p. 144.

25. See Vicente Molina Foix, 'Il cineasta della vita moderna', in Sergio Naitza and Valeria Patané, *¡Folle, folle, folle, Pedro!*, Cagliari 1992, pp. 13–19.

6

LA LEY DEL DESEO

(THE LAW OF DESIRE, 1987)

A Talent for Production

THE DESIRE TO DESIRE

Hablar de estas cosas no es fácil. Hay que ser muy sincero, muy
hábil, y tener mucho talento.
Speaking of these things isn't easy. You have to be very sincere,
very skilful, and very talented.[1]

La ley del deseo is generally cited as Almodóvar's most autobiographical film. Like
Almodóvar, Pablo (Eusebio Poncela) is a successful film director, author of a number of
shocking films with bizarre titles ('The Paradigm of the Mussel'). He is also provided
with a glamorous transsexual sister, Tina (Carmen Maura), whose name mimics that of
Almodóvar's own much-loved brother and business partner, Agustín ('Tinín').
Almodóvar himself has declared that only two moments in the film derive from his own
life: the first is when Tina confronts the choirmaster who had abused her as a child; the
second is when Pablo sends his lover Juan (Miguel Molina) a perfect love-letter which
he asks Juan to sign and return to him (Vidal, p. 196). While Almodóvar claims that he
himself thought better of sending such a letter (thus distancing himself once more
from his narcissistic protagonist) he is clearly teasing his audience, daring them to
associate the director within the film with the one outside it, who had now achieved
such celebrity in Spain. The unpublished script[2] contains wry and ironic references to

the approach of middle age and the dubious advantages of celebrity (predicaments shared by Pablo and Pedro), which can be meant only for himself.

Spanish press coverage of the film suggests an eagerness to assert that auteur and object were one and the same. One critic calls it a 'shameless and unbridled manifesto', in which Almodóvar is 'stripped bare'.[3] Another calls it a 'desahogo', an 'outlet' or 'purging' of that which has previously been bottled up inside.[4] A third suggests that the film's 'exorbitance' seeks to undo repression by passing 'through scandal to freedom'.[5] This fantasy of immediate expression (of film as bodily discharge or psychic release) is perhaps paralleled by the material conditions under which *La ley del deseo* was made. Unable to find commercial funding, Almodóvar and his brother finally secured a largish budget given as ninety million pesetas (as compared to *Matador*'s seventy million); and, exploiting the newly instituted Miró Law, set up their own production company, El Deseo, S.A. As quite literally a self-production (albeit with a government advance subsidy of 40 per cent, secured with some difficulty),[6] *La ley del deseo* clearly offers itself as an auteurist work, one in which the figure of the director informs and transforms the audience's reception of the film. The production of a self suspended between life and cinema continued in Almodóvar's dealings with the press. In an important interview with well-known journalist and novelist Rosa Montero (called, characteristically, 'A Boy Like Me'), Almodóvar compares the making of *La ley del deseo* to a love affair: 'When you're madly in love with a boy and someone asks you: "Do you like him?", you don't know. All you know is that that's the only thing in your head right now, and that it includes every imaginable state of mind, from delight to despair.'[7] 'Architect of himself', in Montero's telling phrase, Almodóvar stresses both the extraordinary discipline his career has required of him and his inability to control his private life, in which (like his creation Pablo) he feels he is not desired as he would wish.

I am not concerned here with verifying such statements. Rather I would suggest that Spanish press coverage (whether sympathetic like Montero or censorious like much of the rest) reveals that far from being repressed, homosexuality was actually promoted by the straight media, anxious to procure 'personal' statements which could be presented as unambiguous testimony to the body of the author. As José Arroyo has suggested, there was thus a desire for homosexuality, an assumption that Almodóvar's career would not reach maturity until he had treated a topic which was assumed to be so intimately linked to him.[8] In this 'gay seduction', it was not at all clear who was the leading partner.

It is no accident that this fantasy of immediacy demanded by straight critics (the identification of director and character) is also played out within the film itself. For example, the closeness of the relation between siblings Pablo and Tina is established through an opening eye-line match: emerging from the cinema in which Pablo's latest erotic epic has been premiered, Tina casts a look out of frame, which is returned in the next shot by Pablo. The two then embrace as the image freezes. The privileged status of fraternity, suspended outside time and place, will be contrasted with the frantic displacements of erotic affairs. And the one character whose relation to the desired object is immediate will prove to be psychotic: after witnessing Pablo's film, young provincial Antonio (Antonio Banderas) descends to the cinema lavatories where, masturbating, he repeats the words he has just heard spoken on screen: 'Fuck me, fuck me'.

Within the film, then, such 'alignments of spectator and subject' are rare indeed, and are displaced by 'circuits for fantasy'.[9] As the prototype of the artist, Pablo's life is a 'double-edged boomerang'; and, unlike Antonio whose passion 'has no intermediaries', he is (in the words of the press book) 'tied to the typewriter with his heart pounding between the keys'. There is thus a certain abstraction or effacement of homosexuality in *La ley del deseo* which belies its relatively graphic sex scenes. For example, the relation between Pablo and the lacklustre Juan is safely displaced into the past from the very beginning of the film. Juan has decided to leave Madrid for the summer. And as the couple undress for a chaste last night together the soundtrack plays Brel's 'Ne me quitte pas'. Juan, who cannot love Pablo as he would wish to be loved, is always already lost, the object to whose absence Pedro must continually reconcile himself. The script stresses the familial relation between the two (Pablo leads Juan to the bedroom 'as one would a child')[10] and their tender chastity (p. 31). As dawn breaks over the capital, an overhead shot shows them naked and intertwined, Juan's leg wrapped around his lover.

The publicity photo corresponding to this scene is much reproduced (Plate 11). But it is perhaps significant that the name of Miguel Molina (whose face is covered by shadow) is often replaced by that of the better-known Antonio Banderas.[11] For part of the de-sexing of homosexuality in this film is the defacement of Pablo's multiple partners, who are presented as interchangeable. Symptomatic here is the ambiguous use of voice-over. While Pablo types the letter he will ask Juan to return to him as his own, the two voices merge on the soundtrack, become indistinguishable. But, as the film's delirious plot will prove, merger has its dangers; and the price of fusion (of overidentification) is death.

In *The Desire to Desire*,[12] Mary Ann Doane has given an excellent account of the complexities of the 'woman's film'. Doane states the characteristics by which audiences were addressed in such films as: 'proximity, passivity, overidentification' (p. 2). As the woman's position in dominant cinema is widely held to be resistant to narrativization per se (because 'aligned with spectacle, space, or image' [p. 5]), female spectators were encouraged to adopt 'the impossible place of a purely passive desire' (p. 7), a place of contiguity in which the body, too close, was 'wrapped up in itself' (p. 12). Founded as it was on 'temporal immediacy, spatial proximity [and the] confounding of desire' (p. 13), feminine fantasy was 'desexualized' (p. 18), confined by 'a dangerous intimacy with the image'. Woman's desire in these films is thus a desire to desire, an inability to accede to that fetishizing distance which grants (heterosexual) men visual pleasure in narrative cinema.

Doane takes care to distinguish between audience address and spectator positioning (p. 34): the responses of empirical women (and men) to actual films are not exhausted by the structures of feeling she analyses. However, Doane's account of the desexualization and dangerous proximity of the woman to the image corresponds uncannily to Almodóvar's representation of gay men in *La ley del deseo*, their bodies so close that they are literally defaced. Almodóvar himself has frequently denied that the film is addressed to a gay audience; it is perhaps more interesting to ask why such disavowals are so persistent.[13] For it is indeed difficult to speak of such matters in a society which is, as Almodóvar acknowledges (Vidal, p. 207), profoundly homophobic. And the playfully ironic and narcissistic appeal to one's 'talent' is a useful strategy in this context, one employed by both the empirical and the fictional director. The action of *La ley del deseo* will suggest, however, that it is only in the moment of merger, in the terrible and pleasurable shattering of the subject, that jouissance is to be found.

STRAIGHTENING OUT

Un hombre no soporta oír que otro le pida: 'Fóllame'.
One man cannot bear to hear another ask him: 'Fuck me'.
(Almodóvar in Vidal, p. 209)

In 'A Gay Seduction', José Arroyo argues that the challenges *La ley del deseo* poses to a straight audience are dissolved, one by one, by narrative means. A plot which objectifies the male body and charts the formation of a homosexual couple (Pablo-Antonio) is offset by 'the affirmation of traditional values such as the family' through the plot line of Pablo's affection for sister Tina and her lesbian lover's daughter Ada

(p. 44). Cross-cutting between dangerous gay eroticism and reassuring if idiosyncratic domestic drama, Almodóvar straightens out his queer characters and offers both the shocking difference and the comfortable similarity required of him by a heterosexual Spanish audience. By the end of the film, argues Arroyo, the traditional narrative requirements of process and closure have been achieved.

I would propose, however, that the character of Antonio remains troubling, unresolved. Miguel Albaladejo notes that, unlike Pablo and Tina whose backstories are exhaustively documented, Antonio is a 'void', without a past (p. 29). As the figure of passion, absolute and unqualified, he is deprived of the gaps or 'fissures' (press book) of the other characters. But, ironically, he is also the only character placed at that intersection of the public and private realms which in English is known as 'the closet': spied on by his obsessive German mother, Antonio insists that Pablo sign love-letters to him with a woman's name.

The framing of the encounters between Pablo and Antonio makes his marginal position clear. When they first meet, Pablo attempts to take Antonio home, but is brushed off. He walks out of frame. But in the very next shot it is Antonio who, having conceded that he has 'lost' the pick-up 'competition', stalks out of frame, leaving a puzzled Pablo behind. Similarly, when later they say goodbye to one another outside a restaurant, Antonio shakes hands formally with Pablo, walks towards the edge of the frame and then rushes back, as the camera moves in on his savage embrace. The script tells us that this passionate kiss is 'compulsive', that Antonio has 'forgotten he is in the middle of the street' (p. 83). Barely bound by the limits of the cinematic frame, Antonio is also progressively unrestrained by social restrictions, even though his bourgeois provincial background makes him more vulnerable to those same restrictions than the glamorous metropolitans amongst whom he moves. Pablo's relaxed acceptance of his homosexuality as open secret (a state of affairs in which the media are shown as happy to collude) is thus troubled by Antonio's refusal to acknowledge boundaries, whether social or sexual.

But there is more. When the two men are about to make love for the first time, neophyte Antonio interrogates the experienced Pablo as to whether his 'promiscuity' has made him vulnerable to sexually transmitted diseases. Pablo denies the charge, irritably, before penetrating Antonio on the latter's request. This scene, which features the use of lubricant but not condoms, was much resented by some North American gay viewers, who held Almodóvar responsible for promoting unsafe sex.[14] Pauline Kael, however, in her perceptive review, suggests rather that as a 'conscious fantasist', Almodóvar is as aware of AIDS as is the audience.[15] Defiantly championing sensuality,

Almodóvar's response to a health crisis which was less familiar in Spain than in the US is not mimetic but redemptive: he refuses to portray the behaviour made necessary by reality, but rather relieves his audience of that reality by conjuring it away.

In an unpublished paper, María Donapetry cites the connection between sodomy and death in a homosexualization of the Pietà found in Genet's *Querelle de Brest*.[16] The image recurs in the final shot of *La ley del deseo* when Pablo will cradle the dead Antonio in his arms. Hence if Almodóvar rejects the historical connection of unprotected anal sex with mortal illness (and thus attempts to console gay men through filmic fantasy for the loss of the unselfconscious pleasures of earlier times), the unconscious association of sodomy and death will reverberate throughout the film in ways which resist strict control.

Almodóvar has claimed in interviews that men cannot bear to hear another ask to be penetrated, however liberated they may think themselves (Vidal, pp. 208–9). While this may not correspond to many gay men's experience, Almodóvar is surely right to call attention to internalized homophobia and to the possibility that such prejudices have not been eliminated even in the most sexually open of societies. Leo Bersani's 'Is the Rectum a Grave?' has investigated similarly disquieting territory, with equally controversial results.[17] Bersani begins by suggesting that there is a pervasive aversion to sex which 'can coexist quite comfortably with, say, the most enthusiastic endorsement of polysexuality with multiple sex partners' (p. 198). This widespread phenomenon is linked to the difficulty in basing a political programme on a sexual practice: sex between men can lead to conservativism as much as to liberalism (p. 205). The peculiar paradox for gay men is that we both struggle against definitions of maleness which oppress us, and incorporate those definitions which we 'carry within us as permanently renewable sources of excitement' (p. 209). It is the violation of our ideal, and of our identification in which we take pleasure. The pathological fear of AIDS is thus a horror of male submission: 'the seductive and intolerable image of a grown man, legs high in the air, unable to refuse the suicidal ecstasy of being a woman' (p. 212).

This is precisely the position of Antonio in *La ley del deseo*, his ankles bent behind the ears. And if, as Bersani argues, 'to be penetrated is to abdicate power' (p. 212) then it is this wilful and pleasurable self-denial that Almodóvar, also, finds 'intolerable'. Response is further complicated, however, when we watch a straight-identified actor (Banderas) submit to his director and play out scenes which (he claimed) initially 'made [him] unsure who [he] was' (Vidal, p. 206). Moreover, the various points made by Bersani are confirmed by the position of Antonio the character (and actor?) in the film.

In spite of his enthusiastic compulsion to perform sex, Antonio clearly shares with Almodóvar a certain aversion to it. As a character branded as 'reactionary' by Pablo (industrious, puritanical, clean-living), he illustrates the fact that there is no necessary connection between homosexuality and political radicalism. Moreover, as a character coded as 'straight-acting' (indifferent to camp and soberly dressed in Lacoste sports shirts) he represents a certain intolerant and inflexible notion of masculinity which is at once hostile and attractive to some gay men, that masculinity whose violation we can most enjoy and regret. If we must urgently resist that fantasy which equates anality and death, then we can, still and more urgently perhaps, take pleasure with Pablo (with Almodóvar?) in that 'internalized phallic male as an infinitely loved object of sacrifice' (Bersani, p. 222). Such is Antonio's role in *La ley del deseo*. It is a role which carries with it the greatest of risks, the risk (in Bersani's words) of 'losing sight of the self'.

TRANSSEXUAL HISTORIES

TINA: Los recuerdos son lo único que tengo.
TINA: All I have left is memories.

Buxom and flame-haired Carmen Maura's Tina squeezes through the railings into her old school (located precisely by Almodóvar in the upmarket calle Serrano). As the organ plays a hymn of praise to the Virgin, Tina advances, singing, to the camera, which pulls back to include the elderly organist. Her red dress with white polka dots[18] contrasts with his dark cassock. When Tina announces that she is the boy who once sang in his choir, we are given a reverse angle of the priest's discomposure. Tina tells him that she was betrayed by the only two men she has really loved: her spiritual father and her natural father, who also abandoned her.

When the priest exclaims, understandably, to Tina: 'How you've changed!' she replies: 'The whole world has changed.' Minimizing her own transformation, Tina seeks to enforce through sheer strength of will a singular and continuous identity: it is the uncompromising 'Soy yo' ('It's me') which precipitates the cut to the priest's reaction shot. The priest urges her to forget their love affair. But Tina replies that all she has now is memories. I will suggest a little later that this cult of memory is more than simple nostalgia. But at this point in the film what is significant is the contrast between image and words. Flagrantly visible in the chapel, Tina is (in Pauline Kael's words) 'overacting womanhood . . . the role of her life'. But if that performance is denaturalized by its very ostentation (if femininity is too clearly a masquerade), then the transsexual cannot 'pass', will be forced to 'crash land' in mid gender flight.

Tina's nostalgia for objects which are (like Pablo's) always already lost recurs in her performance of the leading role in Pablo's version of Cocteau's *La Voix humaine*. Acting out her life once more (for her lesbian lover is watching from the wings), Tina proclaims into the prop telephone to her absent lover: 'Before when we had problems, we made it up with nothing but a look. By telephone, it's different.' Here she and Cocteau's Voice reveal a longing for that unmediated communication achieved through sight, so different from the mechanical alienation of the telephone. But the irony is that, condemned as she is to the realm of the visible, Tina is a living icon of the falseness of appearance, a flagrant example of that cinema specularization which condemns those coded as feminine to mute and fetishistic devotion. The fact that Bibi Andersen, the actress playing the 'GG' (genuine girl) in this sequence, is well known in Spain as a transsexual and was frequently misrecognized as a transvestite by foreign critics only heightens this tyranny of the visual. A look is no guarantee of mutual comprehension. Indeed it can be deadly.

Later Tina, Pablo, and child Ada are returning home after a performance, through a city ominously cloaked by the hoardings common in summer. They come across a cleaner hosing down the street, his jet of water arching, luminous, across the screen. In a clinging orange knit dress, with a zip down the front, Tina begs for the water to be turned on her. It is a scene of orgasmic pleasure, and one in which the other characters are delighted voyeurs. It is perhaps characteristic that a review which castigates Almodóvar for his supposed 'excesses' in the film, for his lack of equilibrium and continuity, should be illustrated with a still from this sequence (Plate 12).[19] And Marvin D'Lugo reads the scene as an erotic spectacle in which transsexual and city coincide as the 'place of a persistent breakdown of the traditional categories of sexual identity in Spanish society'.[20] It is not clear, however, whether such jouissance really stages the breakdown of distinctions between male and female, hetero and homo in a city of constant renovation. For (as in the chapel scene) by escaping into ever more flagrant exhibitionism, Tina is also reconfirming that closeness to the image which has such fatal effects in the woman's film.

The press book describes Tina as a 'self-fabrication'. And as in the case of Banderas's Antonio, Maura's performance as Tina brings a new inflection to the character. She describes to Nuria Vidal how, in such scenes as the hosing-down in the street, she 'gave' herself entirely to the character, was unable to separate herself from her (p. 211). Going to the extreme of taking up weight training (which she detested) for the part, Maura attempted to transform her own body as Tina had also. Moreover, the audience's knowledge that she is a GG (like their awareness that Banderas is married) works against the role, to achieve a certain bracketing of gender identity.

It seems unlikely that Almodóvar has a great interest in transsexuals per se; rather he is concerned with suspending that distinction between artifice and truth which has so oppressed sexual dissidents of all kinds (Vidal, p. 213). However, his portrayal of Tina coincides with Sandy Stone's recent 'Posttranssexual Manifesto'.[21] Resisting radical feminists' accounts of transsexualism as 'rape' of women's bodies, Stone nonetheless criticizes some gender-reassignment narratives whose 'denial of mixture' and erection of an 'impenetrable barrier' between pre- and post-operative gender identities she cannot accept (p. 288). Rather than projecting a potentially irruptive male principle onto 'God-like' figures of surgeon or father, Stone suggests transgendered people embrace the whole of their personal history and reject that wilful amnesia required of them if they are to pass (p. 295). The brave move of taking responsibility for such a history would enable a possibility of political action based on 'reclaiming the power of the refigured and reinscribed body' (pp. 298–9).

In spite of her nostalgia for a singular and unfissured identity and her willingness to project masculine identifications onto God-like father figures, Tina may by read as just such a posttranssexual. In thrall to memories of the past, she cannot bear that her history be erased. And in spite of her ostentatious femininity, Almodóvar has her breach the 'impenetrable' gender divides at key moments in the narrative. For example, when accused by a policeman of 'not being a woman' she floors him with a very virile punch. The assumption of mixture may indeed be a source of political agency.

Most important however is Tina's grand confession towards the end of the film. The jealous Antonio has killed Juan. Suspected of the murder, Pablo has crashed his car and been hospitalized with amnesia in Madrid. Dressed with unusual modesty (white dress and earrings), Tina retells their life stories, of which the siblings have not spoken before, in an effort to jog Pablo's memory. As a boy Tina had an affair with their father. Fleeing to Morocco, he had encouraged her to change sex, before abandoning her. Tina confronts Pablo with photos of themselves as children, and both begin to weep.

Of course, the family romance is absurdly extravagant, typically Almodóvarian. However, its comedy is qualified by Maura's gravely underplayed performance, so different from her acting style elsewhere in the film. And one vital line here is Tina's: 'Your amnesia deprives me of memory.' In this acknowledgement that history is a communal project, that the past (in the family, in society) is an intersubjective process, lies the posttranssexual resolution to shun the hard-earned pleasure of passing, and take responsibility for historical change. It is a challenge which is not taken up by *La ley del deseo*'s gay male characters.

PRODUCING ONESELF

ANTONIO: Quererte de este modo es un delito; pero estoy dis-
puesto a pagar por ello.
ANTONIO: Loving you like this is a crime; but I'm ready to pay for
it.

When Almodóvar and his brother presented the script of *La ley del deseo* to the Ministry of Culture, they were refused funding by the advisory boards (*comisiones*) on the grounds that the film had no 'story' (Vidal, p. 245). Eventually, the government nominee responsible for film production, Fernando Méndez-Leite, was obliged to give the go-ahead himself. On its release *La ley del deseo* became the fourth biggest grossing film in Spain for 1987, making over two hundred million pesetas and winning a domestic audience of over six hundred thousand.[22] More importantly perhaps, *La ley del deseo* confirmed Almodóvar's breakthrough abroad. It was reported to be the film which most represented Spain at foreign film festivals that year,[23] frequently shown alongside Mario Camus's scrupulous adaptation of García Lorca's *La casa de Bernarda Alba* (The House of Bernarda Alba). There could be no more telling juxtaposition of old and new Spains, rural austerity and urban extravagance. *La ley del deseo* earned much praise in the US, where after screening at the Miami film festival it was premiered at commercial theatres only twelve days after its Madrid release, an unprecedented achievement for a Spanish film.[24] Later in the year, Almodóvar won the Los Angeles critics' prize for 'best new director' for this his sixth feature.[25]

The first film of Almodóvar's to be shown commercially in Britain, *La ley del deseo* had the dubious distinction of pigeon-holing Almodóvar as a 'gay director' and creating a frame of reference in which the other, earlier films were read. It also involved him in debates around censorship and the 'promotion' of homosexuality which had little meaning in a Spanish context: he could only throw up his hands in horror at British puritanism.[26] But there seems little doubt that one reason for *La ley del deseo*'s success abroad was the emergence of Antonio Banderas as a sex symbol, a new Joe Dallesandro to Almodóvar's Warhol. However, here as so often, Spanish responses were more complex than those of foreigners. When, after two more films for Almodóvar, Banderas began an English-language career in Hollywood with Arnie Glimcher's *The Mambo Kings* (1992), even the hippest of the British press knew him only as the 'Latin lover', the former Almodóvar star who had appeared as Madonna's love interest in the 1991 documentary *In Bed with Madonna* (US title *Truth or Dare*).[27] But a lengthy cover feature in the Madrid *El Europeo* undertook a critical examination of the same myth: 'Antonio Banderas: el mito del latin-lover'.[28] Angel López Soto's full-page photos frame Banderas, ironically and iconically, as Valentino; formal in tails; or 'natural' with bare chest and beads. And the accompanying text makes something of the incongruity that a Spaniard's first English-speaking role should be as a Cuban. Thus while foreigners were free to take the 'Latin' image straight and to identify the actor with the passionate roles he played, Spaniards were more reflective, taking pleasure in picturing Banderas's foreign success, but qualifying it by what they knew of North American ignorance of and indifference to their culture.

Ambiguous testimony to this cross-cultural pay-off was Banderas's chaperoning of Sharon Stone at the Oscar awards (both sported red ribbons for AIDS solidarity); and his subsequent appearance with her in a lavish Spanish commercial for Freixenet sparkling wine, filmed on the *Queen Mary* at Long Beach and directed by the currently fashionable cineaste Bigas Luna.[29] Stone's faltering Spanish in this spot (so similar to Banderas's inadequate English) attests to the curious and mutual exploitation linking Hollywood glamour to 'Latin' romance.

Few would begrudge Banderas his US success; and he is rumoured to be playing a gay man with AIDS in his next US film. But the continuing resonance in Spain of the provocations caused by *La ley del deseo* are by no means clear. Almodóvar has made no films since *La ley del deseo* in a recognizable gay milieu; and far fewer gay-themed films are produced in contemporary Spain than in the late seventies.[30] Even today the film's admirers seem unhappy to mention the word 'homosexuality'. Enthusiast Angel S. Harguindey (who played the cameo role of a journalist in *Entre tinieblas*) wrote recently that the 'small scandal' the film caused on its cinematic release would not be repeated when it was shown on television. But he speaks, coyly, of 'forbidden loves'.[31] And when next *La ley del deseo* was networked the press ad talked more mysteriously yet of 'impossible loves' and 'unexpected situations'.[32] Almodóvar would no doubt concur with this abstract framing of the film's *amour fou*, which is by no means unique to gays. But, by coincidence, on the same page of the newspaper maverick columnist Eduardo Haro Tecglen prints a passionate call for an end to the repression of Spanish lesbians and gays.[33] Claiming, most unusually for Spain, that the homosexual question has not been resolved and that only a tiny fraction of society is without prejudice, Haro writes that women and men are condemned to a 'clandestinity' worse even than that of opponents to the Franco regime long ago. And writing shortly before the national elections, Haro's fears are whetted by the threat of a return to an unspeakable pre-democratic past.

It may perhaps be relevant to note that Haro's late son, a casualty of the *movida*, was one of the tiny number in Spain to have written openly on homosexuality and popular culture.[34] What is clearly the case is that the libertarian ethic of *La ley del deseo*, so typical of its time, has not proved able to contribute to a political or cultural space for the continuing discussion of homosexuality in Spain. One grave symptom of this is that lacking, until very recently, effective communal organization around AIDS, Spaniards, including gay men, have suffered the highest rate of infection in Europe.[35]

When Antonio leaves the bed after last making love with Pablo, the latter is shot from behind a sheet which is like a shroud. It is Antonio, the obsessive lover, who is about to shoot himself, choosing to pay the price of a criminal passion. But it is as if Pablo is dead already, in life. It is an ominous image for gay men in Spain, an unnerving pointer to the pleasures and perils of a shattered or effaced subjectivity, sceptical of a community or a politics founded on sexual practice. But if in its disavowal of AIDS and homo-phobia *La ley del deseo* reveals a refusal to deal with the everyday life of lesbians and gays in Spain, it is because Almodóvar seeks to intervene at the more potent and fluid level of fantasy, of the constitution of new cinematic subjects. And his self-producing characters, scornful of fixed gender identity and object choice, have earned him attacks from both the homophobic right, who would enforce silence, and the moralistic left, who would insist on more positive images. Almodóvar has thus also paid a certain price in incomprehension for his own passion without limits, the love of cinema.[36]

NOTES

1. Spanish press book, Madrid 1987.

2. 'La ley del deseo: guión', Madrid 1987.

3. Antonio Gutti, '*La ley del deseo*: Almodóvar al desnudo', *Cinco Días*, 19 February 1987.

4. Pedro Crespo, '*La ley del deseo*, un desahogo en la carrera de Pedro Almodóvar', *ABC*, 8 February 1987.

5. Josep Maria López i Llaví, 'Per l'escàndol, a la llibertat', *Avui*, 20 February 1987.

6. Francisco Llinàs, *Cuatro años de cine español*, Madrid 1987, pp. 112–13, 161–17; Angeles García, 'Amor con sangre y lágrimas: Pedro Almodóvar estrena *La ley del deseo*', *El País* (Barcelona), 30 January 1987.

7. Rosa Montero, 'Entrevista: Pedro Almodóvar, "un chiquito como yo"', *El País Semanal*, 28 September 1986, p. 21. When Nuria Vidal reproduces these words from the interview (p. 247) she omits the words 'with a boy' ('de un chico').

8. José Arroyo, '*La ley del deseo*: A Gay Seduction', in Richard Dyer and Ginette Vincendeau, *European Popular Cinema*, New York and London 1992, pp. 31–46.

9. The phrases come from Mark Finch's review in *Monthly Film Bulletin*, vol. 55, no. 658, November 1988, pp. 334–5.

10. '*La ley del deseo*', Madrid 1986, p. 27.

11. e.g. Arroyo, p. 40.

12. *The Desire to Desire: The Woman's Film of the 1940s*, Bloomington 1987.

13. The question is posed by Ellis Hanson in an unpublished paper on *La ley del deseo* and Kubrick's *2001*, 'Technology, Paranoia, and the Voice'.

14. Enrique Fernández, 'Desire Under the Palms', *The Village Voice*, 17 March 1987.

15. *New Yorker*, 20 April 1987, pp. 80–1.

16. 'Almodóvar: márgenes y centros'.

17. *October*, 43, 1987, pp. 197–222.

18. Tina's typically Spanish *lunares* suggest a connection with the overblown femininity of the similarly costumed queens of Andalusian song; see Daniel Pineda Novo's celebratory *Las folklóricas y el cine*, Huelva 1991.

19. Angel Fernández Santos, 'La ley del exceso', *El País* (Barcelona), 15 February 1987.

20. 'Almodóvar's City of Desire', *Quarterly Review of Film and Video*, 13.4 (1991), 47–65, p. 58. Likewise the unusual family celebrated by Almodóvar in such sequences may not be as subversive of current Spanish norms as might be supposed; in *Estructuras familiares en España*, Madrid 1990, Rocío Treviño suggests that what is now typical of Spain is precisely what we find in *La ley del deseo*: the preservation of 'old [familial] forms' but with 'new contents' (p. 135).

21. 'The Empire Strikes Back: A Posttranssexual Manifesto', in *Body Guards: The Cultural Politics of Gender Ambiguity*, Julia Epstein and Kristina Straub, eds., New York and London 1991, pp. 280–304. I take the transsexual slang 'GG' and 'crash land' from this article.

22. J. M. Caparrós Lera, *El cine español de la democracia*, Barcelona 1992, p. 416.

23. Anon., '*La ley del deseo*, película que más veces representó a España en festivales extranjeros en 1987', *La Vanguardia*, 13 October 1987.

24. José Luis Guarner, 'El cine de Pedro Almodóvar y la música de Pegasus, grandes triunfadores del Festival de Cine de Miami', *La Vanguardia*, 21 February 1987.

25. Anon., 'Pedro Almodóvar, premiado por la crítica de Los Angeles como mejor nuevo realizador', *La Vanguardia*, 22 December 1987.

26. Tim Clark, 'Pedro Almodóvar: Desperado Living', *Time Out*, 2–9 November 1988.

27. James Ryan, 'Latin Lover', *The Face*, 45, June 1992, pp. 64–7.

28. Text by Jesús Beltrán and Juan I. Francia, *El Europeo*, 37, November 1991.

29. Lucía Argos, 'Ponte un lazo rojo', *El País*, 30 September 1992; Rocío García, 'Por Navidad, Sharon Stone', *El País*, 29 November 1992.

30. See my *Laws of Desire*, chapter 4.

31. 'El deseo cumplido', *El País*, 18 April 1991.

32. Anon., 'La estrella es . . . Pedro Almodóvar: *La ley del deseo*', *El País*, 3 May 1993.

33. 'Sexo prohibido'.

34. Eduardo Haro Ibars, 'La homosexualidad como problema sociopolítico en el cine español del postfranquismo', *Tiempo de Historia*, 52, March 1979, pp 88–91. Haro Ibars's book *Gay Rock* was a great influence on *movida* luminaries such as Alaska; see José Luis Gallero, *Sólo se vive una vez*, Madrid 1991, p. 331.

35. For an account of and a call for AIDS activism in Spain, see Jordi Esteva and Oscar Fontrodona, 'Tú sí puedes parar el SIDA', *Ajoblanco*, 47, December 1992, pp. 25–30.

36. See Jean Douchet, 'L'Amour du cinéma', *Cahiers du Cinéma*, 435, 1990, pp. 52–3.

7

MUJERES AL BORDE DE UN ATAQUE DE NERVIOS (WOMEN ON THE VERGE OF A NERVOUS BREAKDOWN, 1988)

Femininity by Design

HIGH COMEDY

> Soy infeliz.
> I am unhappy.[1]

SCENE ONE. LARGE TERRACE. PEPA'S PENTHOUSE. DAWN. INTERIOR.
Stealthily, as it does every day, dawn breaks over Madrid. The sun fights its way through the pollution floating over the city. With an imperceptible magic it bestows its light on the large terrace of the penthouse in which Pepa lives. The sun must enjoy rising each day in order to take up its place on this terrace. Here Pepa has brought together her desire to live in the jungle, in the country, and in a farm: there are palms, a hammock, trees with birds in them, and even a little yard with hens, a cock, and a rabbit. There are also a great number of more familiar plants. Everything is put together with cheerfulness and good taste. Silhouetted against the Madrid skyline, a cock crows its early cock-a-doodle-do.[2]

Almodóvar's description of the main set of *Mujeres* illustrates the 'theory of contentment' that pervades his most successful film. Its utopian thesis is that 'society has now adapted itself to individuals', and all their social and professional needs have been met.[3] As José A. Hergueta notes, in the penthouse on calle Montalbán we are far indeed from the M-30.[4] But the synthetic space of the terrace (which unites country and city, upper and lower class, Spain and abroad) is also the abstract space of a genre which Almodóvar calls 'alta comedia': 'high comedy' or 'comedy of manners'. According to the film's stylish press book, high comedy is characterized by anti-naturalism: the sets are flagrantly artificial, performance and speech excessively rapid, and the deepest human ambitions treated in an abstract, almost synthetic manner. The most common ambition, writes Almodóvar, is to be happy or unhappy with the person you love.

How, then, is emotion combined with abstraction, sentimental distress with material ease? The opening sequence of the film (which differs somewhat from the original script) provides a clue. As Carmen Maura's Pepa tells in voice-over of the failure of her relationship with Iván (Ricardo Gullón) we see successive shots of a block of flats (which will prove to be an estate agent's model); a chicken coop; and a record sleeve with a scrawled message (a gift from Iván). The camera tracks slowly over Pepa's chaotic, candy-coloured bedroom to linger on her motionless head, screened by auburn hair. The image dissolves into a black and white sequence in an unestablished location: Iván, an ageing Romeo, walks down an uncannily empty street whispering words of love into an old-fashioned microphone to a bevy of exotic women. The sound is curiously unnatural, studio-like in spite of the exterior location. If the penthouse suggests a certain fixity of place (and Pepa will return to it throughout the film) then the discontinuity editing of the opening sequence suggests a restless dislocation which threatens to confuse all boundaries. It is only later that we discover that the monochrome sequence is a dream of the sleeping Pepa, one which repeats her fears of betrayal by the philandering Iván.

Moreover, there is another technique here typical of the film: the disjunction between image and soundtrack. Pepa talks over a shot of her sleeping self; Iván's voice, 'amplified' by a microphone without a lead, sounds hollow in the empty street. Yet even here in Pepa's nightmare there is a quite specific urban reference. Reflected in the windows which Iván passes we see the skyscrapers of Azca, the development in north central Madrid intended by urban planners to rival Manhattan. Almodóvar here ironizes, even historicizes, modernity itself in the juxtaposition of an ageing lover and an 'aggressively modern' architectural project planned in the now distant 1960s. The setting is thus somewhat incongruous: even guidebooks are forced to admit that Azca is a 'disaster',[5] the last place sociable Madrileños are likely to go for a walk or to meet one another in the open air. The synthetic or abstract ambitions of high comedy are thus contaminated by the history of the city in which that comedy takes place. Indeed, Almodóvar has noted that the highly stylized Madrid of the film (with the skyline on view from the terrace impossible to see in real life) was prompted in part by the recent renovations carried out by the City Council, which had revealed once more the beauty of the historic buildings (Vidal, p. 264).

The competing regimes of the visual and the auditory are highlighted in the next sequences. Iván and Pepa are dubbing artists; and at work in the studio each is cross-cut with images from the film they are looping: *Johnny Guitar*, with Joan Crawford and Sterling Hayden. The staggering of the two sequences suggests the lack of reciprocity between the lovers: each addresses only the screen. But the content of the dialogue also serves as an ironic commentary on the main narrative. Hayden is begging Crawford to deceive him, to tell him that she loves him just as he loves her. In the 'acoustic mirror'[6] of the dubbing studio this old dream of symmetry can be achieved even at successive moments (Pepa and Iván are not physically present to each other). But it is a technological supplement that also nourishes a desire that proves to be insatiable: attenuated by microphone or answerphone, the dwindling male lover, reduced to a Voice (albeit capitalized in the script), can no longer measure up to the unhappy woman, who will confront him only in the final sequence of the film.

Kaja Silverman has suggested that 'classic' (narrative) cinema is 'a textual model which holds the female voice and body insistently to the interior of the diegesis, while relegating the male subject to a position of apparent discursive exteriority by identifying him with mastering speech, vision or hearing.'[7] I will suggest later that to a large extent *Mujeres* reverses these binaries, blurring the boundaries between 'classic' positions. It remains the case, however, that Pepa's voice and body remain confined within the internal spaces of the film and are intermittently ironized or pathologized by its 'abstract' discourse on love. Thus the camera tracks along the beam of light from the projector before coming to rest on Pepa's face (Plate 13); and the reverse angles with the screen encourage the spectator to take up her point of view. But the script emphasizes that she is 'trapped' in the 'cage' of the dubbing theatre, dwarfed by the projectors which reduce her to 'just another piece of that impenetrable and extraordinary machinery.' (p. 12) As we shall see, in *Mujeres* Almodóvar targets the cinematic mechanism (most explicitly in the dubbing sequences) as the designing force of women: of their pleasure and their pain.

SPIKE HEELS AND TUBE SKIRTS

PEPA (al policía): Comentábamos el modelo de la señora.
CANDELA (llorando): Es horroroso, horroroso.

PEPA (to the policeman):   We were discussing the lady's dress.
CANDELA (weeping):   It's dreadful, dreadful.

As the comedy of complication (Spanish *enredo*) develops, the alternation between place and displacement speeds up. Thus typically *Mujeres* alternates between Pepa's confrontations with other characters in the flat and her solitary journeys across Madrid in a taxi (enlivened by a burlesque driver as sensitive as herself to the emotions). As the script notes, the taxi is an intermediate zone 'between two places without being in any place', in which Pepa can take cognizance of her situation, weeping 'without dramatic effect' (p. 76). Cinematography also reinforces the distinction between Pepa and the minor characters who descend on her flat. The camera consistently takes up her point of view. In an unusually explicit homage to Hitchcock, Pepa spies on the building in which Iván's ex-wife Lucía (Julieta Serrano) lives, the camera passing from one illuminated window to another, revealing a Madrileña 'Miss Torso' as it goes. Likewise, the bar opposite Lucía's flat is the 'privileged place' (script, p. 48) from which Pepa watches Lucía's shy son Carlos (bespectacled Antonio Banderas) and his snobbish fiancée Marisa (the hieratic Rossy de Palma). The spectator is only intermittently allowed more knowledge than Pepa and is led to watch her 'joining up the dots' ('atando cabos') of an intricately complex plot.

In one of the few scenes in the film in which Pepa is not present the camera holds still on a television news programme (read by Almodóvar's mother, Francisca Caballero) as daffy Candela (María Barranco) rushes backwards and forwards in and out of frame. Candela has been compared by one critic to Olive Oyle.[8] And her frantic movements here are certainly cartoon-like. There is thus a certain tension in both plot, cinematography, and direction of sympathy between the representation of Pepa and her fellow women. It is a tension that might be summed up as that between fragmentation (fetishization) and specular wholeness (narcissism).

The celebrated title sequence (by the Studio Gatti) consists of fragments of women's costumes and bodies cut up and distorted. Vicente Sánchez Biosca has called this tendency of the film 'the conquest of design',[9] a somewhat ambiguous phrase. Publicity shots also include close-ups of unidentified feet; and in the film itself Almodóvar frequently uses extreme close-ups of clothes or parts of the body (Iván's mouth, Pepa's shoes once more) which serve to disorientate the spectator, to foreground aspects of design which generally pass unnoticed. But this fragmentation of the (mainly female) body is counterbalanced by a narcissistic concern for self-imaging. Pepa herself is frequently shown dressing and making herself up in a mirror (in one case in front of her lover's son Carlos); the crazy Lucía, Iván's ex-wife, is shown adjusting her 1960s wig and Courreges leopard-print hat, insisting that time has not passed since Iván abandoned her, that the mirror image transcends all.

This emphasis on fragmentation and narcissism has proved controversial. At least one Spanish woman critic (María Asunción Balonga) holds that Almodóvar is making fun of women in general, that the joke is on the female spectator. And she goes on to suggest that in their curious combination of modernity and traditionalism Almodóvar's 'girls' ('chicas') are 'incomplete': 'modern but naive, liberated but sentimental, always anxious to be loved, looked after, taken notice of'.[10] It is an accusation of misogyny that is more characteristic of British critics, especially (and ironically) those writing for the most reactionary newspapers.[11]

Much has been made of Almodóvar's avowed debt to the Hollywood sex comedies of Doris Day and Frank Tashlin.[12] If we seek a Spanish context for such accounts of femininity, however, it may be in the representations of women current in the 1960s at the time of Almodóvar's adolescence. Thus even Catholic pamphlets with titles like 'Women's World' and 'Spinsters Today'[13] proclaim the rights of modern women to work outside the home and to a certain autonomy: the unmarried woman, we are told, 'works and earns her own living . . . dresses well, travels, reads, and has male and female friends' (Salas, p. 8). But, on the other hand, it is universally acknowledged that women's essence is sentimental. A sociological study of the same period proclaims: 'There is no doubt that woman was created to love and be loved . . . love is woman's reason for being, her framework and the threshold within which her personality is projected.'[14] The same authors define 'feminine frivolity' as 'a fragmentary personality which projects its affectivity over a wide field of trivial interests, a kind of superficiality which acts as a screen' (p. 38). It is a language which recurs in hostile criticism of Almodóvar himself.

It is clear, nonetheless, that fragmentation and superficiality, however disparaged they may be, are also a threat and a lure. One Catholic sex manual illustrates the 'arousing effect of sexuality' with a line drawing of a bottle of perfume, a pair of gloves, and a lipstick with the top suggestively removed, warning that the 'memory of [such] images' produces arousal.[15] It is an illustration reminiscent of *Mujeres*'s credit sequence, where the paraphernalia of the feminine masquerade is also depicted in resonant and seductive isolation. Alternatively, a pamphlet in a series targeted at young Catholic girls suggests that a discreet exploitation of Max Factor and Royal Ambrée will help a young woman to 'bring to light' the femininity which she bears within herself.[16] Most reminiscent of Almodóvar is the three-volume *Enciclopedia de la mujer*, first published in 1962.[17] This recommends a minute discipline of the body, divided into fragments ('different kinds of hair') and subject to a rigorous daily regime. Some illustrations have now taken on a deadpan surrealism which might well be called Almodóvarian: modern women smile as they soak their elbows in hot olive oil or as their heads emerge from a portable Turkish bath, said to 'dissolve fat' (I, pp. 53, 71).

Almodóvar has often been accused of subjecting his women actors to similar humiliations. And there is no doubt that in his stress on the emotionalism of women (in his belief, stated in the press book, that 'women weep better') he repeats the stereotypes of the 'modern woman' of the 1960s. But as the *Enciclopedia de la mujer* reminds us, 'true elegance pays attention to detail' (I, p. 308). And I would suggest that it is precisely in his attention to detail that Almodóvar denaturalizes the totalizing, specular imagos foisted on women in his youth. Thus two of the most empathetic US critics (Pauline Kael and Vito Russo) both call attention to an item of clothing which has no significance in the plot: Candela's earrings in the shape of coffee pots (which Almodóvar claims to have had made specially for the film).[18] Both Kael and Russo are highly sensitive to the visual pleasures of the film, its delight in colour and costume. Kael in particular notes that it is 'no small thing' for these women to know that they look good. And in one of the few positive British reviews Margaret Walters vindicates Almodóvar's 'saving insight into why women still need to dramatize their femininity and . . . the very real pleasures to be found in dressing and making up.'[19]

Mary Ann Doane has suggested that masquerade is a 'glitch in the [cinematic] system . . . insofar as it attributes to the woman the distance, alienation, and divisiveness of self (which is constitutive of subjectivity in psychoanalysis) rather than the closeness and expressive presence which are the logical outcome of the psychoanalytic drama of sexualized linguistic difference.'[20] We shall see in a moment that Almodóvar himself has been criticized for a pathological 'closeness' to his women, an inability to distinguish between self and cinema. But it remains possible nonetheless to acknowledge the candy-coloured pleasures of his versions of women while admitting the regressive implications they might have in both psychic and historical terms. As a 'glitch' in the cinematic system himself (a Spanish director who has achieved international renown; an openly gay director known for his love of women) Almodóvar crosses the borders of institutionalized affect, confuses the boundaries of the filmic apparatus.

HER MASTER'S VOICE?

PEPA: Me puede engañar con todo menos que con la voz.
PEPA: He can deceive me with anything except his voice.

If Almodóvar's 'girls' are caught within the frame, bound by the cinematic image, they are also delimited by their relation to language. Candela's speech is fast and breathless, marked by a pronounced Andalusian accent. She is given to comic disproportions, as when, abandoned by her Shiite terrorist lover, she complains at how unjustly she has been treated by 'the Arab world'. The script confirms that she is 'unselfconscious and vital' (p. 41). Lucía, the abandoned wife, speaks fluently; but (as she tells us herself) she is only pretending to be sane. In the final sequence of the film, when she pursues Iván to the airport on a hijacked motorbike, she is reduced to a silent head, wig blown out of place and mascara running. Marisa, Carlos's fiancée, is a snooty rich girl (*pija*) from the wealthy barrio of Salamanca, who spends most of the film asleep on the terrace after accidentally drinking spiked gazpacho. Initially a virgin, she achieves a mystical (and silent) orgasm in her sleep. All of these characters are thus marked and disabled by a certain jouissance outside language: ingenuous vitalism, obsessive neurosis, unconscious sexuality. The auditory regime would thus tend to reinforce the visual in which each is dressed in idiosyncratic costume. But what is striking in the performances (by María Barranco, Julieta Serrano, and Rossy de Palma respectively) is the seriousness with which the actors play their roles and their refusal to stoop to cheap gags. This is confirmed by the script which repeatedly affirms that even Lucía is not to be seen as a figure of fun: 'her personality is stronger than her clothes, however bizarre they may be. She never appears grotesque' (p. 21) (Plate 14). Lucía faces the final scene at the airport 'with that seriousness which fate lends the countenance of a tragic heroine' (p. 137).

This sense of a psychological depth realized in performance (of a 'personality' which appears to transcend costume and situation) is related to Almodóvar's newly assured exploitation of spatial depth. Thus the most deftly farcical of *Mujeres*'s scenes involve multiple planes of action. For example, as Iván makes a phone call to Pepa from a box in the foreground, Pepa herself walks behind him in the middle ground to dump his suitcase in the rubbish, while in the far distance a rapidly advancing pink blur announces the approach of Lucía, who will also remain oblivious to the man she seeks and with whom she shares the frame. Such scenes exploit the street corner as a place of intersection, a locale used by Almodóvar as early as *Pepi, Luci, Bom*. But they also reveal a much greater depth of field than earlier films and a skilful exploitation of movement and colour to distinguish multiple planes of simultaneous action. Such formal 'prompts', which encourage spectators to read the flat screen as a three-dimensional space, are known as 'depth cues'.[21] I would suggest that just as Almodóvar exploits depth of field to lend greater complexity to both cinematography and plot, so he elicits from his actors subtle modes of performance which also suggest multiple motivation, seamless simultaneity. And Almodóvar does so without wholly abandoning that cult of the surface (of design and of detail) for which he is so well known.

It is often reported that during shooting Almodóvar acts out the roles to the actors and instructs them to imitate his delivery of the dialogue. The question arises of whether the women characters are mere female impersonators, imitating their master's voice. In *Mujeres* it is clear, however, that the male dominion over language is as fragile as the female's. If Iván is Voice (capitalized) then he is frequently reduced to a part-object: lips shown in extreme close-up. The fantasy sequence at the beginning of the film is one of the very few in which he is shown as a full-length figure. And if his voice is all-pervasive, compared by the script to 'the smell of cooking carried by the wind' (p. 6), it is curiously insubstantial or immaterial, and wholly untrustworthy. His is an 'anonymous body which moves without showing its face at all' (p. 3).

Pepa complains that it is easier to understand mechanics than male psychology, that motorbikes make more sense than men. In the traffic of farce, then, there is a certain gender inversion in which, from the (generalized) perspective of the woman, the man is set up in his specificity as mutability, mendaciousness, enigma. And there is also a trouble in filiation here: Carlos, the shy son of the smooth-talking Iván, suffers from a stammer which Candela satirically refers to as his 'facility with speech'. Exiled from an image track given up to extravagant and colourful women, men are also excluded from a soundtrack devoted to women's stories (and, indeed, women's songs).

In publicity shots for *Mujeres*, Almodóvar takes up his place amongst the cast (Plate 15). Sometimes he is shot pretending to read the script. Unlike Saura, say, who tends to be shown behind the camera directing the action,[22] Almodóvar chooses more often to present himself as part of that action, to place himself within the frame. It is perhaps significant that one of Almodóvar's most unsympathetic critics should stress the supposed 'closeness' of the director to his work, which (he claims) is unprecedented.[23] I would suggest, then, that what critics find disturbing is the 'overidentification' of a filmmaker with the women in his films. In *The Women Who Knew Too Much*, Tania Modleski argues for just such an overidentification in the less likely case of Hitchcock.[24] Films such as *Vertigo*, in which the heroine is almost literally designed by the male protagonist, suggest that 'a fascination with femininity . . . throws masculine identity into question and crisis' (p. 87). This leads to a '"boundary confusion" [which] can be intimidating to the male who, unlike the female, appears to achieve his identity through establishing a firm boundary between himself and woman' (p. 99). The line between desire and identification is thus highly precarious.

In a recent reading of *Mujeres*, Stuart Hall claims that Almodóvar 'breaks boundaries' that are at once sexual and national. In Almodóvar's 'hybridized' Spain, it is 'impossible to see Europe as male and magisterial. Everything has been transposed into the "feminine" register [and] feminine disorder is simply what life is like.'[25] Hall goes on to argue, as I have myself, for a certain depth which he dares to call 'authenticity': 'something that pierces the surface of the narrative and takes it to another level . . . an oblique approach to the grand narratives of love and art and culture and cinema.' He is referring here to the final sequence in which Pepa simply says goodbye to the man she has been chasing so relentlessly throughout the film. But whatever the status of this new-found 'authenticity', it seems likely that Almodóvar has been punished by male critics for placing himself so consistently on the side of the woman (on the side of sentiment and of spectacle). In spite of its success, *Mujeres* was awarded neither the Spanish Goya for best director nor the Oscar for best foreign-language film: the prizes went to more 'serious' (more 'masculine') works. While actual women may not thank Almodóvar for his overidentification with feminine stereotypes which they may well wish to challenge, there is cause to welcome that boundary confusion brought about by his cinematic narcissism. It suggests an unfixing of identities (both sexual and national) which can only tend to support that feminism which is committed to social and to psychic change.

FIGURES OF FUN[26]

Teatro; es puro teatro.
Theatre; it's just theatre.[27]

There seems little doubt that *Mujeres* is Almodóvar's most popular work. It remains at the time of writing the only Spanish film to have grossed more than one thousand million pesetas in the domestic market;[28] and it was sold to Spanish television (with *La ley del deseo*) for the unprecedented sum of two hundred million pesetas.[29] The commercial success of *Mujeres* abroad was also exceptional, making Almodóvar the biggest-grossing foreign-language director in the US for 1989.[30] When the film was first shown on British network television it was scheduled for one of the prime slots of the year: mid-evening Christmas Eve.[31] We will return in a minute to the secrets of foreign success; but it is important to recognize that evidence of foreign popularity changed the perception of Almodóvar at home, lending credence to his claim to represent post-Franco Spain to the outside world. Almodóvar pointedly compared his own profitable project (based on a relatively small budget) to the commercial disasters of his fellow filmmakers, claiming as *Mujeres* was about to be premiered in Hollywood that he could have made Saura's historical epic *El Dorado* for half the price and without the benefit of exotic locations.[32]

As Richard Dyer and Ginette Vincendeau remind us, 'popular' is a slippery term; and it makes sense to read Almodóvar not with reference to the Anglo-American dichotomy of 'art' and 'entertainment' but with reference to the distinction which Dyer and Vincendeau claim is common in France and Italy: 'auteur' versus 'mainstream'.[33] This would explain how Almodóvar's films could still remain artistically distinctive (auteurist), while achieving a mass audience. But if *Mujeres* is as cinematically ambitious as any of Almodóvar's earlier films (an impression confirmed by the number of awards it garnered from critics and festival juries), its profitability was all the more spectacular because it took place at a uniquely grim moment in the history of Spanish cinema. As Pedro Crespo noted at the time in an article entitled 'Political Economy of the Cinema', the generous grants offered under the so-called Miró Law had left the government purse empty; few films were made in 1988, and even fewer were announced for 1989.[34] In spite of the notorious unreliability of the official figures for film budgets and grosses, *Mujeres* was the one indisputable success of its year. It was thus seized on as an antidote to national humiliation in the cinematic arena.

One cause of *Mujeres*'s success must be Almodóvar's attempt to theatricalize the publicity process on a much wider scale than had hitherto been attempted. It is symptomatic that *La Repubblica* should describe the press conference at the Venice Festival, graced by the director and his now celebrated 'girls', as a 'spectacle'.[35] Almodóvar's commitment to a full year of such promotional spectacles around the world was undoubtedly decisive in the film's performance. However, if *Mujeres* is generally taken to be the film with which Almodóvar left behind his cult following and learned to please a wider audience (as the positive review in *Variety* predicted),[36] the strategies employed by the film's US distributors and exhibitors suggest that this impression must be qualified. It was *Variety*, again, that reported that Orion, which had paid an unprecedented $350,000 for the North American rights, 'plan[ned] a 50-city push for Spanish-lingo film'; and that 'research show[ed] women, Hispanics attracted to pic'.[37] The 'mainstream-style' release was thus in fact 'segmented' to attract quite specific audiences according to differences of gender, demography, and region. When the film broke house records in one cinema on New York City's Upper West Side, the general manager explained that many of the audience did not even know that it was Spanish and had never seen a film with subtitles. The advertising tagline used on the radio station with the strongest female ratings in New York ('a new comedy about someone you know') also stressed the proximity of the film to English-speaking North American audiences and played down its Spanish origins.

Variety credits Carmen Maura with a 'heroic' effort in the promotional campaign which targeted Hispanics in such population centres as Los Angeles, Miami, and Texas. And there also seems little doubt that her performance in the film (her last and most expert for Almodóvar) contributed immeasurably to its success. Persistent rumours of a Hollywood remake starring Jane Fonda led indignant Spanish critics to contrast the latter's strident mannerisms with the former's more subtle and affecting irony.[38] While foreign audiences found Maura's performance at once comic and moving, Spanish response was rendered more complex by an awareness of her long career in television and in films of variable quality. To see Maura indisputably glamorous and successful at last was to experience mixed emotions: just as her character Pepa effortlessly combined domesticity and career, so Maura (the 'plain' girl who had come so much further than her prettier rivals) served to reconcile the contradiction between familiarity and novelty, between the old Spain of chickens and rabbits and the new Spain of Islamic terrorists and telephone answering machines. Maura's subtly modulated performance and its intersection with what was known of her career and public 'persona' thus facilitated an identification on the part of the female audience which was not always encouraged by Almodóvar's original conception of the film.

The cover of the Spanish press book for *Mujeres* shows a stylized 1960s-style woman's face (as if from the *Enciclopedia de la mujer*) cut vertically in half and replaced on the left-hand side by unidentified mechanical structures. It seems emblematic of the ambivalence of a film which alternates between paying loving attention to women and offering them up to the merciless mechanisms of farce. One name for this hybrid of machine and organism is 'cyborg'. And in a brilliant essay, Donna Haraway has offered the cyborg, ironically, as a manifesto for feminist futures.[39] The 'fractured identity' of the cyborg rejects organicism and reproduction, refuses the division between natural and artificial, and (like Almodóvar and Maura) 'takes irony for granted' (pp. 153, 180). The enmeshing of femininity and mechanicity in *Mujeres* (the twin focus on machines and fetishized female bodies) might thus be seen as pointing the way to a sophisticated and disabused account of gender and technology, an attempt, in Haraway's words, to 'reconstruct the boundaries of daily life, in partial connection with others, in communication with all our parts.' (p. 181)

The final scene of *Mujeres*, however, has Pepa confessing her pregnancy to Rossy de Palma's Marisa, who has finally recovered from the effects of spiked gazpacho. It is a scene of quiet communion between women whose pleasure is, as the script notes, 'not hysterical but liberating' (p. 141). This stress on maternity may seem retrograde when compared to the cyborg's love of mechanical replication; but, just as Marisa has achieved solitary orgasm in her drugged sleep, so Pepa's pregnancy is self-sufficient, requires no male mediation: the vapid Iván has been definitively dismissed from her life. The maternal body and the libidinal body are thus separate but juxtaposed in the privileged space of Pepa's magical terrace. But if Almodóvar's 'theory of contentment' seems to have little resonance in the wider world outside, we should not denigrate the pleasures he finally permits his figures of fun. For like all utopias, the penthouse on calle Montalbán has clearly historical origins and unmistakably political implications, if we but choose to look for them.

NOTES

1. This is the title of the extravagantly masochistic song sung over the opening credits by Lola Beltrán.

2. 'Argumento original y guión', Madrid 1987, p. 1.

3. These quotations are derived from lengthy texts by Almodóvar in the press book.

4. 'A vueltas con P. A.', in Albaladejo, pp. 10–13 (p. 11).

5. See Javier Martínez Reverte and ANAYA staff, *Guía de Madrid hoy*, Madrid 1991, which claims Azca 'symbolizes an aggressively modern present' but acknowledges that its pedestrian areas are 'disastrous' (pp. 13, 106).

6. The phrase is Kaja Silverman's: *The Acoustic Mirror: The Female Voice in Psychoanalysis and Cinema*, Bloomington 1988.

7. Silverman, p. ix.

8. Sheila Johnston, review, *Independent* (London), 15 June 1989.

9. 'El elixir aromático de la postmodernidad o la comedia según Pedro Almodóvar', in José A. Hurtado and Francisco M. Picó, eds., *Escritos sobre el cine español 1973–87*, Valencia 1989, pp. 111–24 (p. 121).

10. Cited by Caparrós Lera in his hostile *El cine español de la democracia*, Barcelona 1992, p. 324.

11. Christopher Tookey claims the film 'reinforces the macho view of . . . women as emotional cripples' in the *Sunday Telegraph*, 18 June 1989.

12. See Bruce Babington and Peter W. Evans, *Affairs to Remember: The Hollywood Comedy of the Sexes*, Manchester 1989.

13. Ana María Calera and Julio C. Acerete, *La mujer de hoy*, Barcelona 1966 (my edn 1972); María Salas, *Solteras de hoy*, Madrid 1966.

14. Francisco Ansón and Vicente Roa, *Mujer y sociedad*, Madrid 1966, p. 11.

15. Dr A. Clavero Núñez, *Antes de que te cases . . .: un texto de formación prenupcial*, Madrid 1961. p. 28. This text, first published in 1946, was frequently reprinted throughout the Dictatorship.

16. María Emilia González Sevilla, *Moderna y mujer*, Madrid 1965, p. 13. The author warns young women not to adopt 'masculine' dress or behaviour (wearing jeans or riding motorbikes) which may prevent them from catching and keeping a man. It is advice that the ultra-feminine women of *Mujeres* have taken to heart.

17. My edn, Barcelona 1969. Volume I treats 'beauty, exercise, fashion, psychology and graphology [*sic*], etiquette, work, and sex life'; volume II 'cooking'; volume III 'hearth and home'. The *Enciclopedia* recommends cinema as a profession for which women are particularly suited (I, p. 327).

18. Pauline Kael, review, *The New Yorker*, 14 November 1988; Vito Russo, 'Man of La Mania', *Film Comment*, vol. 24, no. 6, November/December 1988, pp. 13–17 (p. 17).

19. The *Listener*, 15 June 1989.

20. *Femmes Fatales*, New York and London 1991, p. 37.

21. See David Bordwell and Kristin Thompson, *Film Art: An Introduction*, New York 1990, p. 143.

22. As in the photo of an imperious Saura directing *El Dorado* in Costa Rica on the cover of Marvin D'Lugo's *The Films of Carlos Saura*, Princeton 1991.

23. See Caparrós Lera, *El cine español*, p. 321.

24. *The Women Who Knew Too Much: Hitchcock and Feminist Theory*, New York and London 1988.

25. 'European Cinema on the Verge of a Nervous Breakdown', in Duncan Petrie, ed., *Screening Europe: Image and Identity in Contemporary European Cinema*, London 1992, pp. 15–53 (p. 52).

26. I take the phrase from Mansel Stimpson's sympathetic review in *What's On* (London), 14 January 1989.

27. This is the title of the extravagantly theatrical song sung over the closing credits by La Lupe.

28. Emilio C. García Fernández, *El cine español contemporáneo*, Barcelona 1992, p. 140.

29. Piedad Sancristóval, 'Pedro Almodóvar vende todas sus películas a Televisión Española', *El País*, 29 December 1990.

30. Anon., 'Almodóvar fue el cineasta extranjero independiente más taquillero en EEUU en 1989', *El País*, 6 January 1990.

31. BBC 2; 24 December 1992.

32. Ramiro Villapadierna, 'Pedro Almodóvar: lo que ha hecho para merecer esto', *ABC*, 11 November 1988.

33. *Popular European Cinema*, London and New York 1992, pp. 3, 8.

34. 'Economía política del cine', *Ya*, 10 January 1989.

35. See Vidal, p. 393.

36. Peter Besas, 6 April 1988.

37. Richard Gold, 'Mainstream-Style Release Set for "Women on the Verge"', 14 December 1988.

38. Angel Fernández Santos, 'El espejo', *El País*, 1 February 1990.

39. 'A Cyborg Manifesto', in *Simians, Cyborgs, and Women: The Reinvention of Nature*, London 1991, pp. 149–81.

PLATE 1   Olvido ('Alaska') Gara (Bom) and Eva Siva (Luci) in
Pepi, Luci, Bom, and Other Girls on the Heap, 1980. Tartan Video
© 1993

PLATE 2   Helga Liné (Toraya) and Fernando Vivanco
(Doctor) in *Labyrinth of Passion*, 1982.
Tartan Video © 1993

Plate 3   Imanol Arias (Riza
Niro) in *Labyrinth of Passion*.
Tartan Video © 1993

PLATE 4   Mari Carrillo (Marquesa) and Julieta Serrano (Mother
Superior) in *Dark Habits*, 1983. Tartan Video © 1993

Plate 5   Chus Lampreave (Sor Rata) and Cristina Sánchez
Pascual (Yolanda) in *Dark Habits*. Tartan Video © 1993

PLATE 6   Carmen Maura (Gloria) and Juan Martínez (Toni) in
What Have I Done to Deserve This?, 1984. Tartan Video © 1993

PLATE 7   Jaime Chávarri (striptease client), Verónica Forqué
(Cristal), and Carmen Maura (Gloria) in *What Have I Done to
Deserve This?* Tartan Video © 1993

PLATE 8   Chus Lampreave (grandmother) in *What Have I Done
to Deserve This?* Tartan Video © 1993

PLATE 9   Assumpta Serna (María) in *Matador*, 1986.
Tartan Video © 1993

PLATE 10   Antonio Banderas (Angel) and Nacho Martínez
(Diego) in *Matador*. Tartan Video © 1993

PLATE 12 Carmen Maura (Tina) in *The Law of Desire.*
Tartan Video © 1993

PLATE 11 Eusebio Poncela
(Pablo) and Miguel Molina
(Juan) in *The Law of Desire,*
1987. Tartan Video © 1993

PLATE 13   Carmen Maura (Pepa) in *Women on the Verge of a
Nervous Breakdown*, 1988.

PLATE 14   Julieta Serrano (Lucía) in *Women on the Verge of a
Nervous Breakdown*.

PLATE 15   Pedro Almodóvar, Carmen Maura (Pepa), Rossy de Palma (Marisa), María Barranco (Candela), Julieta Serrano (Lucía), and Antonio Banderas (Carlos) in a publicity shot for *Women on the Verge of a Nervous Breakdown.*

PLATE 16　Victoria Abril (Marina) in *Tie Me Up! Tie Me Down!*, 1990.

PLATE 17　Antonio Banderas (Ricky) and Victoria Abril (Marina) in *Tie Me Up! Tie Me Down!*.

PLATE 18   Marisa Paredes (Becky) and Victoria Abril (Rebeca)
in *High Heels*, 1991.

PLATE 19   Miguel Bosé (Femme Letal) in *High Heels.*

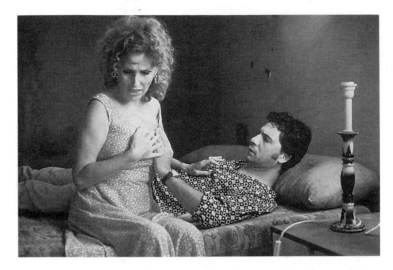

PLATE 20   Verónica Forqué (Kika) and Alex Casanovas (Ramón)
in *Kika*, 1993.

PLATE 21   Verónica Forqué (Kika) and Rossy de Palma (Juana)
in *Kika*.

PLATE 22   Imanol Arias (Paco) and Marisa Paredes (Leo) in
The Flower of My Secret, 1995.

PLATE 23   Marisa Paredes (Leo) in *The Flower of My Secret*.

PLATE 24   Francesca Neri (Elena) in *Live Flesh*, 1997.

PLATE 25   Javier Bardem (David) and Liberto Rabal (Victor)
in *Live Flesh*.

PLATE 26   Cecilia Roth (Manuela) and Eloy Azorín (Esteban) in
All About My Mother, 1999.

PLATE 27   Pedro Almodóvar directing Antonia San Juan (La Agrado) in
All About My Mother.

8

¡ATAME!

(TIE ME UP! TIE ME DOWN!, 1990)

Not a Love Story?

ADDICTED TO LOVE

MÉDICA (a Marina):   Eres una toxicómana nata.
DOCTOR (to Marina):   You're a born drug addict.

¡Atame! is essentially a love story, or rather a story of how someone attempts to construct a love story in the same way as he might study for a degree: by means of effort, will power, and persistence. Can passion be sketched out [*diseñada*] in advance, can it be calculated and brought about [*provocada*] in another? When you have nothing, like my main character, you have to force [*forzar*] everything. Including love. Ricki, the character played by Antonio Banderas, is a boy who has spent his life in public institutions. Orphaned at age three, his whole life has been an unending trek through orphanages, borstals, and mental homes. When they let him out on the street, Ricki has only (as the flamenco singers say) the night, the day, and the vitality of an animal.[1]

These words are taken from a newspaper article written by Almodóvar himself and published on the day he began shooting *¡Atame!* in the psychiatric hospital at Leganés, south of Madrid. The passage raises a number of problems explored by the finished film. First is the problem of desire: is it instinctive or learned, animal-like or premeditated? Second is the problem of power: can Almodóvar's abstracted desire escape the gender hierarchies which inform heterosexual relations, implicit in the use of a verb such as *forzar* with its overtones of 'rape'? Finally, there is the question of humour: seasoning his obsessive narrative with ironic references (in this case to the clichés of popular Spanish song) can Almodóvar sustain the tone of grand passion or will his most focused love story be sabotaged by the intrusion of the crazy humour so characteristic of his earlier comedies?

On *¡Atame!*'s release, Spanish critics rarely seemed to question Almodóvar's idealizing view of his most daring film yet, proclaiming it a 'terribly tender love story'[2] and agreeing with the director that the best scene was that in which junkie and porno actress Marina (Victoria Abril), initially held hostage by Ricki against her will, finally asks to be tied up by him; this is so she will not be tempted to flee from the love he has successfully provoked in her. One critic calls this desire for bondage 'the greatest intensity of love', a 'feminist' statement.[3] It was left to Rossy de Palma (who plays a drug dealer in *¡Atame!*) to confirm that the film's kidnapping was not to be imitated in real life and was only justified by the 'exceptional' nature of the characters.[4] Well received by the Spanish trade press,[5] *¡Atame!* was (like *Mujeres al borde de un ataque de nervios*) the biggest-grossing domestic film of its year, reaching an audience of over a million by August 1990. If we compare this figure to that of Almodóvar's main rivals, this was twice the audience of Carlos Saura's comeback movie *¡Ay Carmela!* and four times that of Fernando Trueba's much lauded international co-production *El sueño del mono loco* (The Dream of the Mad Monkey). Both of these lower-grossing films had larger budgets than *¡Atame!*[6]

As we shall see later, foreign audiences did not share this unanimity. When Antonio Banderas compares his character to Tarzan in a US interview ('Tarzan grabs Jane, he hits her a couple of times . . . He's got her up [his tree], tied with vines'),[7] he seems shocked to hear that some women might find such victimization less than ideal. Banderas repeats Almodóvar's contention that in accepting her bonds, Marina assumes her amorous destiny. The photos that accompany this interview (of Banderas drenched with water and smeared with motor oil) suggest that such stereotypical images of masculinity hold a certain attraction for US audiences also, who may share with Spaniards a soft spot for apemen.

The opening sequence would infer, however, that the spectator is not to identify with Ricki. Called to see the lady director of the psychiatric hospital in which he has been confined (played by veteran Lola Cardona), Ricki states his intention of 'working and starting a family, like a normal person'. The director states quite clearly that he is not a normal person. And throughout the film it is apparent that his actions are, if not insane, certainly infantile. The script specifies that Ricki's drawings (a leitmotif) are 'childish' and that his 'smile is that of an innocent child, his eyes those of a tiger'.[8] Regressive and elemental, Ricki is also placed in the feminine position of exchanging his body for material favours: he thanks the tearful director for treating him so well by making love to her in her office.

With his crewcut and jeans, Ricki is a parody of a standard masculinity which seeks only to be 'integrated' into the society that has sponsored it. But just as Ricki is the perfect male love object (attracting lascivious gazes from women wherever he goes), so Marina is the recipient of heavily loaded looks. First shown as a photograph in a glossy magazine (the sign of a conspicuous alienation from her image), Marina is next glimpsed making up in the dressing-room of the studio where she is filming a horror B movie ('Midnight Phantom') with director Máximo Espejo (Francisco Rabal). The visceral narcissist Ricki, having followed her to the studio, dons a heavy-metal wig and plays an air guitar in the dressing-room mirror when Marina has left.

In Victoria Abril's subtle performance, Marina is initially presented as a woman confident enough to survive male voyeurism: troubled by a visible panty-line, she is happy to remove her knickers before shooting a sequence. But she is subjected to a barrage of looks in the studio as filming begins: reverse angles show her to be the object of the fascinated gaze of the film crew, her obsessive director, and the incognito Ricki, ostentatiously odd in his long wig. A publicity still shows Marina-Abril crouching on all fours, hair dishevelled and dress seductively clinging, at once vulnerable and defiant (Plate 16). In this sequence she tells director Máximo not to look at her 'like that'. He replies that he is not looking, but admiring ('No te miro; te admiro'); to which she retorts that she needs no such admiration. Máximo, who uses an electric wheelchair after a stroke, is left mutely and helplessly circling, the image of male impotence before female mastery.

Hence, as always in Almodóvar, the parody of the male gaze is supplemented by a space between-women, which is not ironized. Thus Marina is first shown with her sister Lola (feisty Loles León); and the script contrasts the former's 'hermeticism and mystery' with the latter's 'explosive', 'gesticulating' femininity (p. 20). Clearly, the two women are complementary; and as a film without fathers (like so many in Almodóvar's oeuvre) ¡Atame! will hint at a matrilinear and parthenogenetic lineage of women, within which men are granted only temporary accommodation. It is not the least of ¡Atame!'s paradoxes that a film often accused of condoning male violence against women should be placed so clearly under the sign of the mother: Lola has a daughter, but no husband; the two sisters are provided with a memorable matriarch, played by Francisca Caballero, Almodóvar's real-life mother.

This female lineage, so comforting in its continuity, is however constantly under threat, menaced with interruption. And one sign of Marina's vulnerability is her addiction. Diagnosed by her unlikely doctor friend (daffy María Barranco) as 'a born drug addict', she is described rightly by one British critic as 'addictive in all things'.[9] A French location report ('Hook Me Up') claims that the dope-passion metaphor sustains the film's gravest moments: drugs are 'a way of loving understood as a progressive habituation [accoutumance] and an art of seeing the object of desire surprisingly similar' to the way in which William Burroughs's narcotics-user sees his connection: 'savouring the feeling of his omnipotence, his power to make you happy or unhappy'.[10]

Marina has a toothache; and for much of the film she will (like Burroughs's junkie cited above) be awaiting that gift of love which will assuage her pain. However, the addiction metaphor (rarely seen by Anglo-American critics, mesmerized by their fascination with sexual violence) goes beyond the equation of passion and dope. For *¡Atame!* bears witness to what Avital Ronell has called a 'toxic drive' which has ambiguous properties.[11] Firstly, addiction is 'non-contingent', generalizable: all of the main characters in the film are addicted. Ricki and Máximo are bound as surely to the image of Marina in magazines or porno videos as Marina is to heroin. Secondly, if drugs, in the extended sense, are in Ronell's words 'the basis of our culture' (p. 13), then they question the integrity of the body and disrupt the policing of boundaries: introjecting alien substances to experience authenticity, the 'body cannot preserve its identity . . . is on the line' (p. 7). There is thus a certain 'crisis in immanence' in narcotics which do not afford the promised escape of exteriority, but rather produce 'fractal interiorities' (p. 15), uncontrollable divisions within the self. Ronell notes that Freud compares addicts to cats in their inaccessibility and apparent libidinal autonomy (p. 53). Marina's pharmacodependency thus at once reveals the 'improper' character of her body (which does not belong to her, which requires external supplementation) and confirms her 'hermeticism' (which divorces her from the world, distances her from the demands of the other). If *¡Atame!* is indeed addicted to love, then it also reveals that bodies and subjects are not as stable as they might initially appear, that the work of art (both stimulant and tranquillizer) permits fluid identifications and boundary confusions.

HOUSE OF HORROR

ANGELINA: Más que una historia de horror parece una historia de amor.

ANGELINA: It's not so much a horror story as a love story.

The most hermetically self-reflexive of Almodóvar's films, *¡Atame!* includes an extended sequence from Máximo's film within the film, *Midnight Phantom*, shot on what is clearly the set previously used for *Mujeres al borde*. Marina, the woman in peril, awaits the appearance of the Phantom in her glamorous flat. Arriving through the window, he is first shown wrapped in a billowing shroud-like curtain. When Marina orders him to come out he tells her that he has come to take her to 'a place without pressures where nobody knows us and we can be happy'. Marina asks him to remove the mask that covers his face, but he refuses, claiming he has no face, that his face is that of a dead man. Suddenly Marina lassoes him with a telephone cable and leaps through the window, thus smashing the Phantom's head against the lower part of the wall and strangling him at the same time. As Marina swings in the void 'like a pendulum' (script, p. 49), the camera pulls back to reveal the wind and rain machines and the edges of the set representing the façade of Marina's house.

This comic *tour de force* is typical of Almodóvar's ironic exploitation of the cinematic apparatus and of his use of crazy humour to relieve tension. But the homage reference to the horror genre (repeated in later allusions to George A. Romero's zombie films) is more than circumstantial and *¡Atame!* coincides at a number of points with the subversive potential discerned by Carol J. Clover in US slasher films.[12] Clover suggests that the genre is an ambiguous response to a feminism which has emphasized both women's victimization by men and their angry response to it (p. 3). Feminist psycho-analytic film theory has generally suggested a gendered division of spectatorship in which male (or male-identified) viewers adopt a sadistic-voyeuristic position in relation to a passive female object (p. 8). This model (which has obvious pertinence to horror movies in which women are most visibly made to weep and suffer) fails to account for a crucial feature of the genre: the rise of the Final Girl, the resourceful heroine who dispatches the monster (until the next sequel) at the end of the film (p. 44). Given that the prime audience for such films is adolescent males, the prominence of the female victim-hero suggests that cross-gender identification is more frequent than has been previously supposed. Indeed, the feminization of the weapon-wielding killer (framed since *Psycho* as a female-identified regressive) prohibits male identification with a nominally male character. Horror thus offers its majority viewers a variety of positions and empathies as a matter of course, allowing young men to 'run [their fantasies] through the figure of a woman', to 'experience forbidden desires and to disavow them' (p. 18). Given such fluidity and mobility it is inadvisable to assume that a 'male gaze' is equivalent to male mastery (p. 19). Rather, if gender is derived from function, not biological sex (femininity from victimhood, not from the sex of the actor), then the audience is 'feminized', terrorized in its victim-identification.

One publicity still for *¡Atame!* shows a grimly determined Ricki holding his hand over the mouth of a terrified Marina (Plate 17). However, even here in its most explicit reference to the horror genre, *¡Atame!*'s traffic of desire is more complex than might at first appear. Like the slasher film whose viewing is (in Clover's words) 'ritualistic and formulaic' (p. 9), Almodóvar's cinema attracts a 'competent' audience ready to anticipate plot moves and acknowledge an ironic complicity between filmmaker and public. And the Midnight Phantom sequence clearly reworks parodically the already parodic excesses of its models. Marina's character is a suitably poised Final Girl, 'intelligent, watchful, level headed' (Clover, p. 44). The Phantom, moreover, for all his extravagant musculature and fetishistic leather drag, is always already unmanned, shrouded like a corpse and de-faced, compared in the script to a toy Master of the Universe (p. 17). Biological sex is thus supplanted by narrative function, with the victim turning hero and killing the monster who had threatened her with death. As a survivor (in Máximo's film, in Almodóvar's film) Marina will disable male mastery, and secure the spectator's identification. Having performed in the backstory at a circus, Marina is proficient at both training horses and tying up men, whose relative 'inflexibility' is only too apparent.[13]

Clover's hypothesis of cross-gender identification thus suggests a way out of the sterile binaries of critical debate on *¡Atame!*, in which English- and German-speaking viewers attack Almodóvar for the 'negative' political content of his images and Spanish and French critics absolve those images of any content, displace them wholly into ironic humour or pastiche.[14] By acknowledging the role of fantasy in filmic pleasure, Clover thus frees up discussion of films (such as Almodóvar's) in which stylized performance and art design clearly signal that a commonsense response is inappropriate; but by paying attention to the specific conditions under which such films are consumed, Clover also argues that such 'figurative' or non-literal readings are, of themselves, inadequate. When Ricki follows Marina to her home, breaks into her flat, and floors her with a vicious head-butt which breaks her tooth, the question remains to be posed with all the more urgency: 'Where does literal end and figurative begin? To which in arriving at a political judgment . . . do we assign priority?' (Clover, p. 44) Almodóvar's house of horror may be more aesthetically designed than those featured in *Friday the Thirteenth* or *Slumber Party Massacre*; the problems it raises are equally disturbing.

THE MASOCHISTIC AESTHETIC

RICKI: ¿Cuánto tiempo vas a tardar en enamorarte de mí?
RICKI: How long will it take you to fall in love with me?

The first shot of *¡Atame!* is of a stylized heart. A heartbeat followed by Ennio Morricone's hypnotic music is heard on the soundtrack. The camera pulls back to reveal kitschy images of Christ and Mary displaying their Sacred Hearts to the spectator. It is a sequence which implies not only that evacuation of content (of the power of grand narratives) for which Almodóvar's playful postmodernism is known,[15] but also that masochistic sensualism thought by some to be characteristic of Catholicism.[16] Less obvious, perhaps, is the bisexuality of such images. One perceptive critic (Suzanne Moore) talks of 'female' masochism in this title sequence, thus erasing the image of Christ, the most feminine of men, who is also prominently pictured on Marina's wall in the guise of Good Shepherd. The hermetic space of the flat in which Marina is held captive is thus not only a theatre for the acting out of the crudest power imbalances between the sexes; it is also a stage for the performance of new and more flexible gender roles by actors and audience.

As the film develops, boundaries come under increasing pressure. For example, Máximo (tyrannical director on the film set) is reduced to a mute spectator when the movie is wrapped and Marina has disappeared. Turning from the TV screen which shows the porno videos to which he is addicted, he faces the window of his flat and speaks into the telephone a message to be recorded by Marina's answering machine. In it he tells the story of how when a bullfighter achieved great success he would be taken to his house on the shoulders of his admirers and then made to appear on the balcony to receive their applause. He claims that he does not know why he is telling her this. But what is interesting here is not simply the nostalgia for a time when virile display might be unambiguously celebrated; it is also Máximo's adoption of the role in which he had previously cast Marina: caught in the light, exposed to the male gaze, suspended at the window. As Máximo gruffly recounts his curious tale, Almodóvar cuts to Marina's flat where his voice is emerging from the machine. The camera pans slowly in an overhead shot over her mute body, bound with green cord and gagged with tape.

Elsewhere Almodóvar uses this cross-cutting to rescue a narrative immobilized by its chosen theme. Thus as Ricki is beaten by narcotics dealers in the Plaza de la Lechuga (just south of the Plaza Mayor in the old heart of Madrid), Marina makes a desperate, but somewhat half-hearted, attempt to escape from her captivity. Generally, however, Almodóvar is content to slow the pace of the action and remove it from that moment of actuality implied by cross-cutting. The framings here (extreme close-ups of the glamorous co-stars immobile in bed) reinforce that sense of a fetishistic frozen moment. When Ricki asks Marina how long she will take to fall in love with him, it is a question that will be echoed by some members of the audience, impatient with such beautifully costumed and immaculately decorated languor.

Almodóvar has consistently denied that *¡Atame!*'s ropes have any link with sado-masochism;[17] and at least one critic has agreed that he 'rigorously refus[es] to give any erotic charge to the ropes and gags'.[18] But this is perhaps to define masochism in too limited a way. For *¡Atame!* clearly coincides with many aspects of the 'masochistic aesthetic' deduced by Gaylyn Studlar from the Dietrich/von Sternberg films.[19] Rejecting (like Carol Clover) a certain feminist view which claims that dominant cinema sets up women as the passive object of a male gaze, Studlar calls attention to the possible pleasures of a male spectatorship situated beyond mastery (pp. 2–3). Criticized (like Almodóvar) for superficiality, inarticulacy, and self-indulgent fantasy, the von Sternberg/Dietrich collaborations combined 'heady visual extremism, ironically inflated melodrama, [and] darkly exotic eroticism' in a masochistic aesthetic in an extended sense (p. 4). Rejecting Freud's Oedipal aetiology of masochism, Studlar follows Deleuze in stressing the role of the mother in masochism and of the oral child's insatiable (addictive?) demand (pp. 14, 15). The chief characteristic of masochism is suspension: the suspension of an orgasm whose arrival is conditioned by pain; the suspension of Masoch's *tableaux vivants* in which suffering brings action to a halt and freezes emotion (pp. 16, 19). As in the bisexual economy of the slasher film, the oral drives of the masochist aesthetic suggest a 'desire for and a fear of symbiotic merging' between the sexes (p. 22), which 'disavow [both] the presence of the father and separation from the mother' (p. 25). The goal is thus (as in the horror film once more) a 'fantasmical parthenogenetic rebirth' (p. 26), but one in which 'ironic humour qualifies melodramatic absurdity' (p. 24).

¡Atame! clearly has more in common with masochism (in Studlar's extended sense)

than the frantically accelerated activity (p. 20) of the Sadian scene. The film takes place under the sign of an archaic mother who (as Spanish audiences know full well) does not merely impersonate Marina's parent but physically produced the film's director. And when Ricki allows Marina to phone Francisca Caballero, the latter is (of course) in the kitchen, making *pisto* (a typically Spanish version of ratatouille) with her grand-daughter. The orality is, however, not so much in the mother's association with food as in the daughter's insatiable demand, typical of the pre-Oedipal child. But Ricki shares that absolute desire, is feminized by the abject nature of his love (which reduces him to tears) and the vigorous beating he receives at the hands of the drug dealers. It is only after this beating (after Ricki's narrative function has cancelled out his biological sex, after pleasure has been suspended and tempered with pain) that the happy couple are permitted an extended and noisy sex scene, which culminates in spectacular orgasm for both. The sequence is framed, moreover, by an ironically humorous perspective which stresses the sheer physical discomfort of any sexual activity performed by a body (Banderas's) attractively blemished by bruises.

Critics have attacked Almodóvar for *¡Atame!*'s supposed dependence on art design.[20] Viewed as part of the masochistic aesthetic, however, Almodóvar's love of colour coordination (with the saturated blues, reds, and oranges of the costumes matching those of the decor) can be read as part of that playful aestheticization so characteristic of the *tableau vivant*: if pleasure is to be deferred it must at least be well dressed and firmly under control. But the visual pleasures of *¡Atame!* need not imply male mastery. On the contrary, as the kidnapping continues and the location becomes ever more baroque (Ricki moves Marina into her neighbour's postmodern fantasia of a flat), masculinity is increasingly under pressure. The lachrymose Ricki is thoroughly domes-ticated, shopping for softer ropes and more malleable tape, urging Marina to eat her breakfast 'before it gets cold'. Ricki's stated ambition is to be a good husband to Marina and a good father to their children; ironically, however, it is by adopting the nurturing, oral role gendered as feminine that he will bind Marina most closely to him and ensure that any escape she makes will be only temporary. Like the cinematic spectator 'suspended in a kind of waking hypnosis' (Studlar, p. 24), victim-hero Marina is left hanging in a space whose status is ambiguous, whose condition is (like that of the feminized Christ on her wall) to be in the world but not of it.

CINEMA, CENSORSHIP, SEXUALITY

Resistiré.
I will survive.

A newsletter for a London group called 'SM Gays' takes as its headline: 'Tie Me Up, Tie Me Down'. It is a salutary reminder that whatever the protestations of their directors, films will always be placed in contexts which their authors did not envisage or are anxious to disavow. SM Gays share with Almodóvar an awareness that bondage carries with it a narrative, but one whose successful completion is by no means guaranteed. They advise newcomers: 'You need to think ahead and explore how to place the bondage within the framework of the whole scene. It's no good tying someone up and then not knowing what to do next.'[21] It is advice that Almodóvar himself might have done well to follow, if we are to believe critics unconvinced by the change of heart which follows Marina's bondage.

¡Atame! is the most extreme case of Almodóvar's inability to control press coverage even as he devoted ever more time to promotion strategies. And it seems likely that the controversies caused by the film derived from differing conceptions of the director's political position, which themselves originated from debates on cinema and censorship peculiar to individual countries. Thus as the film was about to be shown at the Berlin Film Festival, Almodóvar himself wrote in the Spanish press comparing the 'marginal' peoples of Eastern Europe to Ricki, anxious to gain access to that 'normal' consumerist lifestyle from which he has been hitherto excluded.[22] And Spanish critics continued to suggest that Almodóvar was 'transgressive' or 'polemical'.[23] However, puzzled foreign reviewers such as Sylvia Velásquez in the British feminist *Spare Rib*[24] were not quite right in assuming that Almodóvar had a 'left-wing reputation'. Closer to the mark was his continued dismissal of the boring, bearded radicals of the 1970s, the *progres* who had gone on to form Spain's Socialist government.[25] It was foreign journalists' erroneous assumption that Almodóvar shared the radical views of the liberal audience he attracted abroad (on feminism and gay liberation in particular) that led to mutual incomprehension at the Berlin Festival. At the 'tense' press conference which followed an inauspicious screening (the projector had broken down), Almodóvar was in the words of one Spanish reporter 'obliged to put up with questions on homosexuality, the supposed excess of drug abuse in Spain, and the "Spanishness" of his cinema, which seem to have been dreamt up by candidates of the [extreme right] Catholic Action party.'[26] Another journalist was indignant about references to 'the supposed homo-

sexual image of Antonio Banderas in his jeans' and the crass question: 'Is there any irony in your film?'[27] Spaniards were thus appalled at the naïveté of the Germans, who seemed incapable of recognizing humour and metaphor; but they reserved the right nonetheless to censor those unauthorized figurative (non-literal) readings which they themselves would prefer to repress, such as the gay-coded register of Ricki's all too masculine image. And in spite of Almodóvar's defiantly apolitical libertarianism (his blanket defence of the artist's right to unlimited free expression), his Spanish supporters at the Festival implicitly appeal to a progressive political programme (in opposition to Catholic Action) whose agenda does not, however, extend to embrace questions of gender and sexuality.

This controversy was but a curtain-raiser for the battle over the Motion Picture Association of America's decision to give *¡Átame!* an X rating (normally reserved for hard-core pornography). When the case came to court in New York it gave rise to a general debate on cinema, censorship, and sexuality in the US. The attorney for Miramax (the film's North American distributors) edited together a sequence of controversial scenes from recent Hollywood films (*Fatal Attraction*; *The Accused*) to show the 'arbitrary' nature of the rating; and as a veteran advocate for Black Panthers and flag-burners, his very presence placed the case within the debate about censorship and liberalism.[28] The judge dismissed Miramax's case; but he made what *Variety* described as 'an unprecedented attack on the current method of classifying films',[29] claiming the MPAA 'impos[ed] censorship, yet all the while facilitat[ed] the marketing of exploitative and violent films [with] an industry seal of approval'. The AAP ('average American parent') was not well served by a system which permitted representations of 'hard violence' and 'drug use', but not 'explicit sex'. Seeking to rebut this critique, the attorney for the MPAA also invoked the family, warning that 'only in nondemocratic countries do governments substitute their collective wisdom in place of parents.' When, finally, the MPAA did introduce the new rating of NC-17 (adult, but non-pornographic), *The Hollywood Reporter* contrasted US restrictions with Spanish licence, noting that 'the new private TV channels [in Spain] compete for audience with parades of topless – and sometimes bottomless – young women.'[30]

It is clear, then, that while Spaniards lamented the puritanism of North Americans, who (like Germans) failed to recognize that Almodóvar was merely 'playing' with the clichés of pornography,[31] more was at stake than this; and not merely the suspicion that the MPAA discriminated in favour of powerful US majors and to the detriment of vulnerable foreign and independent producers. The rating controversy revealed the conflict between two national ideologies, each of which pledged allegiance to freedom of expression; but it also confronted US literalist readings of the text (in which a film could be reduced to fragments of unambiguous content) to Spanish figurative readings, in which context was all and content at best ambivalent.

This is a crucial distinction for a censorship debate in which, as Annette Kuhn has proposed, moralists and libertarians alike tend to subordinate representation to 'reality' and to justify images on the adequacy with which they correspond to a 'life' which remains unexamined.[32] Questioning the 'prohibition/institutions model', Kuhn argues that censorship should not or not only be seen as an 'agency of exclusion or limitation' (p. 3), but is itself productive: 'active in its own right in the construction of a public sphere of cinema', whose 'objects of regulation' would include 'modes of consumption of films, consumers of films, categories of films, and last – and quite possibly least – contents of films' (pp. 10–11). The ¡Atame! controversy is testimony to this productive function of censorship which not only generated a public debate around sexuality and nationality, but also enabled a small-budget foreign film to help effect a change in the regulatory body of the globally dominant cinema market. In this unlikely encounter between Almodóvar and the Average American Parent it is by no means clear who came out on top.

Aided by sister Lola, Marina slips the bonds she has grown to love and escapes from captivity, only to follow Ricki to the ruined village in Extremadura which had been his home as a child and now is no more. After being grilled by the suspicious Lola, Ricki is allowed into the women's car and driven by Marina back to Madrid where he will be incorporated, temporarily at least, into their all-female family. As they go, the three sing along to a song on the car radio-cassette: 'Resistiré' (I Will Survive). It is a moral that is clearly as close to Almodóvar's heart as it is to Marina's. But it seems only fair to note that many victims of male sexual violence do not survive. On the day that I finished writing this chapter I read a newspaper report of a young woman bound, beaten, and murdered in a London alleyway.[33] Arguments about the distinction between literal and figurative readings, about cross-gender identification and pre-Oedipal fluidity, would seem to have little purchase here. Yet, as we saw from the censorship debate, if we insist that representations are not to be subordinated to reality (that the filmic image is not to be equated with the thing itself) it is not because cinema deserves to be abstracted from the social world and absolved of all responsibility; it is because film and the discourses in which it is enmeshed form a public sphere which is itself part of the real, but whose relation to other discourses and practices is highly complex. Pitting power against humour, Almodóvar's answer (in ¡Atame! at least) is a defiant utopianism, an appeal to a cinematic no-place like Ricki's village, in which history is erased or reduced to the status of a picturesque backdrop. If *¡Atame!* will remain for some viewers more of a horror story than a love story, by placing fantasy so firmly in the centre of the frame Almodóvar challenges his diverse audience (from German feminist to AAP) to acknowledge the power of unconscious drives and their irreducibility to conscious control.

NOTES

1. Pedro Almodóvar, 'A veces hay que forzarlo todo, incluso el amor', *El País*, 4 July 1989.

2. Lluís Bonet Mojica, 'Romper las ataduras del éxito fácil', *La Vanguardia*, 1 February 1990.

3. Javier Maqua, 'Almodóvar, lo sublime y lo grotesco', *Cinco Días*, 30 January 1990.

4. Rossy de Palma, 'Atame, sí, pero átame bien', *El Periódico*, 27 January 1990.

5. See the anonymous review in *Cineinforme*, vol. 29, no. 575–6, February 1990, pp. 34, 36.

6. Alberich, *Cuatro años*, pp. 133, 161, 162, 180, 190.

7. Frederick Kaufman, 'Antonio Banderas', *Interview*, vol. 20, no. 5, May 1990, p. 114.

8. 'Guión original', Madrid 1989.

9. Rupert Smith, review, *Time Out*, no. 1037, 4 July 1990.

10. Philippe Vecchi, 'Accroche-moi', *Libération*, 23–4 June 1990.

11. Avital Ronell, *Crack Wars: Literature, Addiction, Mania*, Lincoln and London 1992, p. 23.

12. Carol J. Clover, *Men, Women, and Chain Saws: Gender in the Modern Horror Film*, London 1992.

13. Almodóvar derives the 'inflexibility' of Spanish men (including actors) from their obligation to play the role of the 'macho hidalgo'; Christine Haas, 'La Passion Almodóvar', *Première*, no. 159, June 1990, pp. 114–16.

14. Compare Adam Mars-Jones's critical review in the *Independent*, 5 July 1990, which argues that the film fails to address sexual hierarchy, with Philippe Rouyer's in *Positif*, 352, June 1990, which argues that sexual scenes in the film are always ironically qualified by kitsch contextualization.

15. See Gonzalo Navajas, 'Lo antisublime posmoderno y el imperativo en *¡Atame!* de Pedro Almodóvar', *España Contemporánea*, vol. 4, 1991, pp. 65–83.

16. See reviews by Mandy Merck, *City Limits* (London), no. 457, 5 July 1990; and Suzanne Moore, *New Statesman and Society*, 13 July 1990 p. 32.

17. See 'Production Notes' in the UK press book distributed by Enterprise Pictures Ltd.

18. Kim Newman, review, *Monthly Film Bulletin*, vol. 57, no. 678, July 1990, pp. 189–90 (p. 190).

19. Gaylyn Studlar, *In the Realm of Pleasure: Von Sternberg, Dietrich, and the Masochistic Aesthetic*, New York 1988.

20. See review by Terrence Rafferty, *New Yorker*, 7 May 1990, pp. 90–1.

21. SM Gays, 'Programme: July–December 1992'.

22. Pedro Almodóvar, 'Madrid-Berlín', *El Mundo*, 8 February 1990.

23. Joan Lorente Costa, 'El transgresor Pedro Almodóvar, entre tenebres', *Avui*, 14 February 1990; Jośe Luis Guarner, '¡*Atame!*: después de la expectación llega la polémica', *La Vanguardia*, 12 February 1990.

24. September 1990, p. 32.

25. Andy Robinson, 'Tenderness and Tyranny', *City Limits*, no. 457, 5 July 1990, pp. 14–15 (p. 15).

26. Fernando Lara, 'Reacciones encontradas ante el estreno de ¡*Atame!*', *El Independiente*, 12 February 1990.

27. Félix Flores, 'Almodóvar topó con el muro', *La Vanguardia*, 12 February 1990.

28. Vicki Sabatini, 'Miramax Sticks to R-Rated Debate in N.Y. High Court', *Hollywood Reporter*, vol. 313, no. 6, 22 June 1990, pp. 1, 56.

29. Will Tusher, '*Up* Loses Fight; Judge Comes Down on MPAA', *Variety*, 25 July 1990, pp. 5, 16, 20 (p. 5).

30. Anon., 'Almodóvar Seeks New Rating, New Release for *Tie Me Up!*', *Hollywood Reporter*, vol. 314, no. 24, 1 October 1990, p. 6.

31. Angel Fernández Santos, 'El ámbito de la libertad', *El País*, 13–14 April 1990.

32. Annette Kuhn, *Cinema, Censorship, and Sexuality 1909–25*, London and New York 1988, p. 2.

33. Edward Pilkington, 'Body of Girl, 12, Found Beaten and Tied in Alleyway Near Home', *Guardian*, 29 May 1993.

9

TACONES LEJANOS

(HIGH HEELS, 1991)

Imitations of Life

MOTHERHOOD AND REPRESENTATION

REBECA (a Becky):   He pasado toda la vida imitándote.
REBECA (to Becky):   I've spent my whole life imitating you.

No film by Almodóvar has received such contradictory responses as *Tacones lejanos*. This drama of sexual rivalry between mother and daughter has been attacked by some critics in the UK and US for its appeal to stereotype (neurotic career woman and sacrificial mother)[1] and 'undercurrent of sexism',[2] while others have praised the way it marginalizes male concerns, placing men quite firmly 'in the supporting role'.[3] One French critic has seen it, in a characteristically more abstract fashion, as a 'story haunted by loss and distanciation, and their corollaries: memory, fetish and trace'. He thus relates *Tacones lejanos*'s heroines to a long tradition of Almodóvarian characters 'worked on by the grief of separation or abandonment, by the quest for complementary other, by the nostalgia for fusion'.[4] And in the most detailed and theorized of readings to date, Marsha Kinder proposes that Almodóvar seeks to 'liberate the maternal' in the style of 'subversive feminist texts'.[5] For Kinder, far from being misogynist, by its closing scene the film vindicates 'the powerful sexual mother' (a fusion of maternity and desire), thus 'providing a new erotic fantasy for empowering a strategic alliance' (p. 44) amongst sexual dissidents of all genders and preferences.

It is a commonplace that the mother–daughter relationship has been under-symbolized (undertheorized) in Christian cultures.[6] And it seems likely that it is Almodóvar's very attempt to focus on maternity to the exclusion of dominant (male) concerns which causes a certain trouble in cinematic and critical discourse: there can be no simple depiction of or response to the representation of a relationship so often repressed. And the film itself suggests from its opening sequences and on both sound and image tracks a certain instability or lack of fixity in relation to its chosen subject matter. Thus as the credits roll (stylized images of guns and shoes) we hear Miles Davis's version of Gil Evans's 'Soleá': an Afro-American interpretation of an Andalusian theme. And this sense of originary, cultural displacement is confirmed by the first scenes. The camera tilts down from a glowering Madrid sky to find TV presenter Rebeca (Victoria Abril), dangerously thin in her prim white Chanel suit, waiting at the airport for the arrival of her glamorous mother Becky (Marisa Paredes), who has abandoned her fifteen years earlier to pursue a singing career in Mexico. Rebeca is first seen reflected in the window, her fragile image superimposed over the aeroplanes outside. It is a distanciating, staticist shot, which will prove typical of the film.

As Rebeca is held in close-up, the image fades to two explanatory flashbacks. The first takes place on a tropical island in 1970. The script specifies that the sequence is to be shot so as to suggest 'a hypnotic atmosphere, a dream or nightmare' reminiscent of the films of Powell and Pressburger. When her hated stepfather pretends to sell her off to the locals, Rebeca runs off amongst the palm trees. Her disappearing image is set against the voice of her mother, off-screen, calling her name. In the second flashback (identified as 'Madrid 1974') Rebeca is shown tampering with her stepfather's pills. She wears a 'mysterious and secret expression'.[7] It is suggested that she is responsible for his subsequent death in a car crash.

Almodóvar has often spoken of his distaste for flashbacks which tend to break the forward dynamism of a narrative. And the main precedent in his oeuvre for their use here is the early *Laberinto de pasiones* (1982), in which the neuroses of adult protagonists are also traced back to infantile traumas, effected once more in the exotic location of the beach. But where the flashbacks in *Laberinto* are framed in the context of a parody of pop psychoanalysis, those of *Tacones lejanos* seem designed to be read as authentic, 'deep' motivation for the characters' subsequent actions: Rebeca's murderous relations with men are caused by her inability to separate from the mother who will abandon her nonetheless. Audience identification is promoted by the unambiguous cinematographic technique of camera height: the child Rebeca is consistently shot at her own level and not 'looked down on' as if by an adult observer.

Douglas Sirk's celebrated maternal melodrama *Imitation of Life* (1959) also begins with a child lost at a holiday location: the would-be actress played by Lana Turner has been separated from her young daughter at Coney Island. And the multiple parallels between the two plots are clear: both focus on the life of a mother-performer, on maternal neglect, mother-daughter strife, and incestuous rivalry over a man:[8] in *Tacones lejanos* Rebeca will marry Becky's ex-lover. And in the murder of a male lover shared by two women Almodóvar may also be drawing on press accounts of Turner's real-life drama which, famously and ambiguously, fed into one of her most commercially successful screen roles. When Almodóvar has Rebeca tell Becky 'Stop acting, mother', he is signalling a quite explicit reference to *Imitation of Life*.[9] And it is worth sketching briefly the changing representations of the mother in US popular culture within and against which Sirk was working.

E. Ann Kaplan traces those representations from 'the cult of true womanhood' (purity, piety, domesticity, and submission)[10] and the 'domestic feminism' of nineteenth-century fiction to the maternal melodrama and woman's film of the first half of the twentieth century. She notes the polarization of 'good' (self-sacrificing) and 'bad' (jealous, rapacious) mothers. Both tend to be seen from the child's point of view; indeed, maternal subjectivity is generally made central only when it is made sexual, and thus requires punishment. Later vulgarizations of psychoanalysis further blame the mother, holding her responsible for the child's psychic health or, more frequently, disorder (p. 123). If the mother steps out of place (either by leaving the home for a career or by valuing her own desires over those of her daughter) she is 'trouble' (p. 131). Alternately sadistic and masochistic, mothers in films such as *Imitation of Life* and *Mildred Pierce* are obliged to sacrifice both their own heterosexual desires and their possibility of pleasure in bonding with their daughter, a bonding now presented as perilously close, even monstrous (p. 134).

I suggest later that we must pay attention to the particularly Spanish reception of Hollywood women's films. But it is clear that Almodóvar's narrative is framed within Kaplan's dichotomies of 'good' and 'bad' mothers, sacrifice and sensuality, identification and desire. Indeed, Marsha Kinder's case for *Tacones lejanos* as an 'oppositional' drama is based on the film's supposed re-evaluation of the mother–daughter dyad: 'the homoerotic desire to love/imitate/become the parent of the same sex (in this case the mother) rather than the heterosexual desire for the other (in this case the father)' (p. 40). And in early sequences of the film Almodóvar uses framing to suggest both the fusion (symmetry) and separation (asymmetry) of the two women. Thus as the couple leave the airport in a limousine they are shown straight on in a two-shot, but with Becky's flamboyant red hat interposing behind and between them. When they reach their destination (the Plaza del Alamillo, where Becky has bought the basement flat in which she was born), the two women are overshadowed once more by the garish posters plastered on the wall behind them (Plate 18). The posters depict Femme Letal (Miguel Bosé), a drag queen who imitates Becky. A much-reproduced still from this sequence shows both actors in profile, gazing into each other's eyes, Becky tenderly touching her daughter under the chin. But (as in the Hollywood women's picture) such fusion is fraught with danger: when they embrace Rebeca's conch-shell earring (bought for her by her mother in the opening flashback) becomes tangled in Becky's platinum coiffure. The mother fails to recognize the earrings as her gift (fails to validate her daughter's memory). The script confirms Victoria Abril's grave, even glum, performance here: Rebeca's passion for her mother is 'inexorable, fatal' (p. 32). But this stress on authenticity (on adult emotion grounded in childhood trauma) is contradicted by the poster of Femme Letal, which announces another, antagonistic theme of the film: the mechanical reproduction of femininity, the ceaseless replication of the real.

THE CHAIN OF SIMULATIONS

LETAL (a Rebeca):   Puedo convertirme en lo que tú quieras. . . .
Dime qué tipo de hombre te gusta y en éste me convertiré.
LETAL (to Rebeca):   I can turn into whatever you want. . . . Tell
me what kind of man you like and I'll turn into him.

When Victoria Abril's Rebeca opens her handbag, Almodóvar cuts to a loving close-up of its Chanel logo. English-language critics have used this attention to costume and detail to attack the supposed triviality of *Tacones lejanos*, obsessed as it would appear to be with accessories.[11] The triumph of *attrezzo* here (more blatant even than in Almodóvar's other films) might be seen as an unwitting testimony to consumerism in post-Franco Spain, to a society in which the cult of nationality has been replaced by the quest for cash, *patria* by *pasta*.[12]

However, Almodóvar is paying homage here to a Hollywood tradition. The production notes for *Imitation of Life* also stress the importance of Lana Turner's gowns and jewels, valued at over a million dollars.[13] And Becky's somewhat severe suits (this time by Armani) serve, like Turner's more improbable costumes, to suggest a geometric hardness and detachment from which a (conventionally maternal) softness, roundness, and warmth are excluded.[14] Moreover, a certain critique of 'accessory theory' is internalized in the film itself: at the emotional reunion of mother and daughter Becky does not neglect to compliment Rebeca on her Chanel suit; the script tells us that Becky is used to her appearance being appraised as dispassionately 'as if she were a cake', not a woman (p. 40). The film thus foregrounds the visual pleasures of costume at the same times as it stresses the ambivalence women may feel in those pleasures, in that costume.

A pre-release cover story for the Madrid monthly *El Europeo* (May 1991) shows Marisa Paredes's mask-like face framed by her gloved hands. It is a pose based on Femme Letal's impersonation of Becky as shown in the poster featured in the film. And as the film develops, the paraphernalia of female accessories are reduplicated in a 'chain of simulations' (the phrase is Kinder's) which focus on Miguel Bosé's triple role as dignified drag queen Letal, mild-mannered Judge Domínguez, and undercover cop Hugo. As the embodiment of what one Italian critic has called Almodóvar's 'dream of metamorphosis',[15] this protean character proclaims once more a favourite Almodóvarian refrain: the primacy of voluntarism, the freedom of the subject to place him/herself on either side of the sexual divide.

Letal is first seen when Rebeca lures mother Becky and unwilling husband Manuel to witness his act at the real-life Villa Rosa nightclub in the Plaza de Santa Ana in central Madrid. Emerging from behind beaded curtains, Letal is followed by the camera in an unusually long and fluid take, as he parades through the audience to take up his place on stage. He is miming to a 'prehistoric' hit of Becky's, 'Un año de amor' (A Year of Love). Already tall, his height is enhanced by a typical 'period' touch: platform shoes. Vocal impersonation is supplemented by the chromatic reminiscence in his costume: Letal's red blouse and glitter miniskirt contrast with his pink lipstick, just as at the start of the film Becky's red Armani suit was accessorized with pink high heels (Plate 19). A comic reverse angle from the stage reveals three drag queens in the audience, perfectly reproducing Letal's stylized gestures: an imitation of an imitation.

As always in Almodóvar the song makes quite specific reference to the narrative: Becky and Manuel are thinking back to the brief affair they enjoyed when Rebeca was a child. But just as Miles Davis's 'Soleá' implies a certain originary displacement (from the native land, from the mother tongue) so the song lip-synched by Letal (and sung in reality by contemporary pop star Luz Casal) points to a primary nostalgia projected into the fluctuating tense of the future in the past: as the singer reminds her faithless lover, when he has left her he will recall the moments they once shared together. And this superimposition of temporal levels (of present imitation of past anticipation of future regret) is matched by what Kinder has called the 'perpetual slippage of identity' (p. 43) of the impersonator: transvestite, judge, and informer imitating a mother for a daughter who has spent her own life perfecting just such a performance. Kinder is perhaps herself overly 'dazzled' by the chain of simulations, as she confuses a number of characters' names and roles.[16] But by taking Almodóvar's multiple substitutions seriously and not treating them as camp throwaways, she opens the way to a new reading of *Tacones lejanos*, which is neither dismissive nor excessively reverent towards the film's mobilization of feminine fetishes.

The script stresses that Letal is one of the 'new wave' of drag queens whose aim is not to be women, but rather to pay parodic homage to them (p. 48). And when Letal is shown offstage after his performance, we are told that he appears 'shy', but not 'effeminate' (p. 50). Refusing to collapse identification and desire, Letal thus preserves a certain awareness of gender roles and of their history. And although s/he claims to be 'whatever people wish to call him/her' and has chosen a name whose gender is in Spanish both masculine and feminine, Letal requires from the audience (in the nightclub, in the cinema) a certain historical self-consciousness (an ability to 'place' miniskirts and platform shoes) which cannot simply be collapsed into a postmodern vertigo of the surface. As Kinder reminds us (p. 44), Bosé is well known to the Spanish public as the son of a famous bullfighter and actress; there is thus a pointed irony in his performing as he does here against a background of stereotyped matadors and gypsies. Moreover, the Villa Rosa itself, with its 'traditional' decor recreated only in the late 1980s, evokes a newly self-confident and ironic appropriation of Spanish iconography, which is by no means ahistorical but rather highly characteristic of contemporary Madrid.

Throughout *Tacones lejanos* actors are framed, like Bosé in the Villa Rosa, against flamboyant backgrounds into which they merge or against which they are forced to compete. As in his use of mirror shots (frequent in *Tacones lejanos*), Almodóvar here coincides with a sense of 'aesthetic distance' held by many critics to be typical of Sirk. Thus Fred Camper has written sympathetically of the 'falseness' and 'flatness' of Sirk's framing, in which actors are 'frozen on to the surface' of static tableaux.[17] Objects are seen 'only in terms of their expressive function within the shot [and are deprived of] worldly physical reality' (p. 253), mere 'masks or reflections of . . . other objects' (p. 263). Paul Willemen has derived Sirk's love of 'distanciation' from his theatrical training which led him to 'set action in an echo chamber',[18] a hermetic space reminiscent of the stage and implying an 'absence behind the diegesis' (pp. 274–5). We find similar spaces in *Tacones lejanos*, and a similar sense of vacuum beyond the world of the narrative: institutions such as the law will prove to be curiously lacking in substance. One critic has chided Almodóvar here for creating a 'world of devoted reference' which allows its characters no access to extra-cinematic concerns.[19]

I would propose, however, that such hermetic, self-reflexive readings of Almodóvar are inadequate; indeed, that where Almodóvar may appear to be most 'devoted to reference' he is also most attentive to history. And just as more recent critics of Sirk, such as Lucy Fischer,[20] have sought to break out of the 'agoraphobic' stress on reflexivity and 'to pay attention to historical changes . . . in the representation of gender, class, and race' (p. 5), so a more sympathetic reading of Almodóvar can interrogate enclosed spaces such as the nightclub without repudiating their maternal dimension or the refuge they offer sexual dissidents. Letal invites Rebeca back to his dressing-room where, half out of costume and his face still smeared with make-up, he engages her in a bout of aerial lovemaking (Rebeca is suspended on a bar high above the floor). Letal gravely informs his partner: 'I want to be more than a mother to you.' Their acrobatic coitus (which will result in Becky's impregnation) attests to a re-evaluation of that maternal excess (that dangerous libidinal supplement) which is the mother's unique contribution to cinematic melodrama.

ALMODRAMA[21]

REBECA: Mamá, deja de montar números.
REBECA: Stop acting, mother.

UK distributors Columbia Tristar advised video rental outlets that *Tacones lejanos* was an 'erotic drama'. Almodóvar himself has described it as a 'slightly serious comedy'; but in a characteristic 'auto-interview' published in *El País*[22] he identified the film as a melodrama in the grand cinematic style, as opposed to the debased Venezuelan television soap operas currently popular in Spain. This question of genre was to dominate Spanish press coverage of the film. In a notice bearing the heavily symbolic title 'Un globo hinchado' (A Swollen Balloon), the chief critic of *El País*, Angel Fernández Santos, claims that Almodóvar is incapable of achieving the three goals of melodrama: dramatic continuity of plot; sentimental identification with characters; 'musical' graduation of sequences. Besides the Everest of *Imitation of Life*, *Tacones lejanos* is but a little Spanish hill.[23] A more sympathetic notice by Francisco Umbral[24] also attacks the lack of 'resolution' in the film, its oscillation between a genre (here taken to be soap opera) and a satirical version of that genre. I suggest in a moment that the film exhibits too much rather than too little continuity; and that this contributes to a certain staticism in its second half. But a look at three masterful sequences (of confession, performance, and confrontation) will reveal that Almodóvar's melodramatic project cannot simply be dismissed, is no fragile balloon to be punctured by the critic's needle.

When Manuel (Rebeca's husband, Becky's lover) is found murdered, the film shifts abruptly into a murder mystery. Interrogated by Judge Domínguez, Rebeca insists at first on her innocence. In a set-piece of comedy and pathos, however, she later confesses to the crime as she reads the network news bulletin, addressing herself (as the script tells us) 'to the camera, to the world, to her mother' (p. 100). As the anxious technicians debate whether or not to pull the plug on her, Rebeca produces photos for the camera, showing it (showing us) her late husband's favourite armchair and closet. Much of the humour of the scene derives from the presence of another woman in the frame beside Rebeca: Isabel (Miriam Díaz de Aroca), Manuel's mistress, who is meant to 'sign' the news bulletin read by Rebeca for deaf viewers. This very particular comic two-shot evokes that ironic commentary on sentimental narrative typical of Almodóvar. But it also points to a certain fracture in femininity, with the fragile, brunette Rebeca standing for voice and affect and the buxom, blonde Isabel for body and gesture. The couple are comically juxtaposed, but do not coincide. The discontinuity of image (the divided frame) is thus echoed in the slippage between image and soundtrack, a slippage which exploits to humorous effect the ambiguities of performance. For in her visual representation of a verbal confession, Isabel is anxious to ensure that viewers do not mistake her as the author of the crime. Moreover, in spite of the affecting gravity and plangency Victoria Abril lends Rebeca in this sequence, the audience cannot be sure that she is telling the truth. Although Rebeca is clearly the identification figure of the first half of the film (the observer of all actions; the recipient of all sympathy) we have not been shown the murder itself and remain, as yet, ignorant of its perpetrator.

There is thus an oscillation between engagement and distanciation which recurs in a second set-piece, Becky's triumphant concert performance (shot at the plush Teatro María Guerrero). Here Becky's emotive torch-song 'Piensa en mí' (Think of Me) is cross-cut with Rebeca's arrival in the prison of Yeserías, where she has been sent after her televised confession and pending investigation by the Judge. The ironic contrast of location is heightened by the use of a sound bridge: the audience's thunderous applause is heard over a shot of the prison gates closing behind Rebeca; and Becky's song is relayed over a transistor radio in the prison dormitory. The divided frame of the confession is here replaced by a critical use of montage in which ironic commentary is displaced from cinematography to editing. But, once more, the question of identification is raised in this sequence. In a gesture at once noble and absurd, Becky kneels to kiss the stage: a single teardrop falls on her lipstick trace, framed in close-up by her red shoes. The script tells us at this point that 'Becky is overwhelmed by emotion . . . she cannot hold back the tears which she dries with her gloved hands' (p. 133). However, in an unusually penetrating interview, Almodóvar claims not to know if Becky's act 'is sincere or if it is an imitation of life'.[25] Citing his own very public gesture of reconciliation with Carmen Maura at the Goya award ceremony in Madrid in 1989, Almodóvar states that there is no simple distinction between theatricality and 'genuine' emotion, that any gesture performed on stage 'becomes spectacle'.

We are back, once again, with the 'chain of simulations'. But the problem with *Tacones lejanos* is that it offers itself up all too easily for facile 'postmodern' readings, which have become generalized in journalism, particularly in the US. Thus in his brief review of the film for *New York* magazine, David Denby lists these commonplaces with telegraphic concision: 'emotion as performance, impersonation as possession, the theatricality of the real, and the authenticity of the theatrical' (16 December 1991). The challenge for the film scholar is thus to break out of the critical 'theatre', to reject cozily 'agoraphobic' readings while remaining true to the constrictions of Almodóvar's incestuous family romance.

At first sight, however, Almodóvar seems merely to have retained and intensified Sirk's formalism (his reflexivity, staticism, 'falseness') while jettisoning his broader social concerns. Thus while *Imitation of Life* contrasted a neglectful, white mother with a sacrificial, black mother, *Tacones lejanos* in a very different Spanish context reveals no concern for race and only a vestigial interest in class. Likewise the career/family dilemma faced by Lana Turner is attenuated by Almodóvar: Becky simply escapes to Mexico to pursue her career, abandoning her daughter; the childless Rebeca's job has required no sacrifice; on the contrary, her husband is the boss of the TV channel where she works. Mother – daughter rivalry is also defused: no one seems surprised that both should sleep with the same man; and when Rebeca finally confesses that she is responsible for the deaths of her stepfather and husband, Becky merely remarks, somewhat ruefully, that she must find another way of settling her differences with men.

In the US of the 1950s melodrama was symptomatic, testifying in spite of itself to the hidden contradictions of a repressive but apparently contented body politic. In the Spain of the 1990s (where nothing is taboo, where anything can be said) the family can no longer serve as the arena for the return of repressed psychic and social traumas: the personal simply remains personal, in an aggressive tautology. The 'draining of dramatic significance' found by Michael Stern in *Imitation of Life*'s white family[26] requires the omission of the collective and social concerns which are posed (but remain conspicuously unresolved) in women's pictures such as those by Sirk. When Becky claims to have done nothing but 'perform' (*actuar*) all her life, she is not referring to that social and economic performance which figures so strongly in maternal melo-dramas in the US.

Almodóvar is insistent on the lack of irony in Sirk's films; curiously so when Sirk himself and most modern critics take ironic distance to be his most characteristic response to the melodramatic material he handled so skilfully.[27] But it seems possible that Almodóvar is engaging with a specifically Spanish reception of the Hollywood women's picture. Carmen Martín Gaite has given an important, if partial and incident-al, testimony to that reception in a Francoist Spain where relations between the sexes were marked by a 'theatricality' or play-acting marked by the necessity of feigning loyalty to a stultifying ideology.[28] Martín Gaite notes how the debate around women's identity and sexuality was inflected by an ambiguous relation to a US cinema which was both feared and envied for its materialism and individualism. Thus the official attempt to valorize sacrificial maternity over vampish sensuality was acted out in 'the battle of the GG's', in which the domesticated Greer Garson was exalted over the tarnished and fading attractions of Greta Garbo (p. 135). Or again, women's films such as *Gaslight* or *Rebecca*, whose protagonists were consumed by obscure psychic traumas, were inter-preted in the light of the state's promotion of endlessly smiling Falangist women and its denigration of those unsociable girls branded as 'odd' ('raras') and heading, irrevoc-ably, for spinsterhood (pp. 38–40). Such films were known significantly as 'películas de complejos' ('films of [psychic] complexes'); they imply that the focus on women's private problems could be read as an oblique form of resistance to the relentless public optimism of the state.

One vital opposition here is that between a Spanish scarcity economy, in which both commodities and emotions were strictly rationed, and US profligacy (Spanish *derroche*), in which both material and psychic resources were conspicuously squandered on screen. Martín Gaite is referring to the 1940s here. But it seems likely that in his love of lavish display (of colour, of costume, of sentiment) Almodóvar is paying homage to a certain Spanish reading of Hollywood in which unlimited excess triumphs over domestic inhibitions. In the climactic confrontation between mother and daughter (a scene located, for dramatic effect, in an empty courtroom), Rebeca tells Becky that her imitation of her mother was also a 'homage', albeit one misread as an insult. In this lengthy sequence the two-shot of the TV confession and the cross-cutting of the theatre/prison performance are replaced by a leisurely succession of tightly framed close-ups. It is a scene in which the intelligence with which Abril and Paredes animate often dull dialogue is transparent; but it is also one in which Almodóvar's version of melodrama (so different from its Hollywood reference point) comes close to a terminal stasis.

ALMODÓVAR ALSO WEEPS[29]

REBECA: Yo tampoco entiendo a Vd.
JUEZ DOMÍNGUEZ: Eso se llama reciprocidad.
REBECA: I don't understand you either.
JUDGE DOMÍNGUEZ: That's called reciprocity.

Released in Spain in mid-October 1991, *Tacones lejanos* had by the end of the year grossed over seven hundred million pesetas and been seen by 1.6 million people. Taking nearly three times as much as the nearest domestic rival of the year, *Tacones lejanos* came second only to Almodóvar's own *Mujeres al borde de un ataque de nervios* in the ranks of most profitable Spanish films of all time.[30] In Barcelona alone it took over one hundred thousand dollars in the first three days of release.[31] Outside Spain the film provoked a blizzard of publicity both before and after its appearance in a bewildering variety of journals. A cover feature in *Cahiers du Cinéma*[32] placed a lengthy location report on Almodóvar next to similar features on art house favourites David Cronenberg and Vitali Kanevski; an interview in *Cosmopolitan* ('The Man Who Loved Women') sought perhaps to reassure a female audience made nervous by *¡Atame!*[33] The new colour pages of one of Britain's most reactionary newspapers were graced by Victoria Abril in her Chanel suit.[34]

In Spain much of the coverage was frankly hostile, as if to testify to the mutual incomprehension of Almodóvar and the local press. Journalists predicted financial disaster and proclaimed that Almodóvar's moment had passed.[35] Even the normally supportive *El Europeo* published a hostile piece to 'balance' a more positive review of Almodóvar's achievements to date.[36] The tone of much of the criticism was personal, with Rafa Fernández in *El Sol* attacking the director for his supposed arrogance.[37] While the predictions of economic decline proved unfounded, the personalization of attacks was perhaps inevitable, given Almodóvar's own choice of promotional strategies: posing moodily in high heels for publicity pictures;[38] proclaiming in the auto-interview that when it came to weeping he was more than a match for his characters.

In a final, protracted death scene, Rebeca tearfully confesses her guilt to her mother, who agrees to incriminate herself and thus save her daughter. The script confirms that this is intended as a scene of redemption and of transcendence, with Rebeca's tears 'cleansing [herself] of years of hate' (p. 216) and a setting sun casting a 'majestic and primitive' light on the moribund Becky (p. 220). It is also the scene where we learn the significance of the title: as a child Rebeca could not sleep until she heard the sound of her errant mother's 'distant heels' clicking on the parquet floor, after her return from some elegant soirée or glamorous performance. The final fade has Rebeca embracing her dead mother as if the two 'form[ed] one body'. It is an ecstatic fusion in which not all spectators will feel able to participate.

Almodóvar seems to abandon here that sense of ironic distance typical of him. And location reports suggest his close proximity to this scene, instructing the actors ever more closely on their delivery, forcing them to imitate his precise tone of voice.[39] *Cahiers* even claims that Almodóvar's normal practice of filming in chronological order extended here to shooting each line of dialogue discretely in order to keep to the sequence as written in the script, rather than filming the whole of each actor's contribution to the scene in one go, as would be normal (p. 23). There is thus a strong investment in continuity here in all senses, a desire for a seamless fusion of actor, director, and audience. It is a desire which tends to abstract the action, immobilize it at that moment of the dying sun when the shadows of high-heeled women are projected, once again, onto the walls of Becky's basement. It is an abstraction which may appear to be geographic as well as temporal. David Thompson claims in *Sight and Sound* that the film is 'strangely adrift [in] a vague Euroland only found in front of a camera' (p. 62). *Cahiers* notes that *Tacones lejanos* is El Deseo's first co-production and that the choice of the mainstream French producer Ciby 2000 is incongruous (p. 6). A sense of glossy deracination pervades the film.

I have argued, however, that a certain awareness of the Spanish background to the film makes visible historical references lost on a foreign audience and often ignored by Spanish critics. And if Almodóvar reiterates stereotypes of the career woman and the sacrificial mother, he also marks a historical advance on his model Sirk by combining the two into a single character; for Becky is not punished for her sensuality and loses nothing by her self-incrimination: she is mortally ill already. However, this new dream of a sexual mother (of a fusion of maternity and desire) drains the plot of tension, creating a ghostly 'imitation of strife' in which generational conflict loses all resonance beyond the immediately personal. The impasse with which the film ends is thus at once ideological and structural: as a self-proclaimed feminist (with this film at least) Almodóvar cannot deny his women satisfaction of all their desires; but by stripping the law of its power (by presenting the judge quite literally as a travesty of justice) he devalues their freedom, undermines their achievement. But as Vicente Molina Foix notes in his perceptive review, it is not Almodóvar but Rebeca who is exiled from history: with her psychedelic sweaters and pop art furniture she remains adrift in the 1960s. Becky on the other hand is forced to come to terms with the present and has learned, perhaps and finally, to stop acting. It may not be as easy as the film implies to fuse identification and desire. But for all its love of surface and simulation, in its brave gesture towards a reevaluation of sentimentality *Tacones lejanos* points, however imperfectly, to a reconciliation with the present which does not reject the past, to an engagement with actuality which does not forget tradition.

NOTES

1. Irene Coffey, *Spare Rib*, May 1992, p. 13.

2. Caryn James, 'Almodóvar, Adrift in Sexism', *New York Times*, 12 January 1992.

3. Carol Sarler, 'Man in the Supporting Role', London *Times*, 21 March 1992.

4. Jacques Valot, 'Talons aiguilles', *Revue du Cinéma*, 478, January 1992, pp. 23–4.

5. *Film Quarterly*, 45.3, spring 1992, pp. 39–44 (pp. 39, 40).

6. This absence has been explored most rigorously by Luce Irigaray; see Margaret Whitford, *Luce Irigaray: Philosophy in the Feminine*, London and New York 1990, pp. 76–84.

7. 'Guión original', Madrid 1990.

8. Lucy Fischer, ed., *Imitation of Life*, New Brunswick 1991, p. 25. The plot of *Tacones lejanos* is perhaps even closer to Sirk's first US melodrama *All I Desire* (1953), in which actress-mother Barbara Stanwyck returns to her beloved daughter after a lengthy absence on the stage.

9. As noted by Anthony Lane in his review in the London *Independent on Sunday*, 24 March 1992, Becky is based on the Lana Turner character in *Imitation of Life*.

10. 'Mothering, Feminism, and Representation: The Maternal in Melodrama and the Woman's Film

1910–40', in *Home Is Where the Heart Is*, Christine Gledhill, ed., London 1987, pp. 113–37 (p. 116); and Kaplan's book-length study, *Motherhood and Representation*, New York and London 1992.

11. See reviews by Anne Billson, *New Statesman and Society*, 27 March 1992; Terrence Rafferty, *New Yorker*, 10 February 1992.

12. *Todo por la pasta* is a TV game show whose name is based on the military motto, 'Todo por la patria'.

13. 'Production Notes' in Fischer, p. 183.

14. Richard Dyer, 'Four Films of Lana Turner', pp. 186–206 (p. 202).

15. Emanuela Imparato, 'Tacchi a spillo' (review and interview), *Cineforum*, 313, 1991, pp. 72–6 (p. 73).

16. Kinder seems to think that 'Juez' (Judge) is Domínguez's name, not his profession; she confuses Isabel (Manuel's mistress) with minor character Luisa; she writes that Bibi Andersen's character has gained access to prison to be with her daughter (rather than her female lover).

17. 'The Films of Douglas Sirk', in Fischer, pp. 251–67 (p. 258).

18. 'Distanciation and Douglas Sirk', in Fischer, pp. 268–72 (p. 270).

19. David Thompson, *Sight and Sound*, April 1992, pp. 61–2.

20. In the introduction to her book *Three Way Mirror*, pp. 3–28.

21. The coinage comes from Vicente Molina Foix's review in *Fotogramas*, 1778, October 1991.

22. 'Almodóvar también llora: autoentrevista de Pedro Almodóvar', *El País: Babelia* (Saturday Supplement), 19 October 1991.

23. *El País* (Barcelona), 27 October 1991.

24. *El Mundo*, 26 October 1991.

25. Nigel Floyd, 'The New Man from La Mancha', *Guardian*, 5 December 1991.

26. See '*Imitation of Life*', in Fischer, pp. 279–88 (p. 285).

27. See, for example, Charles Affron, 'Performing Performing: Irony and Affect', in Fischer (pp. 207–16). Sirk frequently complained that US audiences were incapable of recognizing irony.

28. *Usos amorosos de la postguerra española*, Barcelona 1987, p. 210.

29. The title of the auto-interview is reminiscent of a song by sixties pop star Raphael cited by Almodóvar in the press book to *Mujeres al borde*: 'Men Also Weep'.

30. Rupert Widdicombe, 'Heels Towers over Spanish Competition', *Screen International*, 851, 3 May 1992, p. 3; see also the recently released figures in Emilio C. García Fernández, *El cine español contemporáneo*, Barcelona 1992, p. 140.

31. Patricia Dobson, 'Domestic Bliss for Spain, Italy's Local Heroes', *Screen International*, 832, 8 November 1991, p. 33.

32. Frédéric Strauss, 'Madrid-sur-scène', 446, July/August 1991, pp. 18–24.

33. Angela Holden, March 1992, pp. 99–100.

34. *Mail on Sunday*, 29 March 1992, p. 39.

35. Eduardo Torres-Dulce, '*Tacones lejanos*: el último saldo', *Expansión*, 2 November 1991.

36. Llatzer Moix's 'La otra transición' is in favour; Pedro Azara's 'Chanzas y chascarrillos' is against; both published in January 1992 (pp. 104 and 105).

37. 'La "novena" de Almodóvar', 29 October 1991.

38. *American Film*, January/February 1992, p. 38. The pictures also ran in the US trade press.

39. Shawn Levy, 'King of Spain', *American Film*, January/February 1992, pp. 38–43, 48.

CONCLUSION:

Screen Memories

We are likely to leave Almodóvar's cinema with a selection of images: the young Alaska peeing on the delighted Eva Siva; Chus Lampreave and the unlucky lizard; Victoria Abril bound to the bed; Miguel Bosé, in red dress and pink lipstick. To borrow a term from psychoanalysis, such images might be called 'screen memories': they are vivid but insubstantial; indeed vivid because insubstantial.[1] Like the analyst's quest for the forgotten trauma of which the screen memory is but a displacement, the critic's search for any substantial meaning in Almodóvar's cinematic images is lengthy and complex. What the images lack is a voice. And what Spanish audiences know is that, beyond the seductive visuals, Almodóvar's films are talking pictures. They will think of Chus Lampreave's comic appropriation of teenage slang; María Barranco's breathy Andalusian accent; the lyrics to the songs which play so large a part in Almodóvar's plots. Indeed, it is in the bolero, central to such films as *Entre tinieblas* and *La ley del deseo*, that we find the sensibility closest to Almodóvar's cinema: one in which sexual difference is subject to aesthetic abstraction and androgynous partners migrate from one position to another.[2] Almodóvar's histories of love also share this curious combination of fluidity and formality.

David Thomson has said of Sirk that he could 'pick out the seriousness in vulgarity without condescension'.[3] It is a suitable judgement also for Almodóvar, who celebrates the virtues of pop culture with ironic but enthusiastic intelligence. But Almodóvar not only sees the seriousness in vulgarity; he also sees the vulgarity in seriousness, and is merciless in his critique of what he perceives to be the pieties of both Left and Right. Hence the confusions of his reception in the English-speaking world: liberals anxious to lionize a self-proclaimed male feminist, who came from a corner of Europe they considered to be underdeveloped, and was associated (by them at least) with an openly gay subculture, were dismayed to discover that Almodóvar cared little for the feminist critique of male violence and pornography, made no apology for the belatedness of a Spain which was now culturally modernized, and was sceptical of attempts to base identity on sexual preference. Foreigners thought Spaniards were apolitical; Spaniards thought foreigners were puritan. In a sense, both were right. Spanish libertarians had failed to tackle problems of gender, nationality, and homosexuality which had been prematurely 'solved' by the victory of the well-meaning Socialists in 1982; foreign liberals were unwilling to accept that their oppositional stance and sometimes moralizing criteria were influenced by their more perilous position in English-speaking countries whose cultural climate was determined to a large extent by powerful conservative governments. However, Almodóvar's unstinting pursuit of pleasure might be read as political for foreigners also, in that it anticipated a more libertarian agenda in the nineties which featured feminists against censorship and SM dykes; national identities posing as performance; and an attempted queer alliance between proliferating categories of self-proclaimed gender and sex deviants.

Meanwhile Spanish cinema continued its decline in the nineties. A conference chaired by Pilar Miró (architect of the state sponsorship which had helped Almodóvar to found El Deseo) proclaimed that there was no more cinema in Spain, that the industry was 'humiliated'.[4] Intermittently journalists claimed implausibly, as they had with more reason in the case of *Mujeres al borde*, that Spanish cinema was about to crack the North American market.[5] As the rhetoric of praise and blame continued, Almodóvar went about his work, diversifying into production by sponsoring the first film from El Deseo directed by an outsider, the young Alex de la Iglesia's well-received science fiction comedy *Acción mutante* (Mutant Action, 1993).[6]

There seems little doubt, also, that Almodóvar was in some measure responsible for a mini-boom of Spanish art-house hits at this time. Films as diverse as Julio Medem's Basque ruralist drama *Vacas* and Bigas Luna's sex comedy *Jamón, jamón* (both 1992) benefited from the frame of legibility that Almodóvar had offered foreign audiences, who now expected stylish eroticism and zany humour from Spain. Indeed, Bigas Luna's film functions almost as an anthology of screen memories from Almodóvar: crotch-shots of trainee matadors; scenes in women's lavatories; a pietà with a murdered lover, all filmed with flashy camera angles and in saturated colour. Bigas Luna's casual heterosexism, however, is a welcome reminder that Almodóvar's 'take' will always be more subtle, less conventional.

It thus remained the case that Almodóvar was without honour in his own country. Winning the award for best foreign language film for *Tacones lejanos* at the French César awards (in competition with Altman, Woody Allen, and James Ivory),[7] Almodóvar was also selected, unofficially, to take part in an exhibition for multi-media artists at the Venice Biennale.[8] In Spain, meanwhile, Fernando Trueba's slight period comedy *Belle époque*, extravagantly praised by critics often hostile to Almodóvar, swept the boards at the annual Goya awards.[9] It was business as usual for the threatened but uncowed establishment of what remained of the Spanish film industry.

In the summer of 1993 Almodóvar began shooting his tenth feature, known variously as *Kika* or *Las uñas del asesino* (Fingernails of the Murderer), an incestuous tragicomedy in which the regular family of actors (Abril, Forqué, de Palma) is supplemented by North American Peter Coyote (Plate 20).[10] The shooting schedule corresponded with a general election campaign in which actors associated with Almodóvar (such as Antonio Banderas) made explicit their support for the embattled Socialists and Felipe González told a sympathetic group of artists that they must struggle with him against 'intolerance'.[11] This was a less than subtle appeal for the so-called 'fear vote', the invocation of the memory of Fascism which for many Spaniards was now distant indeed.

Almodóvar had based his career on this distance. No political engagement was necessary while Spaniards appeared to share a certain consensus about emancipation and modernity. Almodóvar's cinema is the most lasting and imaginative tribute to an era which became, suddenly, historicized with the Socialists' loss of overall power after twelve years of near-uncontested dominance. And while Spain had spent the eighties in thrall to a dream of Europe which had remained for many a fantasy, his cinema had indeed made that artistic and commercial commitment with conspicuous success. It remains to be seen how Almodóvar will adapt to a new and more complex cultural environment, in which the limits of desire may be more visible than hitherto. He has already produced, however, a body of work that is both visually dazzling and conceptually challenging. Extravagantly, even excessively, inventive, Almodóvar has many more tales to tell, many more lives to live.

NOTES

1. J. Laplanche and J.-B. Pontalis, *The Language of Psychoanalysis*, London 1988, pp. 410–11.

2. Iris M. Zavala, *El bolero: historia de un amor*, Madrid 1991, pp. 33, 73.

3. *A Biographical Dictionary of the Cinema*, London 1975, p. 569.

4. Regina Valenzuela, 'El cine español, humillado: Pilar Miró reunió a los profesionales descontentos', *El Mundo*, 16 August 1992.

5. Angel Gil Orrios, 'Nueva York descubre el cine español', *El País*, 12 October 1992.

6. Rocío García, 'Alex de la Iglesia: "Almodóvar como productor es único"', *El País*, 22 January 1993.

7. Borja Hermoso, 'El cine francés corona a Almodóvar', *El Mundo*, 9 March 1993.

8. Antonio Astorga, 'Tàpies, Cristina Iglesias y Pedro Almodóvar, presencia española en la XLV Bienal de Venecia', *ABC*, 27 March 1993.

9. Diego Muñoz, '*Belle époque* arrasa en los premios Goya 1993', *El País*, 14 March 1993.

10. Anon., 'Reality Kills', *Guardian Europe* (from *El Mundo*), 3 June 1993.

11. Rocío García, 'Felipe González pide a los artistas que luchen contra la intolerancia', *El País*, 4 June 1993.

FILMOGRAPHY

AND PLOT SYNOPSES

Before his first feature, Almodóvar made a number of shorts, mainly on Super-8 without sound. These were screened informally in the late 1970s with the director providing a live soundtrack. None of these shorts has been shown recently, with the exception of *Salome* (1978), which played at the Seville Expo 1992 on a videotape which includes the made-for-TV *Trailer para amantes de lo prohibido* (Trailer for Lovers of the Forbidden, 1985) and an unshown publicity spot for Volkswagen. My thanks to El Deseo for kindly letting me view this tape.

Plot synopses are taken from *Monthly Film Bulletin* or *Sight and Sound*. My thanks are due to the British Film Institute for permission to reproduce this material.

1. *Pepi, Luci, Bom, y otras chicas del montón* (Pepi, Luci, Bom . . . , 1980)

Production company	Fígaro Films
Producer	Pepón Corominas
Executive producer	Félix Rotaeta
Screenplay	Pedro Almodóvar
Director of photography	Paco Femenia
Editor	José Salcedo

Wardrobe   Manuela Camacho
Sound editor   Miguel Polo

80 mins

CAST

Carmen Maura	Pepi
Félix Rotaeta	Policeman
Olvido Gara 'Alaska'	Bom
Eva Siva	Luci
Kitti Manver	Singer
Julieta Serrano	Actress
Cristina S. Pascual	Bearded lady
Fabio de Miguel (Fanny McNamara)	Roxy

After being raped by a policeman who has spotted her marijuana plants from his flat in a block across the road, Pepi enlists the help of her friends in the punk rock group, Bomitoni, to exact retribution for her lost virginity. On discovering that they have mistakenly beaten up the rapist's twin brother, Juan, Pepi embarks on another revenge plot by taking knitting lessons from the policeman's drab wife, Luci. Luci's masochistic tastes soon become apparent and, when she meets Pepi's friend Bom – from Bomitoni – she finds her sadistic match.

The friendship of the three women then develops through outrageous antics at parties and concerts, wild games and coincidental meetings with their quirky network of acquaintances. When Pepi's allowance from her father is stopped to encourage her to earn her own living, she makes a snap decision to go into publicity, creating a wacky series of television ads, while also writing Luci and Bom's story. When Luci leaves her retrograde husband to move to Cuenca as Bom's 'groupie', Pepi joins them with the idea of turning their story into a film in which they will play themselves. In Luci's absence, her husband has clocked up another rape – this time their neighbour Charo – by posing as his own twin brother.

Still smarting from his wife's departure and the backfiring of his attempt to have Pepi arrested in revenge, he tracks Luci down to a disco where the three women are spending the evening. When Bom sends Luci on an errand, her husband abducts her, winning her admiration and devotion in a violent struggle which results in Luci's hospitalization. Pepi's friendship consoles Bom after Luci's disappearance and, after their visit to the hospital confirms that Luci is reconciled with her husband, they plan a new life together and a future for Bom as a bolero singer. (Rikki Morgan)[1]

2. *Laberinto de pasiones* (Labyrinth of Passion, 1982)

Production company	Alphaville
Production manager	Andrés Santana
Screenplay	Pedro Almodóvar
Director of photography	Angel Luis Fernández
Editor	José Salcedo
Production design	Pedro Almodóvar
Costume design	Helga Liné
	Alfredo Caral
Sound editor	Martin Müller

100 mins

CAST

Cecilia Roth	Sexilia
Imanol Arias	Riza Niro
Helga Liné	Toraya
Antonio Banderas	Sadec
Marta Fernández-Muro	Queti
Fernando Vivanco	Doctor
Ofelia Angélica	Susana
Fanny McNamara	Patty Diphusa
Luis Ciges	Dry-cleaner

Sexilia is a pop star and nymphomaniac with a chronic hatred of the sun; Riza is the gay son of the Emperor of Tiran. Both are strolling in the Madrid Rastro, aiming to pick up boys. Toraya, the ex-Empress of Tiran, is in town to consult Sexilia's father, a famous gynaecologist. She attempts to track Riza down, while he enjoys amorous encounters with Patty Diphusa, a photonovel porn queen, and Sadec, a Moslem freedom fighter from Tiran. Riza finally meets Sexilia when, disguised as 'Johnny', he is performing with a punk band. They fall in love, but are unable to have sex.

Making time in her busy schedule to pick up the dry-cleaning, Sexilia counsels Queti, the dry-cleaner's daughter, on how to free herself from her father's sexual advances. Queti agrees to transform herself into Sexilia through plastic surgery, and thus exchange one amorous father for another. Toraya finally catches up with Riza, and Sexilia discovers they have slept together. Fleeing to her psychiatrist, who has a passion for Sexilia's father, she finally confesses the cause of her nymphomania: a childhood trauma which also made Riza gay: rejected by her father, she had had sex with boys on the beach, while Riza looked on. Sexilia meets up with Queti, who has now taken her place, and decides to forgive Riza and flee with him to Contadora, in the Caribbean. Eusebio, the punk singer whom 'Johnny' has been standing in for, discovers that he is really Riza, and gives him away to Sadec and his fellow Tiranians. Sadec and his group arrive at the airport to find that Riza and Sexilia have already caught their plane, so they kidnap Toraya instead. Queti, disguised as Sexilia, sleeps with Sexilia's father and cures him of his fear of sex. On the flight to Contadora, Sexilia and Riza finally consummate their passion. (Paul Julian Smith)[2]

3. *Entre tinieblas* (Dark Habits, 1983)

Production company	Tesauro
Producer	Luis Calvo
Production manager	Luis Briales
Screenplay	Pedro Almodóvar
Director of photography	Angel Luis Fernández
Editor	José Salcedo
Production design	Pin Morales
	Román Arango
Costume design	Francis Montesinos
(Yolanda and the Virgins)	
Sound editors	Martin Müller
	Armin Fausten

115 mins

CAST

Cristina S. Pascual	Yolanda
Julieta Serrano	Mother Superior
Mari Carrillo	Marquesa
Marisa Paredes	Sister Manure
Chus Lampreave	Sister Rat
Carmen Maura	Sister Damned
Lina Canalejas	Sister Snake
Manuel Zarzo	Chaplain

Madrid. Yolanda Bell, a singer and part-time heroin dealer-cum-addict whose boy-friend has just died of a mysterious overdose, is on the run from the police. She takes refuge in a convent run by the Humble Redeemers, a small order of nuns who purportedly do charitable work with the 'fallen'. Following the recent death of an aristocrat who supported the order because his daughter Virginia – who went to Africa as a missionary and was eaten by cannibals – belonged to it, his widow, the Marquesa, has withdrawn their funding. The Mother Superior, a heroin-user and sentimental lesbian, is struggling to keep the convent going. Yolanda meets the other nuns: Sister Rat, who writes sensationalist novels under a pseudonym, drawing on the experiences of 'fallen' women; Sister Damned, who is devoted to a tiger she has raised from a cub; Sister Manure, an acid casualty; and Sister Snake, a fashion designer who has fallen in love with a priest.

A letter arrives from Africa for the Mother Superior, containing information about Virginia which she tries to sell to the Marquesa. In honour of the Mother Superior, and expecting a visit from their mother order, the nuns throw a party at which Yolanda agrees to sing. Yolanda, who has become friendly with the Mother Superior and cured her drug habit, betrays her by helping the Marquesa to find the letter, which reveals that Virginia died after giving birth to a son, who has been reared in the jungle by apes. Yolanda sings, scandalizing the visiting nuns, who insist that the order be disbanded. Yolanda leaves, and most of the sisters drift away, leaving the Mother Superior devastated.[3]

4. *¿Qué he hecho yo para merecer esto?* (What Have I Done to Deserve This?, 1984)

Production company	Tesauro
Production manager	Luis Briales
Screenplay	Pedro Almodóvar
Director of photography	Angel Luis Fernández
Editor	José Salcedo
Set decoration	Pin Morales
	Román Arango
Costume design	Cecilia Roth
Music	Bernardo Bonezzi
Sound editor	Bernardo Menz

102 mins

CAST

Carmen Maura	Gloria
Angel de Andrés López	Antonio
Chus Lampreave	Grandmother
Juan Martínez	Toni
Miguel Angel Herranz	Miguel
Verónica Forqué	Cristal
Kitti Manver	Juani
Luis Hostalot	Polo
Gonzalo Suárez	Lucas
Amparo Soler Leal	Patricia
Javier Gurruchaga	Dentist

Madrid. In a small tower-block apartment, Gloria lives with her husband Antonio, a taxi driver, fourteen-year-old son Toni and twelve-year-old Miguel, and her mother-in-law. Gloria works as a cleaner (in a kendo academy, she surprises one of the students in the shower and they attempt to have sex); often refused money by Antonio, she is forced to take on extra work, and uses amphetamines to keep her going. Toni, meanwhile, deals in cannabis (the proceeds of which are banked by his grandmother), and Miguel sleeps with male friends of his father's. Gloria negotiates his unofficial adoption by a dentist, which relieves the pressure on her. Also in the block is Cristal, a prostitute, who is saving for a trip to US and a career as an actress (she provides Gloria with extra cleaning clients), and Juani, a dressmaker, and her daughter, Vanessa, whom she mistreats and who wreaks psychokinetic revenge on household objects and the block's elevator.

Antonio has meanwhile picked up a fare, the middle-aged writer Lucas Villalba, who is intrigued by Antonio's story of having once worked in Berlin as a chauffeur to the singer Ingrid Müller, and how he helped her to forge some letters supposedly written by Hitler. Inspired to commit his own forgery, with his kleptomaniac girlfriend Patricia, Lucas flies to Berlin, prevents Ingrid from committing suicide, and blackmails her (by threatening to reveal the original forgery) into calling Antonio. He and Patricia then try to appropriate funds for their scheme through Patricia's ex-husband, a psychotherapist and reformed alcoholic (one of whose patients, Polo, turns up with Cristal as his 'girlfriend'). They fail to get the signature they need, but Patricia's kleptomania saves the day.

Transformed by Ingrid's phone call, Antonio orders Gloria to iron his shirt so he can look his best; she refuses, and during a fight kendo-chops her husband with a hambone. He is killed, but Gloria continues with her cooking as if nothing had happened; only when Cristal visits the apartment is the body discovered and the police called (the inspector, Polo, is also the man who attempted to have sex with Gloria at the kendo academy). At the airport, Lucas and Patricia learn that Ingrid has successfully committed suicide and that Antonio is dead. Toni and his grandmother decide to return to their village on Toni's savings; left alone in the apartment, Gloria redecorates it with the help of Vanessa whom she temporarily adopts. Faced with its emptiness, she leans over the balcony contemplating suicide, only to see Miguel returning, so that there can be 'a man in the family'. (Mark Nash)[4]

5. *Matador* (1986)

Production company	Iberoamericana, with TVE
Executive producer	Andrés Vicente Gómez
Screenplay	Pedro Almodóvar
	Jesús Ferrero
Director of photography	Angel Luis Fernández
Editor	José Salcedo

Art directors   Román Arango
                                 José Morales
                                 Josep Rosell
Costume design   José María Cossío
Music   Bernardo Bonezzi
Sound editors   Bernard Orthion
                                 Tino Azores

96 mins

CAST

Assumpta Serna   María
Nacho Martínez   Diego
Antonio Banderas   Angel
Eva Cobo   Eva
Eusebio Poncela   Police inspector
Julieta Serrano   Berta
Chus Lampreave   Pilar
Carmen Maura   Julia

Diego Montes, a bullfighter forced into early retirement through injury, runs a bullfighting school. He finds sexual solace in sadistic videotapes. Lawyer María Cardenal is a long-time fan of his. She seduces men whom she then kills at the point of orgasm, matador-style, with a long hairpin. Among Diego's pupils is Angel, who suffers from vertigo and faints at the sight of blood. He lives with his mother, a fervent member of *Opus Dei*. Diego's fashion model love Eva lives nearby with her mother Pilar.

To prove to Diego that he is not homosexual, Angel attempts to rape Eva one evening. He later confesses to the police, but Eva and her mother refuse to press charges. Angel then confesses to the murder of four men, killed mysteriously with a long pin. The detective is sceptical. María Cardenal is appointed to defend Angel and police psychiatrist Julia is also put on the case. On leaving Angel's apartment, María glimpses Diego in his car. The two find themselves in a cinema watching the last moments of *Duel in the Sun*. They return to his house where they embrace, but María fumbles and drops her pin. Meanwhile, Julia learns that Angel is subject to trances during which he is able to see the crimes that are committed in the city.

When the detective discovers the bodies of two women in the grounds of Diego's house, María becomes aware that Diego is a killer. She takes him to her cottage, arranged as a shrine to his prowess in the ring. They realize they are destined for each other. Diego breaks off his relationship with Eva but, hoping to change his mind, Eva hides in his house. There she overhears him and María admitting their guilt. She, Julia, Angel, and the detective, goaded by Angel's foreseeing of twin deaths, set out to apprehend María and Diego. As they make for Diego's house, they are overtaken by an eclipse of the sun. A shot rings out. They find Diego and María dead, united in the act of love. (Verina Glaessner)[5]

6. *La ley del deseo* (The Law of Desire, 1987)

Production company	El Deseo, with Lauren Films
Executive producer	Miguel Angel Pérez Campos
Associate producer	Agustín Almodóvar
Screenplay	Pedro Almodóvar
Director of photography	Angel Luis Fernández
Editor	José Salcedo
Set design	Javier Fernández
Costume design	José María Cossío
Music	Bernardo Bonezzi
Sound editor	James Willis

100 mins

CAST

Eusebio Poncela	Pablo Quintero
Carmen Maura	Tina Quintero
Antonio Banderas	Antonio
Miguel Molina	Juan
Manuela Velasco	Ada
Bibi Andersen	Ada's mother
Fernando Guillén	Police inspector
Helga Liné	Antonio's mother

After the premiere of his latest film, director Pablo Quintero is abandoned by his boyfriend, Juan, for the retreat of a small coastal village. Trying to forget him, Pablo pursues his next project: a theatrical production of Cocteau's *La Voix humaine*, featuring his vivacious but lonely sister Tina and her adopted charge Ada, daughter of one of Tina's past girlfriends. Celebrating the play's success, Pablo is seduced by Antonio, a government minister's son who, in the course of the night, goes from having his first homosexual experience to becoming a demanding lover. In order to get rid of him, Pablo agrees to write to him using the pseudonym Laura P. (a character from his next film). Nevertheless, learning of Pablo's love for Juan, Antonio drives to the village and pushes Juan from a clifftop. At first the police suspect Pablo, but later become convinced of Tina's guilt, mistaking her for the fictional 'Laura P.'.

Grief-stricken, Pablo is seriously hurt in a car crash and loses his memory; as the police wait outside his hospital room, Tina – impassioned by her relationship with an unnamed, handsome stranger – tries to cure Pablo's amnesia by recalling her sex change as a teenage boy and her love affair with their father. Finally recovering his memory, Pablo realizes that Tina's new lover is the insane Antonio. He races to her home and offers himself in exchange for the killer's hostages, Tina and Ada. Pablo and Antonio make love before Antonio shoots himself and, as the police look on, the apartment is engulfed in flames from Tina's liturgical candles. (Mark Finch)[6]

7. *Mujeres al borde de un ataque de nervios* (Women on the Verge of a Nervous Breakdown, 1988)

Production company	El Deseo
Executive producer	Agustín Almodóvar
Screenplay	Pedro Almodóvar
Director of photography	José Luis Alcaine
Editor	José Salcedo
Set design	Félix Murcia
Titles/graphic design	Studio Gatti
Costume design	José María Cossío
Music	Bernardo Bonezzi
Sound editor	Gilles Orthion

95 mins

CAST

Carmen Maura	Pepa
Fernando Guillén	Iván
Julieta Serrano	Lucía
Antonio Banderas	Carlos
María Barranco	Candela
Rossy de Palma	Marisa
Kitti Manver	Paulina

Madrid. Pepa awakes from drug-induced sleep to find that her long-term lover Iván has gone, leaving only an answer-machine message asking her to pack his bags. Pepa, who has just learned that she is pregnant, becomes near-hysterical while she waits for Iván to call again, and then impulsively puts their penthouse up for rent. By a series of accidents, she finds herself on the trail of Iván's insane ex-wife Lucía, and discovers that Iván has a twenty-year-old son, Carlos. Back at the apartment Iván has left another message, and so has Pepa's desperate friend Candela. Early the next day, Candela arrives and claims that she is on the run from the police because of her relationship with a Shiite terrorist; coincidentally, Carlos and his bored girlfriend Marisa arrive with a view to rent the penthouse (which Pepa has partly destroyed in her anguish). When Pepa reveals her connection to Iván, Carlos agrees to wait for Iván's call while she goes in search of a good lawyer for Candela. Meanwhile, Marisa falls victim to some tranquillizer-laden gazpacho prepared by Pepa for Iván, and Carlos calls the police with a warning that the Shiites plan to bomb that evening's flight to Stockholm.

Downtown, Pepa has a furious row with the unsympathetic feminist lawyer Paulina de Moralis; she arrives back at the apartment moments ahead of Lucía and two detectives investigating the terrorist tip-off. As Carlos serves the spiked gazpacho to an expanding number of visitors, Pepa deduces that Iván is leaving with new mistress Paulina on the doomed Stockholm flight. Pepa and Lucía race each other to the airport, where Pepa saves Iván from Lucía's attempt to shoot him. Remorseful, Iván suggests that maybe they could get back together, but Pepa realizes that now she has no desire to see or even speak to him. (Mark Finch)[7]

8. ¡Atame! (Tie Me Up! Tie Me Down!, 1989)

Production company	El Deseo
Executive producer	Agustín Almodóvar
Production manager	Esther García
Screenplay	Pedro Almodóvar
Director of photography	José Luis Alcaine
Editor	José Salcedo
Set design	Ferrán Sánchez
Costume design	José María Cossío
Music	Ennio Morricone

101 mins

CAST

Victoria Abril	Marina
Antonio Banderas	Ricki
Francisco Rabal	Máximo Espejo
Loles León	Lola
Julieta Serrano	Alma
María Barranco	Berta
Rossy de Palma	Motorcycle girl
Lola Cardona	Director of psychiatric hospital

Ricki, a young man raised in institutions, is released from psychiatric hospital after being declared sane by a judge. Infatuated by Marina, a porno actress/B-movie queen with whom he had a one-night stand during one of his earlier escapes, he traces her to a film studio where she is starring in *Midnight Phantom*, a horror movie directed by ageing obsessive Máximo Espejo. Returning to her flat to change for a post-filming party, Marina unwittingly lets Ricki in and he kidnaps her, roughing her up and tying her to the bed. He is considerate enough to take her to see her doctor, and to procure black-market drugs for her bruises, since she is an ex-addict and needs strong pain-killers to overcome her tolerance. Marina resists Ricki, but he declares his intention of marrying her and looking after her, demonstrating his affection by procuring the finest rope and most comfortable gag tape.

Lola, Marina's sister, who is also working with Máximo, is mildly concerned about Marina's disappearance, especially when she receives a message Ricki has forced Marina to send claiming that she is going to the country. Marina's neighbour is on holiday, leaving his flat empty, and Ricki takes Marina there. While Ricki is out getting more drugs, he is badly beaten up by a dealer whom he had earlier robbed, and Marina manages to free herself from her bonds, although she does not go through with the escape. When Ricki returns, she treats his wounds and they make love. Lola, who has agreed to water Marina's neighbour's plants, turns up while Ricki is out stealing a car, and the sisters escape from him. However, Marina has fallen in love with Ricki, and traces him to the derelict village where he was born. Ricki and Lola make friends, and Marina drives them back to the city. (Kim Newman)[8]

9. *Tacones lejanos* (High Heels, 1991)

Production company	El Deseo/Ciby 2000
Executive producer	Agustín Almodóvar
Production manager	Esther García
Screenplay	Pedro Almodóvar
Director of photography	Alfredo Mayo
Editor	José Salcedo
Set design	Pierre-Louis Thevenet
Costume design	José María Cossío
Sound editor	Jean-Paul Mugel
Music	Ryuichi Sakamoto

113 mins

CAST

Victoria Abril	Rebeca
Marisa Paredes	Becky
Miguel Bosé	Judge Domínguez/Femme Letal/Hugo
Feodor Atkine	Manuel
Bibi Andersen	Chon

Miriam Díaz Aroca   Isabel
Mairata O'Wisiedo   Judge's mother

Becky del Páramo, once a famous pop singer in the 1960s, returns to Madrid after fifteen years, anxiously awaited by Rebeca, her daughter from her first marriage. Painful memories return to Rebeca of a childhood spent trailing after her mother and assorted lovers – including a second husband, brusquely indifferent to Rebeca, whose 'accidental' death she engineered – before a journalist, Manuel, persuaded Becky to stay in Mexico. Rebeca meets her mother and after a nostalgic stopover at the basement flat where Becky lived as a child with her caretaker father, takes her home. There Becky is shocked to find that Rebeca is now married to Manuel – who is shocked in his turn because he had been unaware of Rebeca's parentage.

Manuel, who is now director of a television station where Rebeca works as a newsreader, tries to revive his old affair with Becky, and tells her that he wants to divorce her daughter. That evening, the three of them attend a performance by a drag artist called Femme Letal, who specializes in miming to Becky's old songs. Manuel is particularly hostile to him, but Rebeca, who has always been a devoted admirer, claiming that Letal has helped to keep her mother's memory alive, goes backstage and secretly has sex with him.

The following morning, Manuel is found murdered, and the investigating Judge Domínguez discovers that three women visited him that night: Becky, Rebeca, and Isabel, who 'signs' the news for deaf viewers with Rebeca on television, and who had begun an affair with Manuel. All three plead their innocence, but later, while announcing the murder on television, Rebeca breaks down and confesses to the crime. Although she is arrested and taken to jail, Domínguez doesn't believe her to be guilty, especially after his own invalid mother's collection of newspaper cuttings reveals that Manuel was once Becky's lover. In jail, Rebeca sees a picture of a fellow inmate's boyfriend, Hugo, a drug dealer who bears a strong resemblance to Femme Letal and who is apparently killed after he turns out to be a police informer. Rebeca also realizes that she is pregnant by Femme Letal.

Becky gives a triumphant return performance in Madrid, dedicating her first song to her daughter. Rebeca is released from jail, and returns home to hide the missing murder weapon, Manuel's gun. Still convinced of Rebeca's innocence, Domínguez reveals to her that he is Femme Letal, one of a number of personas he has adopted to penetrate the criminal world, and that he is in love with her. After an emotional encounter with Rebeca, who confesses her childhood 'homicide', Becky collapses on stage. In hospital it emerges that she returned home because of a mortal illness, and mother and daughter are finally reconciled, Becky confesses to Domínguez that she was the murderer, but then tells a priest that she lied. She returns to die in the basement flat where she has taken up residence again, and Rebeca hands her the murder weapon to plant her fingerprints on it, so that their secret will go with her to the grave. (David Thomson)[9]

NOTES

1. *SS*, vol. 2, no. 4, August 1992.

2. *SS*, vol. 3, no. 10, February 1993.

3. *MFB*, vol. 57, no. 651, October 1990.

4. *MFB*, vol. 56, no. 668, September 1989.

5. *SS*, vol. 1, no. 9, January 1992.

6. *MFB*, vol. 55, no. 658, November 1988.

7. *MFB*, vol. 56, no. 665, June 1989.

8. *MFB*, vol. 57, no. 678, July 1990.

9. *SS*, vol. 1, no. 12, April 1992.

SELECT BIBLIOGRAPHY

This bibliography does not include scripts, reviews, interviews, or press material, which can be found in the endnotes to the appropriate chapter.

1. ALMODÓVAR

Albaladejo, Miguel et al., *Los fantasmas del deseo: el cine de Pedro Almodóvar*, Madrid 1988.

Almodóvar, Pedro, *Patty Diphusa y otros textos*, Barcelona 1991; translated by Kirk Anderson as *The Patty Diphusa Stories and Other Writings*, London 1992.

---- , 'Relatos', Madrid 1975 (unpublished ms).

Arroyo, José, '*La ley del deseo*: A Gay Seduction', in Richard Dyer and Ginette Vincendeau, *European Popular Cinema*, New York and London 1992, pp. 31–46.

D'Lugo, Marvin, 'Almodóvar's City of Desire', *Quarterly Review of Film and Video*, 13.4, 1991, pp. 47–65.

Donapetry, María, 'Almodóvar: márgenes y centros', unpub. paper.

Douchet, Jean, 'L'Amour du cinéma', *Cahiers du Cinéma*, 435, 1990, pp. 52–3.

Evans, Peter, 'Almodóvar's *Matador*: Genre, Subjectivity, and Desire', *Bulletin of Hispanic Studies* (forthcoming).

Francia, Juan I. and Pérez Perucha, Julio, 'Primera película: Pedro Almodóvar', *Contracampo*, no. 23, September 1981, pp. 5–7.

García de León, María Antonia and Maldonado, Teresa, *Pedro Almodóvar: la otra España cañí*, Ciudad Real 1989.

Hall, Stuart, 'European Cinema on the Verge of a Nervous Breakdown', in Duncan Petrie, ed., *Screening Europe: Image and Identity in Contemporary European Cinema*, London 1992, pp. 15–53.

Hergueta, José A., 'A vueltas con P. A.', in Miguel Albaladejo et al., *Los fantasmas del deseo: el cine de Pedro Almodóvar*, Madrid 1988, pp. 10–13.

Molina Foix, Vicente, 'Il cineasta della vita moderna', in Sergio Naitza and Valeria Patané, *¡Folle, folle, folle, Pedro!*, Cagliari 1992, pp. 13–19.

Naitza, Sergio and Patané, Valeria, eds., *¡Folle folle, folle, Pedro! Il cinema di Pedro Almodóvar*, Cagliari 1992.

Navajas, Gonzalo, 'Lo antisublime posmoderno y el imperativo en *¡Atame!* de Pedro Almodóvar', *España Contemporánea*, vol. 4, 1991, pp. 65–83.

Olla, Gianni, 'L'impossibilità di essere banale', in Sergio Naitza and Valeria Patané, eds., *¡Folle, folle, folle, Pedro!*, Cagliari 1992, pp. 25–32.

Sánchez-Biosca, Vicente, 'El elixir aromático de la postmodernidad o la comedia según Pedro Almodóvar', in José A. Hurtado and Francisco M. Picó, eds., *Escritos sobre el cine español 1973–87*, Valencia 1989, pp. 111–24.

Vidal, Nuria, *El cine de Pedro Almodóvar*, Barcelona 1989.

2. SPANISH CINEMA

Alberich, Ferrán, *Cuatro años de cine español*, Madrid 1991.

Besas, Peter, *Behind the Spanish Lens: Spanish Cinema under Fascism and Democracy*, Denver 1985.

Caparrós Lera, J. M., *El cine español de la democracia*, Barcelona 1992.

D'Lugo, Marvin, *The Films of Carlos Saura*, Princeton 1991.

Fernàndez, Lluís, prologue to the Spanish trans. of Richard Dyer's *Gays and Cinema: Cine y homosexualidad*, Barcelona 1982.

Gallero, José Luis, *Sólo se vive una vez: esplendor y ruina de la movida madrileña*, Madrid 1991.

García Fernández, Emilio C., *El cine español contemporáneo*, Barcelona 1992.

Gómez B. de Castro, Ramiro, *La producción cinematográfica española: de la transición a la democracia*, Bilbao 1989.

González Ballesteros, Teodoro, *Aspectos jurídicos de la censura cinematográfica en España*, Madrid 1981.

Haro Ibars, Eduardo, 'La homosexualidad como problema sociopolítico en el cine español del postfranquismo', *Tiempo de Historia*, 52, March 1979, pp. 88–91.

Higginbotham, Virginia, *Spanish Film Under Franco*, Austin 1988.

Hopewell, John, *Out of the Past: Spanish Cinema after Franco*, London 1986.

---- , *El cine español después de Franco*, Madrid 1989.

---- , '"Art and a Lack of Money": The Crises of the Spanish Film Industry, 1977–1990', *Quarterly Review of Film and Video*, vol. 13 (4), 1991, pp. 113–22.

Llinàs, Francisco, *Cuatro años de cine español*, Madrid 1987.

Luqui, Joaquín, *Treinta años de diseño gráfico en el cine español*, Madrid 1987.

Pineda Novo, Danicl, *Las folklóricas y el cine*, Huelva 1991.

Smith, Paul Julian, *Laws of Desire: Questions of Homosexuality in Spanish Literature and Film, 1960–1990*, Oxford 1992.

Soria, Florentino and González Requena, Jesús, *La comedia en el cine español*, Madrid 1986.

Vallés Copeiro del Villa, Antonio, *Historia de la política de fomento del cine español*, Valencia 1992.

Zulueta, Iván, *Pausas de papel: carteles de cine de Iván Zulueta*, Valencia 1990.

3. GENERAL AND THEORETICAL

Babington, Bruce and Evans, Peter W., *Affairs to Remember: The Hollywood Comedy of the Sexes*, Manchester 1989.

Bersani, Leo, 'Is the Rectum a Grave?', *October*, 43, 1987, pp. 197–222.

Bordwell, David and Thompson, Kristin, *Film Art: An Introduction*, New York 1990.

Clover, Carol J., *Men, Women, and Chain Saws: Gender in the Modern Horror Film*, London 1992.

de Lauretis, Teresa, 'Sexual Indifference and Lesbian Representation', *Theater Journal*, 40, May 1988, pp. 155–77.

Doane, Mary Ann, *The Desire to Desire: The Woman's Film of the 1940s*, Bloomington 1987.

---- , *Femmes Fatales*, New York 1991.

Dyer, Richard, 'Four Films of Lana Turner', in Lucy Fischer, ed., *Imitation of Life*, New Brunswick 1991, pp. 186–206.

---- and Vincendeau, Ginette, eds., *Popular European Cinema*, London and New York 1992.

Fischer, Lucy, ed., *Imitation of Life*, New Brunswick 1991.

Gledhill, Christine, ed., *Home Is Where the Heart Is: Studies in Melodrama and the Woman's Film*, London 1987.

Haraway, Donna J., 'A Cyborg Manifesto', in *Simians, Cyborgs, and Women: The Re-invention of Nature*, London 1991, pp. 149–81.

Kaplan, E. Ann, 'Mothering, Feminism, and Representation: The Maternal in Melodrama and the Woman's Film 1910–40', in *Home Is Where the Heart Is*, Christine Gledhill, ed., London 1987, pp. 113–37.

---- , *Motherhood and Representation*, New York and London 1992.

Kuhn, Annette, *Cinema, Censorship, and Sexuality 1909–25*, London and New York 1988.

Laplanche, J. and Pontalis, J.-B., *The Language of Psychoanalysis*, London 1988.

Mayne, Judith, *Cinema and Spectatorship*, New York and London 1993.

Merck, Mandy, '*Lianna* and the Lesbians of Art Cinema', in *Perversions: Deviant Readings*, London 1993, pp. 162–76.

Miller, D. A., 'Anal Rope', in Diana Fuss, ed., *Inside/Out: Lesbian Theories, Gay Theories*, London 1991, pp. 119–41.

Modleski, Tania, *The Women Who Knew Too Much: Hitchcock and Feminist Theory*, New York and London 1988.

Mulvey, Laura, 'Notes on Sirk and Melodrama', in Christine Gledhill, ed., *Home Is Where the Heart Is* , London 1987, pp. 75–79.

Ronell, Avital, *Crack Wars: Literature, Addiction, Mania*, Lincoln and London 1992.

Savage, Jon, *England's Dreaming: Sex Pistols and Punk Rock*, London 1991.

Segal, Lynne and McIntosh, Mary, eds., *Sex Exposed: Sexuality and the Pornography Debate*, London 1992.

Silverman, Kaja, *The Acoustic Mirror: The Female Voice in Psychoanalysis and Cinema*, Bloomington 1988.

Stone, Sandy, 'The Empire Strikes Back: A Posttranssexual Manifesto', in Julia Epstein and Kristina Straub, eds., *Body Guards: The Cultural Politics of Gender Ambiguity*, New York and London 1991, pp. 280–304.

Studlar, Gaylyn, 'Midnight S/Excess: Cult Configurations of "Femininity" and the Perverse', in J. P. Telotte, *The Cult Film Experience*, Austin 1987, pp. 138–55.

---- , *In the Realm of Pleasure: Von Sternberg, Dietrich, and the Masochistic Aesthetic*, New York 1988.

Telotte, J. P., *The Cult Film Experience*, Austin 1987.

Thomson, David, *A Biographical Dictionary of the Cinema*, London 1975.

Whitford, Margaret, *Luce Irigaray: Philosophy in the Feminine*, London and New York 1990.

Williams, Linda, '"Something Else Besides a Mother": *Stella Dallas* and the Maternal Melodrama', in *Home Is Where the Heart Is*, Christine Gledhill, ed., London 1987, pp. 299–325.

---- , *Hard Core: Power, Pleasure, and the 'Frenzy of the Visible'*, London 1991.

Wright, Elizabeth, ed., *Feminism and Psychoanalysis: A Critical Dictionary*, Oxford 1992.

PART II

1 0

KIKA

(1 9 9 3)

Future Chic

(HI)STORIES OF CINEMA

DOÑA PACA: Como España no hay nada.
DOÑA PACA: Nothing compares to Spain.

It promises to be a cold winter in Madrid. As the long hangover from the Olympic *annus mirabilis* of 1992 drags on, Spain is facing up to record unemployment, continuing political scandal, and mounting concern over the intrusions of the newly deregulated media. In a mirror image of the UK, a long-serving government, incapable of managing either the budget deficit or the rising tide of crime, is confronted by an ineffectual opposition and an alienated electorate. The only difference is that in Spain the government is Socialist and the opposition back-to-basics conservatives. The winter would also seem to mark a new low for the once promising Spanish film industry. Now the high hopes inspired by the generous state subsidies of the 80s have gone unfulfilled, policy has shifted to protectionism, with the government passing panic measures to reduce the dubbing licences granted to US-hungry distributors and vigorously campaigning for film and television to be excluded from the GATT agreement.

At this inauspicious moment comes *Kika*, the longest awaited and biggest budget film of the year, and the tenth feature from Pedro Almodóvar, the most profitable Spanish director of all time in both domestic and foreign markets. Three questions arise. First, how will Almodóvar adjust to the end of the wonder years of the 80s, the decade of conspicuous pleasures and quick profits with which he is so closely identified? Second, what is his relationship to a Spanish film industry whose perpetual crisis now seems in danger of becoming terminal? And finally, why has his undisputed commercial success attracted such critical derision, both abroad where he is often dismissed as 'crazy' or 'camp', and at home where the attacks are more personal, increasingly bitter? The answers are not quite what we might expect; and they derive ultimately from a suspicion of identity politics which is typically Spanish and frequently mystifying to foreigners.

In the week *Kika* was released 17,000 people applied for two hundred clerical jobs in Madrid city council. They sat competitive exams in the former municipal abattoir. When Almodóvar had shot a bizarre fashion show in the same location for *Matador* (1986) it had been a campy joke; but as unemployment heads for a ten-year high, no one is laughing now. Ever sensitive to the mood of the moment, Almodóvar's latest feature offers evidence of a new pessimism clouding a famously sunny outlook; and the erstwhile muse of Madrid now proclaims the city to be 'unlivable', swamped by drug-related crime. Thus *Kika* offers fans the frantic farce and gloriously saturated colours and costumes we have come to expect from its director; and in the title character we find the incorrigible optimist typical of Almodóvar's heroines. As played by Verónica Forqué (Plate 20) (previously cast as the perky prostitute in *What Have I Done to Deserve This?*, 1984), Kika confronts the vicissitudes of urban rape and multiple murder with disturbing equanimity. By turns naive, sexy, and vigorously independent, Forqué, known to Spanish audiences for her appearance in domestic farces with titles like *Salsa rosa* ('Pink Sauce', Manuel Gómez Pereira, 1991), suggests a curious combination of Judy Holliday and Barbara Windsor.

The benevolent Kika is, however, matched by Victoria Abril's malevolent Andrea Caracortada ('Cutface'), the presenter of an exploitative real-life crime show entitled 'The Worst of the Day'. This is sponsored, with conspicuous incongruity, by a milk manufacturer. Abril clearly relishes the role, sporting much-publicized black rubber outfits by Gaultier and revealing what must be the bushiest female armpits ever shown on screen. In the central scene of the film Kika is raped by an escaped convict who has grown tired of screwing 'queers' ('maricones') in prison (Plate 21). The crime is presented as a comic tour de force; certainly it provoked much hilarity from the young, mainly female audience on the night I saw it in the massive Palace of Music theatre in Madrid. However, Kika's humiliation comes not so much from the act itself (which she vigorously resists), but from its TV screening by the wicked dominatrix Andrea, who has procured graphic video footage from a mysterious voyeur.

While such sequences will surely try the patience of UK audiences, they hint at a new social concern in Almodóvar, one which is, however, typically ironized and distanced.

Once more, in the very week of *Kika*'s release, a Spanish family who were victims of a kidnapping complained of the 'disgusting' exploitation of their case by a private TV channel. And the newly hostile press coverage of Almodóvar himself has revealed hitherto unplumbed depths of that combination of unhealthy curiosity and ghoulish delight known in Spanish as *morbo*. Thus the film prompted reports of Almodóvar's supposed marriage to long-time collaborator Bibi Andersen, now celebrated as a chat show hostess and once billed as the tallest transsexual in Europe. Denying he was the source of the wedding rumours, Almodóvar compared the press coverage he has nurtured so carefully throughout his career to a 'bomb', liable to explode in his face at the worst possible moment. *Morbo* is, however, a two-way street. And by including gleefully gratuitous frontal nude shots of Andersen in *Kika* Almodóvar might be seen as not upholding the highest standards of cinematic propriety himself.

The typically stylish credit sequence of *Kika* features a spotlight, a keyhole, and a camera shutter. This can be read socially as a reference to the increasingly intrusive voyeurism of the Spanish media; but it also points quite clearly to that reflexive and ironic attention to the cinematic apparatus that has run through Almodóvar's work since his first feature *Pepi, Luci, Bom* (1980) had its three eponymous heroines make a video version of their own lives. An unlikely Spanish Godard, Almodóvar uses *Kika* to rub our faces in the self-conscious (hi)stories of cinema held to be typical of a postmodern culture.

Indeed, all of *Kika*'s characters are shown to fictionalize their experience: Kika herself is a make-up artist, shown at one point adding 'natural colour' to a corpse; Andrea circles Madrid with a camera on her futuristic helmet and arc lights in place of breasts; and the two male leads, Kika's boyfriend Ramón (Alex Casanovas, in the Antonio Banderas role of the attractive and sensitive young man) and his stepfather Nicholas (Peter Coyote, dubbed unconvincingly into Spanish) play a voyeuristic photographer and an autobiographical novelist respectively. Most gratuitously and intrusively, Almodóvar casts his own octogenarian mother as a TV presenter and has her drop knowing references to her son's profession. The viewer can only agree with her when she tells expatriate American Nicholas in this sequence, 'Nothing compares to Spain.'

IDENTITY PARADES

JUANA: ¡Soy auténtica!
JUANA: I'm authentic!

The commercial back story of *Kika* is, however, perhaps more important than these emphatically self-conscious elements. The second co-production between Almodóvar's own company El Deseo, S.A. (Desire Ltd) and mainstream French producer Ciby 2000, *Kika*'s generous budget enables glossy production values which few films could aspire to outside Hollywood. If European cinema is in Stuart Hall's words 'on the verge of a nervous breakdown', the continuing success of the Almodóvar 'trademark', most spectacularly in France, might provide a model elsewhere for a film practice which is both grounded in domestic concerns and attractive to foreign audiences. In the Spanish capital where *Kika* is currently the most conspicuous local film playing the vast picture palaces of the Gran Vía (Madrid's Shaftesbury Avenue) and the only domestic product to figure in the top ten grosses (bringing in a healthy $300,000 in the first three weeks), El Deseo's dominance is such that it is claimed that industry insiders are unwilling even to criticize King Pedro the Cruel.

It seems likely, however, that Almodóvar has been a victim of his own success. Foreign audiences now expect stylish eroticism and furious farce from Spanish films; and they now have other directors such as Bigas Luna (*Jamón, jamón* [1992]; *Huevos de oro* [Golden Balls, 1993]) to provide it for them. In Spain itself, the newly cautious mood has made Fernando Trueba's bland period comedy *Belle Epoque* (1992) the most critically and commercially popular film of the year preceding *Kika*'s release. And an ill-timed announcement has just awarded the earnestly highbrow Víctor Erice (*El espíritu de la colmena* [The Spirit of the Beehive, 1973]; *El sur* [The South, 1983]; and *El sol del membrillo* [The Quince Tree Sun, 1992]) the National Prize for Cinematography. *Kika*'s gorgeous art design and consistently inventive cinematography (by Alfredo Mayo, Almodóvar regular and lenser of Vicente Aranda's *Amantes* [Lovers, 1991]) produce pleasure, but no longer surprise. It seems only fair to ask: has Almodóvar painted himself into a corner?

Almodóvar once claimed, facetiously, that he could not wait to go out of fashion so that he could become a classic. It would seem that only the first part of his wish has been granted. *Kika* was greeted in Spain by a crescendo of critical abuse, in which Almodóvar served as an unwilling and perhaps unwitting litmus test for the problems of misogyny and homophobia which continue to dog Spain more than a decade after the socially progressive Socialists took power. These responses relate both to the film itself and to Almodóvar's typically idiosyncratic promotion of it. Based, as ever, on a cavalcade of strong women (from 'good' Kika to 'bad' Andrea by way of Rossy de Palma's gloriously 'ugly' turn as Juana, the lesbian maid in love with her mistress), *Kika* shamelessly proclaims itself a woman's film and one whose female characters are granted both the 'ultra feminine' visual pleasure characteristic of mainstream film and the central narrative position generally occupied by men. This implicit threat to masculinity is confirmed by the male leads who, as so often in Almodóvar, are comparatively dull: the cataleptic Casanovas is muted; the saturnine Coyote merely bemused.

Moreover, as a consummate female impersonator, Almodóvar has clearly placed himself on that side of the cinematic gender division which is coded as feminine. Thus he posed cheekily for Spain's best-selling daily *El País* peeking out from behind a pair of curtains, an oversized polka-dotted bow in his bushy hair. The same paper carried pictures of the director in costume for all the principal roles of the film, male and female. Even *Cahiers du Cinéma* ran a spread of parallel shots of director and actors acting out scenes on the set, with Almodóvar vigorously ironing the laundry or firmly bound to a chair like Rossy de Palma's maid before and during the rape sequence. Such antics seem to have provoked the latent homophobia of the Spanish press, normally liberal by UK standards. Indeed one paper accused Almodóvar of promoting 'a homosexual fashion', an accusation he proved over-eager to refute.

At a deeper level, the threat of Almodóvar's professions of performance is in their hints of subjective merger and fluidity. Just as his films are full of characters unable to separate from their parents or lovers (in this case the mother-obsessed Ramón), so Almodóvar's over-identification with his creations, his compulsion to repeat and act out their dilemmas both on and off the set, puts fixed individual boundaries into crisis and throws the rigid divisions of gender binaries into confusion. Wilfully frivolous and superficial, Almodóvar's films can be read as identity parades, an acting out of roles with no depth or essence. This cult of the surface is nowhere more evident than in *Kika*. Gloriously shot, beautifully dressed, and skilfully acted, it is poorly plotted and characterized, its rogues' gallery of grotesques provoking little of the audience identification Almodóvar was clearly hoping for.

But if *Kika* may well be seen as a midpoint in Almodóvar's career, in which the maestro treads water between the unselfconscious pleasures of the 80s and the more critical climate of the 90s, there can be no doubt as to the importance of that career as a whole. For as Almodóvar's films clearly reveal, far from being belated, the Spain that offers a mocking reflection of the UK's political and economic decline reveals no sign of the regressions signalled by Major's cynical appeal to 'traditional values' or indeed Clinton's disingenuous call for 'security'. In spite of domestic horror stories, still less do we find in Spain the turn to neo-Fascism exemplified by Italy. Indeed, Madrid may well be ahead of London or New York in the sexual arena. Thus in his love of sex and gender fluidity, in his hostility to fixed positions of all kinds, Almodóvar anticipated by a full decade the critique of identity politics now commonplace in Anglo-American feminist and queer theory.

Once we are weaned from the reassuring comforts of gay/straight, female/male dichotomies, Almodóvar's cinema thus offers English-speakers the promise of a nightmare and a dream for the nineties. The nightmare is a future of powerlessness in which (as in Spain) feminists and gay men prove unable to organize and unwilling to found a sense of community on the experiences they have in common. The dream is a future of fluidity in which (as in Spain, perhaps, once more) sexual practices are not constrained by fixed allegiances and each of us negotiates our own price in the libidinal economy. The financial metaphor is apt. For as Almodóvar's constant concern for the bottom line has shown, economic clout is essential if any dissonant voice wishes to make itself heard in an increasingly globalized entertainment industry.

Kika ends with its plucky heroine, having sped in her car from the scene of multiple murders, picking up a handsome young stranger at random from the side of the road. The scene is shot against a glorious blaze of sunflowers. Relentlessly optimistic even in extremis, Almodóvar may also, like his heroine in this sequence, have lost his sense of direction for the time being. It seems very likely, however, that the future journey will be well worth making, the cinematic and sexual adventure characteristically unpredictable. In the meantime *Kika* remains gloriously flashy fun. And Almodóvar's combination of uncompromising modernity and unabashed visual pleasure could teach the more timid and tasteful UK film industry a thing or two.

Sight and Sound (January 1994)

11

LA FLOR DE MI SECRETO

(THE FLOWER OF MY SECRET, 1995)

An Interview with Pedro Almodóvar

MASTER OF SOLITUDE

Rosa y negro (pressbook)
The pink and the black (pressbook)

London, the first, freezing days of winter. Pedro Almodóvar is in town for the UK premiere of his new feature, the masterful *The Flower of My Secret*. Five months into a world promotional tour with actresses Marisa Paredes (the sacrificial mother from *High Heels*) and Rossi de Palma (the Cubist beauty from *Women on the Verge*), the strain is telling and he is coming down with the flu. But in the discreet, airless luxury of Brown's Hotel off Piccadilly, he is charm itself: funny, smart, and endlessly voluble. He is dressed in basic black.

Almodóvar has a lot to be happy about. After the spurious scandal over the supposed excesses of his last feature *Kika*, *The Flower of My Secret* has already proved itself an unqualified critical and commercial success. New York Festival-goers are ecstatic; France has seen some 400,000 admissions in two months; and, crucially, crusty domestic critics in Madrid, who have hitherto failed to bestow their blessing on Spain's most celebrated export, have finally been won over. Even the famously frosty British audiences seem to have lost their cool: later that day a packed Odeon West End will greet Pedro, Marisa, and Rossi with very un-English whoops and cheers.

Clowning through a Guardian Lecture at the NFT, Almodóvar offers burlesque guidance to neophyte cineastes: don't fuck the actors; they won't take direction the next day when they know the size of your dick. For *Sight and Sound*, however, Almodóvar is uncharacteristically serious, as befits the newly sombre theme and austere style of *The Flower of My Secret*, concerned as it is with love, loss, literature, and the work of mourning. After a trick beginning, in which a grieving mother is revealed to be an actress coaching doctors on how to break the news of a loved one's death, *The Flower of My Secret* becomes the story of Leo (Paredes), a middle-aged romantic novelist, who, neglected by her soldier husband (heartthrob Imanol Arias, from *Labyrinth of Passion*) (Plate 22), finds she can no longer write the way she once did. Darkly comic relief is provided by her feuding sister and mother, played by the expertly matched de Palma and Chus Lampreave (the stingy grandmother in *What Have I Done to Deserve This?*). The story of a woman abandoned in the city, *The Flower of My Secret* is also a story of solidarity amongst women in the country: Leo and her mother return to the red earth of Almodóvar's native La Mancha, the depopulated agricultural region south of Madrid. Leo is helped by a male friend with the emblematic name Angel (genial, tubby Juan Echanove). By the end of the film Leo has become, in Almodóvar's words, 'the mistress of her solitude'. As if this were not enough, *The Flower of My Secret* also boasts an explosive contribution by Spain's hottest young flamenco dancer, teenage sex symbol Joaquín Cortés.

In this interview Almodóvar speaks of the necessary collusion between realism and artifice; the expressive potential of word and image; and the practice and the business of film-making in Europe. He also takes up an unusually explicit political position in the face of the current, unprecedented parliamentary crisis in Spain. Finally he suggests that, in *The Flower of My Secret* at least, a girl's best girlfriend can be a boy. Pedro Almodóvar spoke in his richly vernacular Spanish, sometimes lapsing into English for emphasis.

Paul Julian Smith: You've told the Spanish press that this is your most La Manchan and most traditional film. But it strikes me that with its references to NATO and Bosnia, to the newspaper *El País* and Prime Minister Felipe González, this is your most European and most contemporary film.

Pedro Almodóvar: When I say the film's La Manchan I mean it's my most realistic film yet. Of course I'm not interested in naturalism: even if I made a documentary it would turn out to be a fictional work on that subject. Between what inspires me and what I actually make, there is always an element of distance, of representation. Even when you decide where to place the camera, you're manipulating reality. So this is my most realist film, but with the proviso that my realism is very personal and that there is always a touch of artifice there. It's also my most contemporary film, with references to political demonstrations and to the tension that people now feel on the street. It's based on the place where I was born: La Mancha; and the place where I now live: Madrid at this particular historical moment.

PJS: You've said that it's your most personal film.

PA: Normally I'm very embarrassed to speak about my roots and my mother, and of myself in the first person. This time the film turned out like that in spite of myself. However, all of my films are absolutely personal; it's just that normally the things that affect me personally are hidden behind the characters. For example, people often say to me: 'Your films are so full of mothers, it's as if you didn't have a father.' But it's not true. In *High Heels*, for example, my father is the model for elements of the mother played by Marisa Paredes: my father had cancer and returned to die in the room in which he had been born, just like the mother in the film. I haven't spoken about this before.

PJS: This is the first time in your films that the village from which the characters originate actually appears. In *What Have I Done to Deserve This?*, the grandmother and grandson are shown leaving for the village; and in *Tie Me Up!* Antonio Banderas returns to his village, but it's in ruins. But in *The Flower of My Secret* there is an idealized view of the village, to which it's in fact impossible to return.

PA: In reality I myself don't go back to my village. I don't know what to do with myself there. But the mere fact of placing the camera in front of the earth, the red earth of La Mancha, is moving for me: there's something atavistic and primitive in that earth of my childhood. In the end I didn't shoot in my own village, which has changed, but in Almagro, some twenty kilometres away. Almagro now looks more like my village than my village does. This is the question of representation again.

PJS: Can we talk about this shoot? This is the first time you've worked with director of photography Affonso Beato.

PA: I liked his work with Glauber Rocha and Jim McBride, but I chose him because, although we have a terrible film-making crisis in Spain, in January 1995 fifteen films were being shot and the cinematographers I like were already fully booked. So I had to bring in someone from abroad. Although this film has a less vivid palette than the others, it still has a colour scheme that's recognizably mine.

PJS: The image remains as stylized as in your previous work. And yet there's a very raw emotionalism also.

PA: The look of the film is stripped down, austere. I had originally imagined the film as being more extravagant, but I gradually discovered that the more sober and austere it was, the more expressive it would be. It's the austerity that gives meaning to this film: I've made films before about abandoned women, but I've never made such an economical film, one which speaks such a simple cinematic language.

PJS: Is it relevant that this is the first time for many years you've shot a film entirely on location and not in a studio?

PA: The fact of working in a real place imposes a certain shooting style. At first it's disconcerting because, of course, you can't knock down walls to get a shot. But it gives a kind of tension and naturalism to the camerawork because you have to invent new solutions all the time.

PJS: You make great use of mirror shots in these interiors.

PA: Mirrors serve a number of functions. First, on a practical level, they make the space seem bigger: a real house is always too small, because you have to fit the crew in too. On the other hand they give an effect of duplication. This links up with the duplicity of the characters (Leo is a writer with several pseudonyms) and the reproductive functions of literature and the mass media: when Leo visits the newspaper *El País*'s printworks, her image is repeated in multiple windows, just as the written word is subject to reproduction. Another key scene in the film is when Leo's husband arrives home. The space was very small and we put a mirror to expand it. But instead of a single mirror I chose one made up of multiple mirrors, so that when the two characters kiss you can't see their lips. This is to show that this couple is already split apart or fragmented, from the very first moment.

PJS: There are also shots through lace, which seem to have a distancing function. And lace-making is a symbol of village life.

PA: Lace-making is a kind of work traditionally carried out by women. I use lace to speak of the solitude of both mother and daughter and in the key scene between them I begin by shooting through lace to show that they are in a wholly female world. La Mancha is perhaps the only place in the world where women still make lace by hand, sitting in the street enjoying the last rays of sunlight (Plate 23). It's an image of the woman alone and of the woman accompanied by other women, a matriarchal society. The whole film is shot from the woman's point of view: even when she's mistaken or unfair to her husband, it's her perspective.

PJS: 'Leo' means 'I read' in Spanish and this is a very literary film, with the main character changing literary genres just as you change cinematic genres in your films.

PA: All my films are literary in the sense that there is a lot of dialogue. But Rohmer's cinema is literary and colloquial at the same time. For me a literary cinema is one in which language is centre stage and is the motive force for the action. This film talks about literature as a means of self-understanding: Leo's writing becomes darker, just as her life does.

PJS: When you start to write a film you begin with the dialogue.

PA: That's right: dialogue is action for me. I've often said and it seems like a joke but it's not: in Europe we make films about people because it's cheaper to put two people in a living room talking than to make a film full of special effects. For me two girls and some good dialogue are as effective as all the FX in *Terminator*.

PJS: Godard said that all you need for a film is a girl and a gun. But you'd rather have two girls?

PA: Maybe they're carrying a gun in their handbag, and you can't see it. Or maybe they use their tongues as guns.

A CINEMA OF WARMTH

LEO (a Paco):   Te fuiste a solucionar una guerra huyendo de la que tenías aquí, en tu casa.
LEO (to Paco):   You went off to keep the peace just to escape from the war you had here, in your home.

PJS: You normally try to shoot in sequence. Did you do this with *The Flower of My Secret*?

PA: I tried, but you can never really do that because it's too expensive. You have to shoot according to the locations and we managed to shoot blocks of action in sequence because they were all set in Leo's flat. This time I began by shooting a scene from the middle of the film: the visit of Leo's husband. I don't mind starting with a tough sequence. It gets the actors into their character and I like to be confronted by difficulties from the very beginning.

PJS: Does shooting more or less in sequence enable you to improvise on set?

PA: There are no changes affecting the production schedule. Once I have the sets ready I rehearse for a week before shooting. That's when I adapt the script. Where the film became much richer was in the role of the mother, played by Chus Lampreave. Chus is my cinematic mother and she understands me perfectly. I gave her a lot more lines five minutes before shooting. She had to learn it quickly. But it's never she who improvises. I'm the one who improvises. Nothing happens for the first time in front of the camera. We've always rehearsed it before.

PJS: In the visually arresting first sequence you cross cut between two unrelated scenes: the grieving mother in the seminar and Leo desperate in her flat. Was this decided in the script or in the editing?

PA: It was written that way.

PJS: The technique is reminiscent of the opening of some of your previous films, especially *Women on the Verge* and *Matador*.

PA: This is a metaphor which is initially hermetic and disconcerting because the audience doesn't yet know what's happening. It involves a sequence that occurs on another level and serves as a premonition of what will happen later: in *Women on the Verge* it's the character's dream; in *Matador* it's the slasher footage. I like to begin like this.

PJS: It's a very cinematic technique, not literary at all.

PA: Yes, it's peculiar to cinema. I'm proposing from the start that this is a representation or performance.

PJS: Marisa Paredes is extraordinary in the main role. She is famous for her work in the theatre as well as on film. How did you collaborate with her here?

PA: Yes, she's worked more in the theatre than in films. Her performance is splendid, but it's one of the easiest jobs I've ever had. The only thing I tried to do was to lead her in a certain direction. This is almost an epic of grief and an actor might tend towards exaggeration. I kept cutting and cutting and led her in the opposite direction. To such an extent that at one point I said: 'Don't move a single muscle in your face.'

And yet this empty mask is enormously expressive. Marisa understood at once that an economy of gesture was essential to this part.

PJS: The scenes with Chus and Rossi are marvellously comic; but they're played with a double edge of emotion also.

PA: It's terrible to see two people who love each other at loggerheads like this. My mother treats my sister just like this and it's destroying my sister. It looks funny but it terrifies me.

PJS: If comedy is serious, is seriousness comic also? Even when Leo attempts suicide, audiences aren't quite sure how to react.

PA: When she comes back to life in the bathtub, she looks like one of the living dead. Of course there's a lot of humour in this. It's a very risky technique, but one I've become a specialist in.

PJS: Can we talk about your first experience of film? You've compared it to the opening of Erice's *The Spirit of the Beehive*, when the travelling cinema comes to the village.

PA: My relationship with cinema started as a child in the village when I'd go with a tin can full of glowing pieces of cheap charcoal: it was right in the middle of the post-War period and to keep warm in the cold you took a tin can with you. I seem to remember that in *The Spirit of the Beehive* the characters went to just this kind of improvised cinema. My conception of cinema is still that it's something that gives me warmth, that comforts me, like that tin can.

PJS: If this is an image of the past of Spanish cinema, what of its future? You've now made three successful features in co-production with the French company Ciby 2000. Is this a model for European film-making?

PA: My relation with Ciby is absolutely free. It's not just that they don't bother me when I'm shooting; they don't even see the film until it's subtitled in French. It's the ideal model because it means that the co-production doesn't become hybrid and deracinated. With us the money doesn't affect the idiosyncrasy of the project and the decisions are artistic, not financial. The film is still Spanish, although the funding is French. Moreover, my films are cheap and Ciby knows they sell all over the world. So it's good business for them. That's why I have so much freedom. If I got involved with a film like *Little Buddha* that cost forty million dollars I'd have more problems.

PJS: But your films are expensive by Spanish standards.

PA: A normal Spanish film costs less than mine, that's true. I spend a lot of money on set design. I won't settle for things you can buy in the shops. I have things brought in from all over. This stylization is expensive. I also rehearse the actors a lot, which is costly. These things are essential for my films.

PJS: What about postproduction? You've made all eleven features with editor José Salcedo.

PA: I'm very fast with editing. I cut every day after shooting and I continue refining the rough-cut as I go. It makes things cheaper, because the day after we finish shooting we have a cut of the whole film and ten days later we always have the final version. I can't shoot and wait until the end to edit. The film is alive and if you cut as you shoot you know what rhythm it's taking on and how the characters are really turning out. You can also sort out problems as you see them coming up in the editing process.

PJS: Leo has a line: 'The country is on the point of exploding.' Do you have any views on the political situation in Spain now?

PA: The country is very tense. It can't stand the Socialist government and it blames Felipe González for not resigning. But when the Socialists go the [extreme right] People's Party will get in. Young people have no memory of political activism; they don't even know what it means to have a political position. They may say they're on the right but they don't realize the right will stop them living the way they live now.

PJS: Will a future right-wing government provoke a reaction against it?

PA: Exactly. We'll all react and become more radical. We will protest once more.

PJS: Critics in the UK and US have often asked you to take up a clearer political position in your films.

PA: My political position is perfectly clear. I've never been a member of a political party because I need to keep my independence. But I'm very much on the left. In films it's not necessary for characters to talk about politics. The politics is implicit in the film.

PJS: To finish: this may strike you as crazy, but there seems to be a connection between two characters called Angel: the one who comes to the aid of Leo in *The Flower of My Secret* and the Angel (played by Antonio Banderas) who plays a similar role in *Matador*. They are both creatures without sex.

PA: This is something that hadn't occurred to me. But it's true that this Angel undergoes a process of feminization throughout the film. By the end he and Leo have become two female writers toasting each other by the fireside, like Candice Bergen and Jacqueline Bisset in *Rich and Famous*. So the man ends up as the woman's best girlfriend. It's a very positive process.

Sight and Sound (February 1996)

1 2

CARNE TRÉMULA

(LIVE FLESH, 1997)

Absolute Precision

A PERFECT PLOT

Ensayo de un crimen (Buñuel)
'Rehearsal for a crime' (Buñuel [English title: *The Criminal Life of Archibaldo Cruz*])

It's 11.30 pm at the London Film Festival and Pedro Almodóvar is getting serious. On stage at a packed Odeon West End after the UK premiere of *Live Flesh*, he has clowned his way through predictable questions on sex, drugs, and comedy from the delighted audience. But now he is speaking of his 'weariness' with the overfamiliar 'Almodóvar style' and of 'the temptations of austerity'. The point is vital to the reception of his twelfth feature, universally proclaimed by critics to be his best yet. For if *Live Flesh* is predictable in its sumptuous visual style and extravagant emotionality, still it strikes new and unfamiliar ground in its restrained approach to plot and character, in its use of new, untested actors, and in its appeal to social and historical issues untouched by Almodóvar's previous films.

This change of mood has proved popular at home, where hostile Spanish critics, who have attacked Almodóvar's supposed unevenness in plotting and scripting over two decades, have finally rolled over for the Manchegan maestro, acclaiming his 'masterpiece' with such unaccustomed adjectives as 'consistent' and 'cohesive'. In France and Italy also, Almodóvar's traditional Latin heartlands, *Live Flesh* took impressive grosses on its release last December. British distributors Pathé are planning to open the film wide, scorning Almodóvar's traditional minority audience (and, incidentally, granting scarce interviews only to national newspapers). And in the US, *Live Flesh* has been picked by major MGM as a spearhead for its new distributing arm Goldwyn Films. But is this confidence in English-speaking audiences misplaced? Accustomed as we are to Almodóvar's heady hedonism and crazy comedy, are we adult enough for a Pedro who has well and truly grown up?

Almodóvar is known for breathtaking beginnings: the shock treatments of *Matador* and *The Law of Desire* spring to mind. And the post-credit sequence of *Live Flesh* is no exception, economically and unforgettably introducing the five main characters. Elena, a skull-faced junkie with a halo of white hair (Plate 24), waits on her dealer in a lush diplomatic apartment: Titians on the walls and Buñuel's *The Criminal Life of Archibaldo Cruz* on the TV. David and Sancho cruise the night streets in their police car: the first young, serious and sober; the second middle-aged, unstable and alcoholic. Clara, Sancho's brutalized and adulterous wife, tends the plants on her terrace. Finally Víctor, the innocent and ignorant sex partner of Elena, seeks access to her apartment, obsessed with the woman who has used him once and thrown him away. By the time the scene is over, David will be twice wounded: physically felled by a bullet from a gun held by Víctor, emotionally pierced by a look of love from Elena.

Conventional wisdom has it that Almodóvar bought the rights to Ruth Rendell's novel and threw it away. But this opening scene is very similar in the book and the film, with the proviso that Almodóvar's version greatly increases its density and intensity. For Almodóvar, unlike Rendell, integrates the plot by making the girl at the stakeout (Elena) fall in love with the wounded policeman (David); and, thinking visually as ever, Almodóvar does not limit himself like Rendell to the single viewpoint of the young, psychotic Víctor, but rather cross-cuts between the perspectives of the five characters, assembling an intimate and intricate collage. The perfect plotting of *Live Flesh* (undoubtedly aided by Almodóvar's co-scriptwriter, tattooed, generation-X novelist Ray Loriga) has the narrative trace a satisfying circle: there will be two fatal shootouts, two deaths, and two births, each event charted with absolute precision.

'Absolute precision' is the ironic advertising slogan displayed on the bus in which, in a pre-credit sequence, Víctor is born at Christmas and to an unmarried mother. This new Nativity (with a bus taking the place of Christ's stable) is played out at a fatal time and in a fatal place: a 'state of exception' in the dying days of the Francoist regime and a spectral, deserted Madrid, lit only by the tawdry glitter of neon decorations. The brief but memorable role of Víctor's mother is played by *jolie laide* Penélope Cruz, an Almodóvar newcomer still best known in the UK as the young pregnant girl in Bigas Luna's *Jamón, Jamón* (1992), and a favourite with the youthful Spanish audience.

Elsewhere the casting is also unexpected. With a nod to the important Italian territory, Elena is played by Francesca Neri, known in Spain for her title role in Bigas Luna's unspeakable *Las edades de Lulú* (The Ages of Lulú, 1990) (notorious for its repeated close-ups of genital shaving). Here she undergoes an extraordinary metamorphosis in the course of the film, from haggard junkie to luminous wife and social worker. Clara is Angela Molina, once the southern temptress of Buñuel's *Cet obscur objet du désir* (That Obscure Object of Desire, 1977), a foil to Carole Bouquet's northern ice queen. The expert Molina, in her first role for Almodóvar in a long and distinguished career, brings a fragile dignity to the abused wife who seeks sexual solace outside a loveless marriage.

If we are asked here, unusually for Almodóvar, fully to engage with these female characters' emotions, then more surprising still is Almodóvar's rediscovery of masculinity. Male roles in *Kika* and *The Flower of My Secret* were crude and flat. Here Pepe Sancho's brutally unsympathetic Sancho is revealed, through a neat plot twist, to have hidden, moving depths; and it was inspired casting against type to have such an uncompromisingly physical actor as Javier Bardem (who starred with Cruz in *Jamón, Jamón*) play a character confined for most of the movie to a wheelchair (Plate 25). Bardem, who is perhaps Spain's most versatile male star, displays a dignity and endurance at the hands of fate which is more moving than the emotional excesses of Almodóvar's earlier films. Finally, the young principal Víctor is played by novice Liberto Rabal. Acclaimed by Almodóvar for the 'fleshiest lips in Spanish cinema', Rabal's walk-ons in previous features reveal little more than a soft-faced youth with a charisma bypass. After Almodóvar's punishing induction and the loss of four kilos, however, he was ready to take the place of the Antonio Banderas whose loss to Hollywood Almodóvar still publicly mourns. An innocent adolescent released from prison to wreak havoc in the world outside, Rabal's Víctor is suspiciously close to Banderas's Ricky who, in *Tie Me Up, Tie Me Down*, bound Victoria Abril to a bed in order to teach her a lesson about love. But, unlike Banderas (and in a nod to Almodóvar's restless gay audience), Rabal generously agrees to frontal nudity: springing from the shower to put out a fat fire in the kitchen with his towel, he flails against the flames, smoky and sweating.

The visual potency of such a scene, which goes far beyond its narrative purpose, is typical of the haunting suggestiveness of the photography by Brazilian Affonso Beato, lenser of Almodóvar's equally stylized *The Flower of My Secret*. But if Beato's camerawork is fluid and restless in such action scenes as the stakeout, it also knows the virtues of stillness and restraint. Thus in the nativity scene the bus is held in extreme long shot as the camera tracks imperceptibly forward, as if hesitating to violate the privacy of the moment. Likewise the lush mise-en-scène of Elena's initial apartment gives way to her stylish but modest married quarters with Víctor, surely the first Almodóvar set to showcase Habitat so prominently. Or again, the soundtrack features a gloriously sentimental ballad from Chavela Vargas, Almodóvar's favourite drink-sodden Latin American chanteuse. But the subtle, probing score is by Alberto Iglesias, whose string arrangements are more associated with the psychological thrillers of a director as intellectually self-conscious as Julio Medem (*La ardilla roja* [The Red Squirrel, 1993]; *Tierra* [1996]). A wheelchair basketball sequence is dynamically edited to a pounding track from Afro Celt Sound System; but one of the simplest and most moving sequences is silent: Víctor's laborious entrance into his car (which involves the folding and stowing of his wheelchair) is shot with a static camera and jumpcuts signalling painful ellipses of time.

Such a scene, unprecedented in Spanish cinema, reveals a new seriousness, even gravity, in Almodóvar's concern for social issues. And his approach to disability is impeccable. Where Rendell makes the handicapped hero incapable of sexually satisfying his wife (an impotence bitterly resented by disabled readers posting their complaints on the internet), Almodóvar, in a delicious bath scene, shows David tenderly pleasuring Elena orally. Just as in, say, *The Law of Desire*, lesbian and gay family units were shown in their casual domesticity, so here the everyday lives of people with disabilities and those who love them are at once represented and respected.

NATIONAL NARRATIVES

VÍCTOR: Hace tiempo que en España la gente ha perdido el miedo.
VÍCTOR: People stopped being afraid in Spain long ago.

Live Flesh's poster shows two perfectly symmetrical bodies and hands embracing, as alike as the 'two drops of water' in the song by Chavela Vargas which plays over the sex sequence from which the image is taken. And *Live Flesh* is also innovatory in Almodóvar's corpus for its stress on the possibility, hard won and fragile, of reciprocity in love. Only, the film seems to suggest, when we have taken responsibility for our actions (when David, Víctor, Elena and Sancho have told the truth about the shooting) can we come to know happiness. It is an ethical approach to sexual relationships, like that between the able-bodied and the handicapped, that is brilliantly fleshed out in the film without need of explanatory dialogue.

Twice, however, Almodóvar does have recourse to voiceover in order to frame the image and direct the audience. This is in the first and the final sequences of *Live Flesh*. The film opens with the ominous tones of Francoist minister Manuel Fraga (still today a leading politician) announcing the suspension of what few civil liberties Spaniards enjoyed under Franco; and it closes, boldly, at Christmas once more a quarter of a century later with a voiceover from Víctor stating that 'A long time ago we stopped being afraid in Spain.' The Almodóvar who has protested for almost twenty years that Spaniards can hardly remember a Dictatorship that has no resonance for his youthful audience, here bravely assumes his country's history and dares to speak on behalf of a nation that is now ruled by a rightist government openly hostile to the cinema made in its own country.

But yet more important than this volte face, breathtaking as it is, are the ambitions to which *Live Flesh* aspires. The political framing of the personal melodrama makes Almodóvar's collective protagonist (the five central figures) the embodiment of a national narrative whose grand theme is reminiscent of a nineteenth-century novel: the definitive shift from dictatorship to democracy. Note here the focus on the birth motif. While previous Almodóvar films (from *Pepi, Luci, Bom* to *Matador* and *Kika*) focused with wearisome insistence on rape between characters too degraded to contemplate relationships, here Almodóvar rejects the rape motif offered him by Rendell (her Víctor, unlike Almodóvar's, is a serial rapist) and with it Rendell's cod psychology (her Víctor is traumatized by witnessing a primal scene of parental sex). By the journey's end, when Elena sets off through the crowded Christmas streets to give birth, just as Víctor's mother had before her, the lost souls are redeemed and Víctor and Elena sanctified by a new ethics of care for one another. Here the difference between novel and film is telling once more: the passing of time in Rendell is marked by such details as the introduction of the 20 pence piece, hardly comparable to the momentous changes which took place in Spain in the same period. Likewise Rendell's London is composed of sleepy suburbs: from Kensal Rise to Theydon Bois. Almodóvar's Madrid, on the other hand, is alive with historical conflict: when Víctor returns home it is to an old prefab district rendered desolate by the brutal shadow of the leaning skyscrapers known as the KIO towers, a dramatic urban development familiar from Alex de la Iglesia's apocalyptic comedy *El día de la bestia* (The Day of the Beast, 1995).

The structural device here is the circle: the son becomes a father, the daughter a mother. Born, as we have seen, on a bus, the baby Víctor is presented in a mischievous black and white parody of the *NoDo* or Francoist newsreel with a lifelong bus pass which he will use to travel Madrid's own circle line. The revolving wheels of the bus and wheelchair match the illuminated star decorations to which Almodóvar's camera tilts up in the opening sequence and from which it tilts down at the close. Circularity is even built into the casting: Buñuel's icon Angela Molina is juxtaposed with the master's Mexican melodrama *Ensayo de un crimen* (The Criminal Life of Archibaldo Cruz, 1955), a fetishistic narrative whose plot turns like that of *Live Flesh* on the responsibility for a shooting. Or again Liberto Rabal, successfully launched as Spain's hot new sex symbol and endlessly photoed in the glossies spread-eagled on a motorbike or lounging provocatively on a sofa, is best known as the real-life grandson of Francisco Rabal, the veteran actor who played the youthful *señorito* in Buñuel's *Viridiana* (1961). Newly mature, Almodóvar can live up to the comparison; indeed his subtle take on Spanish institutions in *Live Flesh* makes Buñuel's casual misogyny and anticlericalism seem as mechanical and lifeless as the mannequin that looms so large in the sequence from *Archibaldo* we glimpse on Elena's TV screen.

Surprisingly, then, this stylistic circularity gives way to a faith in linearity, even progress: both Spain and Víctor are decidedly different and better at the end of the film than they were at the beginning. And so Almodóvar, proclaimed for so long as the quintessential postmodernist, seems to have rediscovered not only masculinity, in his newly tough and tender male characters, but also modernity. While a comedy like *Women on the Verge of a Nervous Breakdown* favoured irony, fragmentation, and superficiality, *Live Flesh* tends rather towards direct engagement with its characters, coherent integration of plot, and a sense of psychological, social and historical depth. And while some in Spain may refute Almodóvar's optimistic view of current conditions, citing the persistence of Basque terrorism as proof that things have not been so wonderful in the post-Franco period, there seems little doubt that, cinematically at least, Almodóvar has produced a miraculous synthesis: without abandoning his trademark glamour and stylishness he has managed to integrate the concerns of an earlier, more sober Spanish cinema characteristic of directors such as Carlos Saura. Central to *Live Flesh* is a Saura-like concern for the development of the individual and society stunted, even mutilated, by the horrors of history. *Live Flesh* is thus flashy but not superficial, serious but not po-faced.

In an industrial context also *Live Flesh* is highly significant. At a time when only tiny numbers of foreign-language films achieve distribution in the UK and US, Almodóvar holds a unique position in his claim to both artistic ambition and commercial clout. Made for a relatively high budget (by European standards) of $4.4 million, through Almodóvar's long-standing production deal with French independent Ciby 2000, *Live Flesh* is an increasingly rare example of aesthetic and industrial autonomy. Indeed Almodóvar's producer-brother Agustín told *Screen International* that his company El

Deseo's films were, unusually, not pre-sold, thus sparing Pedro financial pressure during the shoot. The varied commercial and critical reception of Ciby's slate of other features, even those with the considerable advantage of English dialogue such as Lynch's *Lost Highway* and Wenders's *The End of Violence*, reveals the increasing isolation of Almodóvar, who is one of the last foreign language auteurs to achieve global distribution. And while a sympathetic Labour government aims to expand the market share of domestic films in the UK from 5 per cent to 10 per cent, a relatively healthy Spanish cinema, albeit openly abused by a right-wing administration, increased its share in the home market last year to an impressive 17 per cent. The stimulus of Almodóvar's success has encouraged local audiences to embrace such mixed local fare as Juanma Bajo Ulloa's manic farce *Airbag* (1997) (pulled from the London Film Festival last year) and de la Iglesia's *Perdita Durango* (1997) (which also stars Javier Bardem). These three films each grossed several million dollars in their opening weeks in Madrid and Barcelona alone. The contrast with once proud producers as Italy and Germany, now almost invisible in international markets, is telling.

It is Almodóvar's achievement, then, to have sustained a European career over two decades while so many others have fallen by the wayside. And with *Live Flesh* he has managed to reinvent himself triumphantly for the late 1990s as a consummate stylist with a serious touch. If his future is by no means certain, with the Ciby production deal up for renegotiation and *Live Flesh* once more passed over by Almodóvar's peers in nominations for the Spanish Oscars (the *Goyas*), then still we can look forward hopefully to two typically idiosyncratic projects: a biopic of Marlene Dietrich, starring Uma Thurman, and a gay Western. The twin motifs of *Live Flesh* thus shine out clearly. The Christmas star and the wheelchair hold the promise, respectively, of renewed hope for a beleaguered European film industry and of artistic mobility even under the gravest of restraints. Looking around at the London Film Festival screening I found as many forty-somethings like myself as young trendies who would have flocked to an Almodóvar premiere a decade ago. Perhaps British audiences who have grown up with Almodóvar and are sated with the excesses of Hollywood will be seduced like him by the subtler temptations of austerity. A brilliant return to form, *Live Flesh* deserves no less.

Sight and Sound (April 1998)

1 3

TODO SOBRE MI MADRE

(ALL ABOUT MY MOTHER, 1999)

Silicone and Sentiment

FROM ROSE TO BLUE

LA AGRADO: Una mujer es más auténtica cuanto más se parece a lo que ha soñado de
sí misma.
LA AGRADO: A woman is authentic only in so far as she resembles her dream of herself.

In the climactic sequence of *All About My Mother*, Manuela (Cecilia Roth) finally confronts Lola (Toni Cantó), the transsexual father of her dead son. The dying Lola, who has indelibly marked the lives of all the film's women, tells her: 'I was always excessive, and now I am very tired.' If Almodóvar also has founded a career on excess, he is clearly by no means exhausted, either creatively or commercially. *All About My Mother* follows hard on the heels of last year's hit *Live Flesh*, and promises to be yet more successful than its predecessor. The first of Almodóvar's thirteen features to be shown in competition at Cannes, *All About My Mother* not only won Almodóvar the prize for best director, it also proved to be the popular hit of the festival, with the often cynical Cannes audience granting him a lengthy standing ovation. Clocking up over one million admissions in France alone, *All About My Mother* has rivalled such mainstream opposition as the Connery/Zeta Jones *Entrapment* all over Europe, thus proving Almodóvar's prediction to the Italian press that the big budgets of Hollywood can only be beaten by something that comes free to Europeans: imagination.

All About My Mother is the final part of what can now be seen as the loose trilogy of Almodóvar's mature 'blue period' (as opposed to the earlier, more florid 'rose' films).

Like *The Flower of My Secret* it focuses on one woman's grief, in this case Manuela's loss of a beloved son; but like *Live Flesh* it boasts a complex plot and gallery of characters whose lives intersect with clockwork precision and to deadly effect. If *All About My Mother* is, then, an 'Almodrama' (Cuban critic Cabrera Infante's coinage for the new genre created by the director), it is one of unusually wide interest: as attractive to film theorists as to fashionistas and as remarkable for its masterful cinematic technique as for its new commitment to social critique. And as in the earlier films of the trilogy, cinematographer Affonso Beato (veteran of the Brazilian cinema novo movement) and composer Alberto Iglesias (longtime collaborator with the cerebral Julio Medem) help to set a tone that is at once gravely austere and powerfully sensual.

The opening credits to *All About My Mother* shimmer and dissolve as the camera pans slowly over medical paraphernalia: drips and dials in blue, red and yellow. In a typical combination of economy and stylishness, this colour coding will continue throughout the film. Manuela (Cecilia Roth) will shelter beneath a primary hued umbrella (Plate 26) on the dark, rainy night in Madrid when her son is run over seeking an autograph from diva Huma Rojo (veteran Marisa Paredes). And after this first medical moment, the second theatrical section of the film is yet more stylized: escaping to the Barcelona she had left when pregnant eighteen years earlier, Manuela encounters in swift succession tranny prostitute La Agrado (newcomer Antonia San Juan), pregnant nun Sister Rosa (young star Penélope Cruz), and Huma herself, whose production of *A Streetcar Named Desire* has transferred to the Catalan capital.

The marginal milieu, if not the glamorous production values, is almost parodically reminiscent of Almodóvar's early 'rose' manner. And *All About My Mother* is densely self-referential. Cecilia Roth, who has worked in her native Argentina for the last decade, has not starred in an Almodóvar feature since *Labyrinth of Passion* in 1982; and memories of her as nymphomaniac Sexilia sit oddly with her brave performance here, at once fiercely emotional and unsentimental. Her character Manuela is a nurse who partici-pates in training seminars to counsel relatives of prospective organ donors. This is a sequence repeated near verbatim from *The Flower of My Secret*, but now with the twist that the simulation of death will be repeated for real. Almodóvar completists will love additional tiny gestures to fans: La Agrado's Chanel suit matches Victoria Abril's in *High Heels*; and her defiant claim 'I'm authentic' echoes Rossy de Palma's lesbian maid in *Kika*. The dubbed inserts of Bette Davis in *All About Eve* (Joseph L. Mankiewicz, 1950) echo the Joan Crawford clips from *Johnny Guitar* (Nicholas Ray, 1954) in *Women on the Verge*, while the theatre scenes of *A Streetcar Named Desire*, shot with an eye for the ironies of on- and off-stage life, recall those of Cocteau's *La Voix Humaine* in *The Law of Desire*.

Self-citation is used as a kind of narrative shorthand, increasing the density and intensity of the new work by calling up the rich, varied and unique universe Almodóvar has created over twenty years of film-making.

But this narrative synthesis (the condensation and displacement of Almodóvar's earlier corpus) is matched by a newly analytic use of cinematic resources. The plot may be melodramatic and the ambiance theatrical, but Almodóvar has coached his actresses to produce what Spanish critics have called a 'Swedish' performance style in which less is more. Prone to tears, in accordance with Almodóvar's belief that 'women weep better', *All About My Mother*'s circle of women also confront death, disease and abandonment with a stoic and static mask of grief, all the more moving because of its impassivity. And there are some pitiless close-ups of transsexual San Juan and diva Paredes, which reveal the trace of time in a ravaged face, however theatrically it is preserved. Yet there is still space in the hybrid 'screwball drama' (Almodóvar's own definition) for nicely judged moments of comedy, as when Sister Rosa claims that 'Prada is perfect for nuns.'

This newly extended range of performance style is matched by Almodóvar's shift of location. Hitherto confined to the old imperial capital Madrid, his films have ignored the decentralization of the Spanish state that has been the great achievement of democracy during the period in which he has worked, a constitutional experiment on which the United Kingdom has only just embarked. And Barcelona, the maritime metropolis, has never been more beautiful than through the lens of this unrepentant son of land-locked La Mancha. Introduced with a swooning helicopter shot from the Tibidabo hill down to the night lights of the bay below, Spain's second city lives up to Almodóvar's claim that it is the 'greatest of film sets'. The distinctive towers of Gaudí's Sagrada Familia (re-lit specially for the film) swim and buckle as reflected in Manuela's taxi window. La Agrado's home beat is the grimy but vibrant, multiracial Raval (formerly known as the Barrio Chino), while Sister Rosa's intolerant mother resides in a glamorous apartment decorated in the ornate *modernismo* of Catalan art nouveau. The steep, cluttered cemetery of Montjuïc is counterbalanced by the sleek glass and steel of the Hospital del Mar, twin ancient and modern faces of the city by the sea.

But just as performance and authenticity are gleefully confused, so location and dislocation go hand in hand. The visually striking scene in which cars slowly cruise prostitutes as if in some lower circle of suburban hell is shot not in Barcelona, but in Madrid, albeit with Catalan trannies (more showy than their Castilian sisters) imported as extras for the occasion. The Sagrada Familia is shown to the swelling chords of the Argentine *bandoneón*, appropriate for the central character Manuela, but highly incongruous in this Catalan context. And the bilingual status of Barcelona is barely acknowledged, with the actors essaying only the barest of greetings in the local language. Indifferent to local politics, still Almodóvar writes a visual love letter to the Catalan capital, one which was welcomed by a Catalan press which has often been friendlier to Almodóvar than that of his home town. As mobile as Manuela, shuttling between Barcelona and Madrid, Almodóvar is also as stable as her, consistent in his focus on love and loss.

A SENSE OF SOLIDARITY

MANUELA (leyendo a Truman Capote):   Cuando Dios te entrega un don, también te da un látigo. Y el látigo es únicamente para autoflagelarte.
MANUELA (reading Truman Capote):   When God hands you a gift, he also hands you a whip; and the whip is intended solely for self-flagellation.

This alternation of motion and stasis is also played out in Almodóvar's shooting and cutting style. Almodóvar has remarked how reluctant he now is to move the camera without good cause. Such key moments as the son Esteban's accident are shot with studied simplicity: the camera merely cants sideways to the ground as, from the dying's son's pov, we see a sodden Manuela come howling into shot. Three subtle features, however, contribute substantially to the film's narrative and aesthetic effect. The first is the slow pans along walls, floors and curtains which introduce many sequences. Like Ozu's interpolated shots of flowers or chimneys, unmotivated by the plot, Almodóvar's pans suggest his characters are caught up in the web of accidents that make up everyday life and cannot be extricated from the highly coloured locations they inhabit. The second technique is the dissolve. The grid of Esteban's notebook fades into the flashing lights of the theatre in which Huma is performing, a reference at once tragic and ironic to the unwitting cause of the youth's death. Or again, Almodóvar cuts from the black mouth of a waste bin to the ever receding railway tunnel through which Manuela flees the city. Narrative pace is quickened by bold, elliptical editing which cuts like a knife: located as we are within Manuela's mind, we see like her only those essential elements that drive forward her drama of primal loss and ultimate redemption.

The final technique here is the two shot. Consistently exploiting the wide screen and scorning TV-friendly square compositions, Almodóvar's framings privilege the relation between characters. In the prologue mother and son are kept constantly together, whether watching Bette Davis on television or Huma Rojo on stage. Later the central figure of Manuela will generously share the frame with the supporting players: Huma, Rosa, La Agrado and Nina, Huma's junkie lover. Superficially similar to *Live Flesh*, which also focused on relationships between multiple characters and boasted sharp shooting and cutting, *All About My Mother* is here significantly different to its predecessor. For, as the two shots suggest, the bond between the characters is not sex, but rather simple solidarity. Perhaps the boldest of Almodóvar's innovations is to secularize Catholic iconography and ideology. Manuela is Mary in a new Holy Family (hence the appearance of the Sagrada Familia), the grieving mother of a son of doubtful paternity. Chic sister Rosa (splendidly underplayed by Spain's favourite young actress Penélope Cruz) will be martyred by the contemporary afflictions of unmarried motherhood and AIDS. And, finally, the Biblical injunction to love thy neighbour will be fully put into practice by Manuela, embracing the lives, loves, and even babies of the women she meets. But she does so in the name not of Christ but of the Blanche Dubois played on stage by Huma: we are all shown to be dependent on the kindness of strangers.

This sense of solidarity is based on the breaking down of barriers. Just as the actors share space within the frame and Manuela touches the lives of all those she so casually encounters, so the themes of the film, weighty but never ponderous, point to a cohabitation without limits. Esteban's heart will beat within another's chest, the ultimate gift of life. Inversely his father Lola (originally known as Esteban also) will transmit a fatal virus to Rosa. Letters, photos and children circulate amongst the cast, eventually reaching their destination. Esteban never sees a photo of his father, but his father will see a photo of the son he never knew, before he too dies in turn. Huma will write the autograph for Esteban that she refused him on the fatal night. And a third Esteban (Rosa's son) will come to take the place of his lost father and brother in Manuela's care. Opaque on the page, such complexities are transparently clear on screen: this is a kind of open heart cinema in which the way we touch one another is shown to have immediate and mortal effects. Creation and procreation (cinema and motherhood) are thus implacable masters, God-given gifts that become self-inflicted scourges.

I take the Lacanian reference to 'letters reaching their destination' from a French feature on the film in *Cahiers du Cinéma*. And one unique aspect of Almodóvar is how his films play to such a wide variety of audiences, many of whom will be unfamiliar with *Cahiers*' psychoanalytic asides. In spite of its popular success, then, *All About My Mother* seems all too easily to offer itself up for academic interpretation, most particularly to the many critics who now see gender not as identity but rather as performance. In a blissfully comic sequence Antonia San Juan's La Agrado takes the stage (Huma's performance has been cancelled) to perform her own life story as a transsexual well endowed in both male and female departments (Plate 27). A modest but generous chick with a dick, she runs through the true costs of 'authenticity': each of her body parts has a price at the plastic surgeon. And she also claims that the truest parts of her are the silicone and sentiments. But it would be wrong to take this monologue as proof of Almodóvar's supposed 'postmodernism', his love of style and surface. Rather, in his loving attention to lives lived at the margins, Almodóvar suggests a respect for others, however rich and strange they may be, that can only be called humanist.

This newly radical humanism has clear political implications in Almodóvar's native Spain. For one final characteristic of the 'blue period' trilogy is their increasing engagement with social issues, even amidst the lushest of visual pleasures. *The Flower of My Secret*'s sentimental drama was set in a Madrid racked by strikes and anti-government protest. *Live Flesh* began with the imposition of a Francoist curfew and ended with a celebration of twenty years of Spanish democracy. *All About My Mother* goes yet further: the birth of Rosa's child coincides, we are told, with the imprisonment of an Argentine general; and the integration of AIDS into Almodóvar's chain of solidarity is hardly casual in a country where HIV transmission is far higher than in the UK. Asked by movie magazine *Fotogramas* for his thoughts for the millennium Almodóvar replied not with holiday hints but with the earnest desire that Pinochet finally be brought to trial. Moreover, while reviews have been generally favourable in Spain, some critics have reacted badly to Almodóvar's marginal characters. The reviewer in the supposedly liberal daily *El Mundo* wrote that he 'failed to recognize himself' as a heterosexual man in Almodóvar's Spain, a nation exclusively composed of lesbians, drag queens and junkies. *All About My Mother* may prove more appetizing to the minority foreign audience who felt *Live Flesh*, too straight by half, was a betrayal of Almodóvar's early genderbending work. But in a home market where Almodóvar remains the only director whose name can 'open' a film, his mainstream status still raises problems of representation, with some audiences claiming to be excluded from an all too distinctive filmic world that has shaped many foreigners' perceptions of modern Spain.

Finally, perhaps, the US influences paraded by *All About My Mother* are red herrings. Unlike Eve Harrington in *All About Eve*, the good-hearted Manuela will not betray the star whose life she infiltrates; and unlike Blanche in *Streetcar*, Almodóvar's heroines hold on to their sanity to the bitter end. *All About My Mother* finishes, moreover, with a very Spanish reference: Huma rehearses the role of the mourning matriarch in

Lorca's *Blood Wedding*. Equally at ease with Prada and Lorca, *All About My Mother* effortlessly fuses style and feeling, silicone and sentiment. Newly mature and boundlessly creative, Almodóvar has proved himself worthy of the comparison with Spain's greatest dramatist.

Sight and Sound (September 1999)

FILMOGRAPHY

AND PLOT SYNOPSES

10. *Kika* (1993)

Production company	El Deseo S.A. and Ciby 2000
Executive producer	Agustín Almodóvar
Production manager	Alejandro Vázquez
Screenplay	Pedro Almodóvar
Director of photography	Alfredo Mayo
Editor	José Salcedo
Set design	Javier Fernández
	Alain Bainée
Costume design	Jean-Paul Gaultier
	José María Cossío
	Gianni Versace
Sound	Jean-Paul Mugel

114 mins

CAST

Verónica Forqué	Kika
Peter Coyote	Nicholas

Victoria Abril	Andrea Caracortada
Alex Casanovas	Ramón
Rossy de Palma	Juana
Santiago Lajusticia	Pablo
Anabel Alonso	Amparo
Bibi Andersen	Susana
Charo López	Ramón's mother

Kika is an ever-optimistic beautician living with Ramón, an introspective and uncommunicative underwear photographer she met when summoned to make up his cataleptic 'corpse'. Returning from abroad, Ramón's stepfather, American novelist Nicholas Pearce, moves into the flat above. Ramón and Nicholas jointly own a country house ('Youkali') bequeathed them by Ramón's mother, with whom Ramón has been obsessed since her suicide. Unsatisfied by her relationship with Ramón, Kika secretly enjoys occasional sex with the mysterious and seductive Nicholas.

Ramón also has his secrets: before Kika, he had been involved with Andrea Caracortada (Scarface), an ex-psychologist turned crime reporter. Their relationship ended dramatically, leaving Andrea with a sizeable grudge and a scar on her face. Equipped with a motorbike and customized black rubber suit, Andrea specializes in on-the-spot crime reports and sensationalist interviews with victims and perpetrators for her TV 'reality show' 'The Worst of the Day'.

Andrea encounters Kika when pursuing mentally deficient convicted rapist Pablo, who escaped while on parole from prison to attend a religious festival in his home village. Unknown to Kika, her maid Juana is Pablo's sister and Kika's flat is his first port of call on the run. Juana, a plain-speaking lesbian who is in love with Kika, does her best to protect her sleeping mistress from Pablo's voracious sexual appetite by promising to satisfy his needs herself. She decides to send Pablo into hiding and tells him to steal some of Ramón's cameras, concealing her role in the theft by getting Pablo to slug her and tie her to a chair. While Juana is bound and unconscious, Pablo repeatedly rapes Kika until the police arrive and pull him away. He escapes as Andrea arrives on the scene. Kika angrily refuses to answer Andrea's intrusive questions and tries to put the incident behind her, only to be further humiliated by the TV screening of a video recording of the rape sent in by a neighbouring voyeur. Discovering that Ramón is the source of the video, she moves out.

Andrea's continuing scrutiny of Ramón's video and Nicholas's latest manuscript lead her to suspect Nicholas of multiple murder and, desperate for the scoop, she pursues him to Youkali, where Ramón has already discovered a dead body and confronted him with the evidence of his mother's murder. While Ramón lies in another cataleptic swoon, Andrea forces her way in and dies in a struggle with Nicholas. Kika, drawn by a letter from Ramón, turns up in time to hear Nicholas's dying confession and revive Ramón. Following the ambulance taking him to hospital, however, she picks up a hitcher, with whom she drives off into the sunset. (Rikki Morgan)[1]

11. *La flor de mi secreto* (The Flower of My Secret, 1995)

Production company	El Deseo S.A. and Ciby 2000
Executive producer	Agustín Almodóvar
Production manager	Esther García
Screenplay	Pedro Almodóvar
Director of photography	Affonso Beato
Editor	José Salcedo
Music	Alberto Iglesias
Set design	Wolfgang Burmann
	Miguel López Pelegrín
Costume design	Hugo Mezcua
	Max Mara and Sportmax
	Ermenegildo Zegna
Sound	Bernardo Menz

107 mins

CAST

Marisa Paredes	Leo
Imanol Arias	Paco
Juan Echanove	Angel
Carmen Elías	Betty
Rossy de Palma	Rosa
Chus Lampreave	Mother
Joaquín Cortés	Antonio
Manuela Vargas	Blanca

Under the pen-name Amanda Gris, Leo Macías has written a series of best-selling romance novels. Lately, however, she feels incapable of delivering the upbeat plots specified by her contract. Instead, she has stated to drink heavily and write grim tales of accidents and murder. Her work has been affected by the tense condition of her marriage to Paco, a NATO official working in Brussels for the Bosnian peacekeeping force. Whenever the two are together, they quarrel bitterly; but most of the time, Leo finds herself abjectly alone.

Over dinner, a psychologist friend Betty advises Leo to try journalism, and suggests that she meet with Angel, editor of the Culture section of *El País*. At her flat, Leo discards some old manuscripts. The loyal housekeeper Blanca is visited by her son Antonio, who tries to persuade her to resume her former career as a flamenco dancer. Antonio steals a manuscript for a novel as well as Leo's onyx earrings.

Leo meets with Angel, bringing with her a different new novel and two essays. Angel proposes that she write a feature on Amanda Gris, but Leo claims to detest the author. She visits her sister Rosa, who lives in a state of perpetual rancour with their querulous, hypochondriac mother. The latter feels adrift in Madrid and longs for her native village; while Rosa has to contend with a shiftless husband. Angel loves Leo's work and offers her a commission; but when she calls Paco to tell him, he is aloof and irritable. Then Leo's publishers threaten to expose her true identity if she doesn't write something more cheerful. Disgusted, Leo pens a brutal critique of Amanda Gris, using another pseudonym.

Paco announces that he has obtained a day's leave, and Leo perks up immediately. However, he stops by the flat merely to shower and press his clothes. The pair argue and Paco leaves, declaring the marriage over. In despair, Leo swallows a half bottle of tranquillizers; but she is jogged back to consciousness by a phone message from her mother, who has decided to return to the village. Staggering out into the middle of a student demonstration, Leo meets Angel and faints in his arms. Leo awakens in Angel's flat, having revealed in her stupor that she is Amanda Gris. Back at Leo's, Betty admits that she and Paco have been having an affair, which she has just ended for Leo's sake. Leo sorrowfully accompanies her mother to the village, where she slowly recovers her strength.

Later, the publisher telephones to enthuse over her new romance novels; perplexed, Leo consults Angel, who confesses to ghosting them. In Madrid, they attend a triumphant flamenco performance by Blanca and Antonio, after which Angel avows his love. On a midnight visit, Antonio admits to having stolen Leo's things, which he sold to finance the show. She accepts his apology, but resists his amorous advances. Soon after, Leo drops by Angel's flat; they toast each other and kiss. (Peter Matthews)[2]

12. *Carne trémula* (Live Flesh, 1997)

Production company	El Deseo S.A. and Ciby 2000/France 3
Executive producer	Agustín Almodóvar
Production manager	Esther García
Screenplay	Pedro Almodóvar, with Ray Loriga and Jorge Guerricaechevarría
Director of photography	Affonso Beato
Editor	José Salcedo
Music	Alberto Iglesias
Art design	Antxón Gómez
Costume design	José María de Cossío
Sound	Bernardo Menz

100 mins

CAST

Francesca Neri	Elena
Javier Bardem	David
Liberto Rabal	Víctor
Angela Molina	Clara
José Sancho	Sancho
Penélope Cruz	Víctor's mother

Madrid, 1970. In the empty streets of the city during a curfew, a young prostitute gives birth on a bus to a son, Víctor. Twenty years later, Víctor shows up for a date with Elena, the drug-addicted daughter of an Italian diplomat, but she barely remembers him. She threatens him with a gun. Two policemen, David and Sancho, arrive. David is shot and Víctor is sent to jail. Two years later, Víctor sees David, now a paraplegic and married to a now-sober Elena, playing basketball in the Barcelona Paralympics. Víctor vows revenge.

After being released from jail, Víctor sees Elena at her father's funeral and meets Clara, Sancho's wife, with whom he begins an affair. Víctor gets a job at the children's shelter Elena works at. When David tries to confront Víctor, Víctor reveals that it was really Sancho – wanting revenge because of David's affair with Clara – who shot him. Elena goes to bed with Víctor. Meanwhile, Clara decides to leave Sancho for Víctor and shoots him when he tries to prevent her from leaving. Elena confesses to her affair with Víctor to David. He goes to tell Sancho of Clara's affair with Víctor and a badly wounded Sancho goes to kill his rival. Instead, he finds Clara at Víctor's and the two of them kill each other. Some time later, Elena gives birth to Víctor's son in a taxi. Víctor tells his child how lucky he is to be born in a new Spain. (José Arroyo)[3]

13. *Todo sobre mi madre* (All About My Mother, 1999)

Production company	El Deseo S.A. and Ciby 2000/France 3
Executive producer	Agustín Almodóvar
Associate producer	Michel Ruben
Production manager	Esther García
Screenplay	Pedro Almodóvar
Director of photography	Affonso Beato
Editor	José Salcedo
Music	Alberto Iglesias
Art design	Antxón Gómez
Costume design	José María de Cossío and Sabine Daigeler
Sound	Miguel Rejas

101 mins

CAST

Cecilia Roth	Manuela
Marisa Paredes	Huma Rojo
Candela Peña	Nina
Antonia San Juan	La Agrado
Penélope Cruz	Sister Rosa

Rosa María Sardá	Rosa's mother
Toni Cantó	Lola, 'la Pionera'
Eloy Azorín	Esteban
Fernando Fernán Gómez	Rosa's father

Manuela is a single mother living in Madrid. She takes her son Esteban on his seventeenth birthday to see a production of *A Streetcar Named Desire* starring Huma Rojo. Moved by the performances, they wait for autographs. Manuela, who has told Esteban nothing about his father except that he died before Esteban was born, confesses she once played Stella to his father's Stanley. She promises she will tell him more once they return home. Huma and her co-star Nina appear and board a taxi. Running after, Esteban is hit by a car. He dies and Manuela donates his organs. Later, she decides to honour Esteban's last wish by going to Barcelona to find his father and tell him about his son.

While looking for Esteban's father at a pick-up place, Manuela helps a transvestite being beaten up by a punter. The transvestite turns out to be La Agrado, who twenty years ago had lived with Manuela and Esteban's father – also called Esteban before he had a sex-change and became Lola the Pioneer. La Agrado tells Manuela she took in the sick Lola only for her to run off with La Agrado's belongings. While Manuela finds a job as Rojo's assistant, La Agrado decides to change her life and goes to see a nun, Sister Rosa, for counselling. Sister Rosa was impregnated and infected with HIV by Lola. Manuela nurses Sister Rosa through her pregnancy, the birth and eventually her death. Lola finally appears ravaged by AIDS. The child is born HIV+. Manuela decides to bring up the child who is named Esteban. Before Lola dies, Manuela presents her with the newborn Esteban and tells her about the dead one. Later, the third Esteban has neutralized the virus naturally. (José Arroyo)[4]

NOTES

1. *SS*, September 1994.

2. *SS*, February 1996.

3. *SS*, May 1998.

4. *SS*, September 1999.

BIBLIOGRAPHICAL UPDATE

Since the first edition of this book, publication on Almodóvar, both popular and academic, has greatly increased. In a welcome development, El Deseo has begun to publish scripts to tie in with the release of each film and one has been translated into English. It has also continued to produce lavish press books, complete with extended texts by Almodóvar, which are not, however, available to the public. This bibliographical update lists only some of the more significant contributions to the field. Vernon and Morris's excellent collection of essays (see below) includes a comprehensive bibliography, limited, however, to publications in the United States.

Almodóvar, Pedro, *The Flower of My Secret* [script], London 1997.

---- , *Todo sobre mi madre* [script], Madrid 1999.

Arroyo, José, 'The Auteur and the National Cinema' [review article], *Tesserae*, 2, 1996, pp. 269–74.

---- , Review of *Live Flesh, Sight and Sound*, May 1998, pp. 50–51.

---- , Review of *All about My Mother, Sight and Sound*, September 1999, p. 40.

Caughie, John, 'Becoming European: Art Cinema, Irony, and Identity', in Duncan Petrie, ed., *Screening Europe: Image and Identity in Contemporary European Cinema*, London 1992, pp. 32–44.

Colmeiro, José F., 'Del rosa al negro: Subtextos culturales en *La flor de mi secreto*', *Arizona Journal of Hispanic Cultural Studies*, 1, 1997, pp. 115–28.

Deleyto, Celestino, 'Postmodernism and Parody in Pedro Almodóvar's *Mujeres al borde de un ataque de nervios*', *Forum for Modern Language Studies*, 31.1, 1995, pp. 49–63.

Eng, David, 'Fractured by Voices: Technologies of Gender in Pedro Almodóvar's *Mujeres al borde de un ataque de nervios*', in George Cabello Castellet, Jaume Martí Olivella, and Guy H. Wood, eds, *Cine-Lit II: Essays on Hispanic Film and Fiction*, Portland, Oregon 1995, pp. 146–54.

Escudero, Javier, 'Rosa Montero y Pedro Almodóvar: miseria y estilización de la movida madrileña', *Arizona Journal of Hispanic Cultural Studies*, 2, 1998, pp. 147–61.

Evans, Peter, 'Almodóvar's *Matador*: Gender, Subjectivity, and Desire', *Bulletin of Hispanic Studies*, 70, 1993, pp. 325–35.

----, *Women on the Verge of a Nervous Breakdown*, London 1996.

Fuentes, Víctor, 'El cine de Almodóvar y la posmodernidad española (logros y límites)', in George Cabello Castellet, Jaume Martí Olivella, and Guy H. Wood, eds, *Cine-Lit: Essays on Hispanic Film and Fiction*, Portland, Oregon 1995, pp. 209–18.

Hanson, Ellis, 'Technology, Paranoia and the Queer Voice', *Screen*, 35.2, 1993, pp. 137–61.

Keown, Dominic, 'Ethics and Aesthetics in Almodóvar's *Matador*', *Bulletin of Hispanic Studies*, 69, 1992, pp. 345–53.

Holguín, Antonio, *Pedro Almodóvar*, Madrid 1994.

Matthews, Peter, Review of *The Flower of My Secret*, *Sight and Sound*, February 1996, p. 40.

Morgan, Rikki, 'Dressed to Kill' [on *Tacones lejanos*], *Sight and Sound*, April 1992, pp. 28–9.

----, Review of *Kika*, *Sight and Sound*, July 1994, p. 48.

Mudrovic, William Michael, 'The Law of the Father in Pedro Almodóvar's *La ley del deseo*', *Letras Peninsulares*, 7.1, 1994, pp. 333–50.

Smith, Paul Julian, 'Almodóvar's Women', in *Vision Machines: Cinema, Literature, and Sexuality in Spain and Cuba, 1983–93*, London and New York 1996, pp. 17–55.

----, 'Pornography, Masculinity, Homosexuality: Almodóvar's *Matador* and *La ley del deseo*', in Marsha Kinder, ed., *Refiguring Spain: Cinema/Media/Representation*, Durham NC 1997, pp. 178–95.

Strauss, Frédéric, ed., *Almodóvar on Almodóvar*, London 1996.

Triana Toribio, Nuria, 'Almodóvar's melodramatic Mise-en-Scène: Madrid as a Setting for Melodrama', *Bulletin of Hispanic Studies*, 73.2, 1997, pp. 179–89.

Varderi, Alejandro, *Severo Sarduy y Pedro Almodóvar: Del barroco al kitsch en la narrativa y el cine postmodernos*, Madrid 1996.

Vernon, Kathleen, 'Melodrama against itself: Pedro Almodóvar's *What Have I Done to Deserve This?*', *Film Quarterly*, 46.3, 1993, pp. 28–40.

----, 'Scripting a Social Imaginary: Hollywood in/and Spanish Cinema', in Jenaro Talens and Santos Zunzunegui, eds, *Modes of Representation in Spanish Cinema*, Minneapolis 1998, pp. 319–29.

----, and Barbara Morris, eds, *Post-Franco, Postmodern: The Films of Pedro Almodóvar*, Westport, Conn. 1995.

INDEX